Be Your Own
Financial Adviser

Jonquil Lowe

Which? Books are commissioned by
Consumers' Association and published by
Which? Ltd, 2 Marylebone Road, London NW1 4DF
Email address: books@which.net

First edition March 1996
Reprinted February 1997, September 1997
Second edition March 1998
Reprinted April 1998, May 1998, November 1999
Third edition July 2000
Fourth edition June 2002
Fifth edition January 2004
This edition May 2005

Copyright © 1996, 1997, 1998, 1999, 2000, 2002, 2004, 2005 Which? Ltd

British Library Cataloguing-in-Publication Data
A catalogue record for this book is available from the British Library

ISBN 1 84490 012 6

Cover photograph by Jeff Smith/getty images
Editorial and production: Joanna Bregosz, Ian Robinson

Typeset by Saxon Graphics Ltd, Derby
Printed and bound in Great Britain by Creative Print and Design (Wales) Ebbw Vale

For information on the latest Budget see www.which.co.uk (click on Bookshop and follow
the links).

Contents

PART 3: THE MAIN INVESTMENT TOOLS

Addresses, telephone numbers and, where applicable, Internet sites for those organisations marked with an asterisk (*) can be found in the address section starting on page 352.

Introduction

Increasingly the state is encouraging people to take responsibility for their own financial well-being. Nowadays you are generally expected to take contingency measures to protect yourself and your family. For example, the state safety net if you cannot work because of illness is too low to cover most people's living costs and bills. If you become unemployed, you usually have to carry on meeting your mortgage costs for several months before state help kicks in. State benefits to help your family if you die are low and not available to unmarried partners. In some regions, you can no longer even rely on the state to provide dental care.

At the same time, you have to meet planned expenditure either by saving up or taking on debt. With the basic state retirement pension standing at less than a fifth of average earnings, without your own savings (either through a scheme at work or your own plan) you will face a meagre old age. Young people must either run up thousands of pounds of debt if they want a university education or look to parents for help.

This culture of self-help has various implications. Firstly, you will have to develop a good understanding of your needs and how you might go about meeting them. This can seem daunting – a quarter of UK adults feel they are not good at managing their money.[1]

Secondly, equipping yourself with life cover, income protection insurance, mortgage payment protection insurance, a pension scheme, and giving your children a helping hand can easily cost hundreds of pounds a month. On top of paying a mortgage, your household bills and day-to-day living, that's a tall

---

[1]Financial Services Authority, Consumer Research 27, *Financial Capability: Consumers views on developing their financial capabilities through schools and workplaces*, May 2004.

order, especially with average earnings standing at just £22,000 a year.[2] Therefore, it is essential to weigh up carefully which financial goals are a priority and to shop around for the products which offer the best deal.

Choosing the best deal implies that you have a reasonable understanding of what's on offer so that you do not buy the wrong products, pay over the odds or run unnecessary risks.

Equally, when it comes to savings and investments, you don't want to play it so safe that you lose all realistic chance of building up enough to meet your goals. Experts agree that for long-term goals it is sensible to put some of your money into share-based investments because the return is linked to economic growth and over the long run tends to outperform the return from safer investments, such as bonds and deposits. Yet, early signs are that most parents looking to invest their children's 18-year child trust fund are choosing low-risk, low-return bank and building society accounts. More generally, private investors continue to shun share-based investments following the stock market slide of 2000 to 2003, even though the market has since risen by 50 per cent.[3] As this suggests, it is all too easy to take a reactive, short-term approach to financial decision-making. By contrast, sound financial planning is about making informed decisions that anticipate potential problems and are robust in the face of short-term changes.

A key aim of *Be Your Own Financial Adviser* is to give you a sound understanding of the issues, risks and opportunities involved in managing your money and the ability to apply that understanding to the financial decisions you make throughout your life. Whether you want to be your own financial adviser or simply to engage more effectively with professionals, *Be Your Own Financial Adviser* aims to put you on the right road. It shows you how to build a financial plan that is tailored to your particular needs, circumstances and attitude towards risk. It explains how and to what extent advisers can help and how to protect yourself from the rogue element who stoop to unscrupulous tactics.

---

[2] Office for National Statistics, *2004 Annual Survey of Hours and Earnings*, October 2004.

[3] The FTSE 100 Index stood at 5007 on 25 February 2005 against a low of 3287 on 12 March 2003.

In plain language with plenty of examples and tips, *Be Your Own Financial Adviser* guides you through the main financial goals: building up an emergency fund, protecting your family in the event of death, protecting your income in case you fall ill, paying for healthcare, buying a home, helping your children, investing for growth, saving for retirement, providing extra income, coping with long-term care and passing on your money tax effectively.

This edition is up-to-date at end-February 2005. As we went to press, the 2005 Budget had just been announced and the main Budget measures are summarised on the next page.

Budget 2005

The following Budget 2005 measures affect material in this book. The measures may be changed by Parliament before becoming law. After a general election, an incoming government might announce further tax changes.

- **Income tax rates and bands in 2005–6** Rates are unchanged. Starting rate band is £2,090 and higher rate tax starts at £32,400.
- **Main income tax allowances for 2005–6** Personal allowance:under 65s £4,895; 65–74 £7,090; 75 plus £7220. Married couple's allowance:lower £5,905; 75 plus £5,975; basic amount £2,280. Income at which age allowances start to be lost £19,500.
- **Couples** From 5 December 2005 couples who register as civil partners will be treated for tax the same as married couples. If you get married or form a civil partnership on or after 5 December 2005, any married couple's allowance will be based on the income of the person with the highest income (not the husband's). Existing marriages are not affected.
- **Capital gains tax** Annual allowance for 2005–6 is £8,500 (previously £8,200).
- **Child trust funds** The government plans to add a further sum to each child trust fund when the child reaches age seven and is consulting on the amount (expected to be a further £250 or for low-income families £500). It is also consulting on whether to make additional payments when the child is secondary school age.
- **Individual savings accounts (ISAs)** Availability extended to 5 April 2010. The investment limits of £7,000 a year overall and £3,000 for cash will apply for the whole period.
- **Inheritance tax** Nil-rate band for 2005–6 is £275,000 (previously £263,000). For the following two tax years it is £285,000 and £300,000.
- **Shari'a-compliant financial products** Mark-ups and profit-sharing are to be taxed in a comparable way to interest.
- **Real estate investment trusts (REITs)** The government is consulting further on this a new type of pooled investment that can be used to invest in a spread of residential as well as commercial property.

Chapter 1

Why be your own financial adviser?

A glance at your local telephone directory or a stroll down the high street will quickly tell you that there is no shortage of firms and individuals eager to help you organise your finances. So why choose to be your own financial adviser? Since you would not be reading this book if you had not already been tempted to handle your financial affairs yourself, one or more of the following reasons for choosing the d-i-y route has probably occurred to you. Some are good reasons, others less so.

Reason 1: I can't afford financial advice

In fact, with many financial products, you don't pay *extra*, because you are already paying for advice even if you haven't had any! Most advisers get paid only if they sell something. They receive commission from the company whose product you have bought or invested in. The commission is financed out of the charges you pay for the product. The advantage of this system is that the cost of advice is spread over the life of the product, making it easy to afford. The snag is, with many products, the charging structure is just the same even if you haven't had any advice. If you definitely don't want advice, it pays to shop around for products which do not have commission payments built in (see page 14) or haggle for a commission rebate (see page 26).

Reason 2: I'm not wealthy enough to have an adviser

However large or small your savings are, you need to invest them wisely. Often, the smaller the amount you have, the more important it is to take the right financial decisions, since you can ill afford to make mistakes. Some financial advisers are willing to give time and attention to even the smallest of clients, but most are not because, if you have only small savings, the most suitable investments for you are likely to be schemes like building society accounts and National Savings & Investments (NS&I). Advisers generally receive little or no commission if they recommend these types of investment. You are also unlikely to take up many of the health and other insurance products which are important sources of income for many advisers.

Some advisers charge you fees, rather than relying on commission income, and so do not suffer the above drawbacks, but the fees charged will often outweigh the benefits of the advice given to a client with only small means.

Reason 3: Financial advisers cannot be trusted

Endowment mortgages, pension transfers, contracting out, with-profits bonds, split capital investment trusts – all are familiar from newspaper headlines and have fuelled the public's general mistrust of financial advisers. But it would be a mistake to tar all advisers with the same brush: there are many skilled, knowledgeable, conscientious and trustworthy advisers the length and breadth of the UK. The trick is to spot and avoid their less honourable colleagues. Certainly, the more you find out about handling your finances, the less likely you are to fall prey to a fraudulent or incompetent adviser.

Reason 4: Advisers are just pushy salespeople

Outright fraud is thankfully rare but, sadly, there are other ways in which an adviser can let you down. The commission system described on page 11 is a less than ideal way of paying an adviser who is supposed to have your best interests at heart. It means there is a built-in incentive for advisers to recommend:

- products or courses of action which produce a commission rather than those which do not: for example, a personal pension rather than membership of an occupational pension scheme, or unnecessary switching from one company to another

- products which pay higher commission than others: for example, endowment mortgages rather than repayment mortgages, investment-type life insurance policies rather than unit trusts
- the product of a company paying higher commission than other companies
- that you invest more, or buy more insurance cover, than might really be ideal for you.

A good adviser will not be swayed by the lure of commission – not only would it be unethical, but it could be bad business if the adviser wants to build up a base of satisfied customers who will generate a steady stream of further business over the years. Unfortunately, not all advisers fit this mould.

You can avoid the possibility of advice biased due to commission by choosing an adviser who is instead paid by fees.

Reason 5: I don't know how to find an adviser

There are different sorts of adviser. Some act as agents of a company whose products they sell. Others act as your agent and can recommend products from the full range on the market – these are 'independent' advisers. Chapter 2 explains the different types of advice in more detail. In surveys, most people say they would prefer to have independent advice, but often they do not know how to find it. By default, many people turn to their trusted and familiar bank or building society for advice, but very few banks and building societies give independent advice and most offer only a narrow range of products. However, finding an independent adviser is not as difficult as you imagine. There are several directories that you can use to search for details of advisers in your area – see page 24.

Finding an adviser is one thing; finding a *good* adviser is quite another. *Which?* magazine keeps a check on the standard of advice being offered to consumers. Although the proportion of advisers giving poor advice has been falling in recent years, it is clear that choosing an adviser can still be something of a lottery (see page 15). *Which?* has generally found that independent advisers give good advice more often than other types of adviser.

Reason 6: The need for financial advice is overrated

There is no reason at all why you should not make an excellent job of handling your own financial affairs. But do not make the mistake of assuming that this is a trivial task. Superficially, your finances may seem simple, but you could be unaware of, or underestimate, the importance of certain aspects. If your circumstances genuinely are straightforward and your resources modest, it might not take long to sort out your finances – this time. But financial planning is not a one-off exercise: as your circumstances change, and as the economic and political climate alters, you will need to revise your affairs, which might become more, or less, complex. If you have substantial wealth or, for example, your family circumstances are complicated, understanding and organising your finances will already be a challenging task. Whatever your situation, proper financial planning requires adequate time, thought and care. If you are unable or disinclined to give the job the attention it demands, you should seriously consider consulting a professional financial adviser instead.

Reason 7: Handling my own finances will save me money

Whether you pay a fee or your adviser receives commission (see page 11), it's true that the cost of advice can run to hundreds or thousands of pounds. So can you save that money by doing the job yourself?

Obviously, if you choose not to go to a fee-charging adviser, you save the fee. The picture is more complicated when you look at commission-based advice.

The cost of paying the adviser commission is passed on to you, the customer, through the charges for the product you have bought. For example, the cost of commission might be taken as an upfront charge, leaving less of your money to be invested. Alternatively, the cost of commission might be taken gradually over the years through a variety of charges, but recouped through a single, large surrender penalty if you cash in or stop the product early.

With many products, these charges are exactly the same whether or not you use an adviser. So opting to buy without advice does not

Income protection advice

Between September 2003 and January 2004, *Which?* sent under-cover researchers, posing as first-time homebuyers, to test the quality of advice that banks, building societies and estate agents offer. It particularly wanted to see what sort of insurance advisers were selling to homebuyers to cover their income if they weren't able to work due to illness or accident. Overall, the advice they received was poor, misleading and generally unhelpful – and could have left them with too little cover, or wasting hundreds of pounds a year on unsuitable policies. Only one out of 39 advisers gave acceptable advice.

One tactic to sell policies *Which?* came across was to shock people with distressing tales of serious illness. An adviser recommending critical illness insurance said: 'I'm going to a funeral later today for someone who was 42 and has died of leukaemia'.

To make sure you end up with the right sort of policy, an adviser should start, not by scaring you, but by asking about your circumstances. However, two-thirds of advisers in the survey didn't do a proper check, and a third didn't take the researchers' income and spending patterns into account at all. In a couple of cases, advisers even fiddled figures, reducing the researchers' outgoings to make insurance seem more affordable.

Which? June 2004

(See Chapters 7 and 9 for information about insurance to protect your income and mortgages, respectively.)

necessarily save you money. However, there are three ways to overcome this problem:

- Go to a 'direct company' – in other words, a provider that sells direct to the public (often by phone or via the Internet), by-passing advisers and other intermediaries. Often, the products from direct companies cost less, in part reflecting the fact that no commission is being paid.

- Even where a company normally does sell through advisers, try approaching it direct and asking if it will refund to you some or all of the commission which would have gone to an adviser.
- Buying through a 'discount broker'. These are independent intermediaries that, as standard practice, rebate a large part of the commission you would normally pay (but don't usually offer advice). This results in lower product charges, ensuring that more of your money is invested. 'Fund supermarkets' (see Chapter 18) – Internet sites where you can buy a range of different companies' unit trusts and similar investments – also rebate commission as standard. Examples of discount brokers and fund supermarkets are given in the Addresses section.

Bear in mind that what you save by not using an adviser could be trivial compared with your losses if you choose the wrong product. If you have any doubts, it is usually better to pay up and take advice. But remember that, even if you use an adviser who gives you a full advice service, he or she might be prepared to cut the cost of the advice if you ask for a rebate (see page 26).

Reason 8: Handling my own finances would be fun

This is the best reason for being your own financial adviser. If you would not find it a satisfying and enjoyable experience, you would do better to concentrate your energies on finding a professional adviser whom you trust.

Chapter 2

What to expect from a professional adviser

Before deciding how far down the d-i-y financial planning road to go, you should have a clear understanding of the services that a professional can offer. You will then be in a position to assess which of those services you can provide for yourself.

Where to go for professional advice and what the advisers offer depends largely on the type of financial products or services you are considering.

Savings advice

'Savings' means deposit-based products where you earn interest on your money and (except in the unlikely event of the provider going bust) get back your capital in full. Savings include bank and building society accounts and National Savings & Investment (NS&I) products.

If you are seeking financial advice in a wider context from an independent financial adviser (see page 19), as part of the advice the adviser may well recommend the best savings accounts for part of your money. But there are no advisers who give only advice about savings and no special rules concerning this sort of advice. A voluntary Banking Code requires providers to give you information about their own products to help you choose whichever is suitable. But, in general, if you want to weigh up different providers' accounts, you usually have little choice but to be your own adviser.

Chapter 16 describes the savings products on offer and where to get information to help you compare them. Chapters 5, 10, 11 and 13 show how savings products can help you achieve various financial goals.

Investment or personal pension advice

Advice about most investments (including personal pensions) is subject to rules set out by the Financial Services Authority (FSA). In general, anyone giving investment advice must be authorised by the FSA (see Chapter 3) and abide by detailed rules governing the way advisers deal with customers. Two important rules are:

- **know the customer** The adviser must find out enough about your personal and financial circumstances to be able to give you sound advice. Usually this is done by taking you through a 'fact find' – a list of questions covering, for example, your age, marital status, whether you have children or other dependants, your work status, how much you earn, what you spend, what savings and financial arrangements you already have, your financial goals, how you feel about taking risks with your money, and so on. You don't have to give all the information asked for but, if you don't, the adviser will only be able to give you limited advice

- **suitable advice** The adviser must recommend only products and courses of action that are appropriate for you given your personal and financial circumstances. An important part of this process is making clear what you are buying and, in particular, any risks involved. For example, if the return from a product depends directly or indirectly on stock-market performance, the adviser should explain this and make sure that you are comfortable with the possibility that the value of your investment might go up and down or fall short of any target amount.

Some of the rules advisers must abide by depend on the type of investment involved: packaged or other.

To see how investments can help you meet your goals, see Chapters 10 to 13. For general guidance on how they work and where to get information about them, see Chapters 16 to 18.

Packaged investments

Packaged investments are branded off-the-shelf products, including: personal pensions (including stakeholder schemes), annuities, insurance-based investments (such as endowment insurance, whole life policies, with-profits bonds and unit-linked insurance), unit trusts, open-ended investment companies (OEICs), investment trust savings schemes and individual savings accounts (ISAs) and personal equity plans (PEPs) that invest in these sorts of investment.

A firm described as an 'independent financial adviser' must be able to recommend suitable products for you from the full range on the market. Other types of adviser, including most banks and building societies, can only advise on and sell you the products of either just one or a handful of providers. If they can recommend just one provider's products they are called 'tied advisers'. If they can recommend several providers' products, they are 'multi-tied'.

If a tied or multi-tied adviser does not have anything suitable for you within their range they must tell you this, but might be able to arrange for you to buy an 'out-of-range' product from another provider.

By mid-2005, on first contact with an adviser, you must be given an Initial Disclosure Document (IDD) – see Chapter 3 – which tells you what type of advice the adviser can give you.

From spring 2005, employers can give you advice about a personal pension or stakeholder scheme at work provided the employer pays into the scheme on your behalf and does not itself derive commercial benefit from the scheme. Employers do not need to be authorised (see page 32) to give this advice.

Changing times

Firms selling or advising on packaged investments used to be covered by rules known as 'polarisation', which meant they either dealt with the products of just one company or were independent and could recommend from the whole market. From 1 December 2004, polarisation is scrapped, though firms have a six-month transitional period during which they must switch to the new rules. The new rules also include a third option ('multi-tied') under which firms can deal with the products of a handful of companies. As part of the changes, firms must issue you with new documents (see Chapter 3) making clear their status and the products they sell.

Other investments

These are assets such as shares, gilts and corporate bonds sold on stock markets and similar trading exchanges. You can think of them as building blocks that you can use if you prefer to build your own investment portfolio rather than buying a ready-made packaged product. The main type of adviser you would use is a stockbroker. Any advice must be independent.

Mortgage advice

Since 31 October 2004, advice about most mortgages is regulated by the FSA. Advisers must comply with rules which are similar to those for investment advice, for example:

- **type of advice**. On first contact, the adviser must tell you whether the advice will be based on products from a single lender (tied advice), a number of lenders (multi-tied advice) or the whole market (independent advice). This information will be included in an Initial Disclosure Document (IDD) – see Chapter 3
- **suitability**. A recommendation by the adviser must be suitable given the information you have provided about yourself and your needs. In assessing suitability, the adviser must be reasonably sure that you can afford the payments and should draw your attention to any risks, such as the possibility of payments increasing if interest rates rise.

Buy-to-let mortgages are not covered by the above rules, nor are mortgages on your own home which are not the first charge. (A 'first charge' is the loan that would have to be paid off first if your home were sold). For information about mortgages, see Chapter 9.

Equity release scheme advice

Equity release schemes are arrangements where you raise a lump sum or extra income by taking out a mortgage on your home (called a lifetime mortgage) or selling part of your home (called a home reversion scheme).

Since 31 October 2004, lifetime mortgages are regulated by the FSA. The rules about type of advice are the same as for mortgages (see above) and they apply also to home reversion schemes if the firm also offers these.

Additional rules set out how advisers are to ensure that any recommended lifetime mortgage is suitable for you. As well as weighing up the features of the lifetime mortgage, including risks inherent in the scheme, the adviser must also take into account the following factors:

- any impact on means-tested state benefits (such as pension credit and council tax benefit)
- any impact on your tax position (through loss of age allowance)
- whether other arrangements, such as a home reversion scheme or local authority grant, would be more suitable, and
- your plans for passing on your estate when you die.

Although the availability and general suitability of home reversion schemes must be taken into account, home reversion schemes are not currently covered by the detailed FSA rules. This means you are not protected in the same way if you are badly advised to take out a home reversion scheme as you would be when taking out a lifetime mortgage (see Chapter 3). The government has announced that the FSA will take over the regulation of home reversion schemes from a future date (unlikely to be before 2006).

For information about equity release schemes, see Chapter 13.

Insurance advice

Any insurance with an investment element (such as an endowment or whole life policy) is covered by the investment advice rules described on page 18.

Advice about long-term care insurance (see Chapter 14) has been subject to FSA rules since 31 October 2004. Since 14 January 2005, the FSA also regulates advice about most other non-investment insurance including, for example, term insurance (see Chapter 6), car, home and travel policies, mortgage payment protection cover (see Chapter 9), income protection insurance (see Chapter 7) and private medical insurance (see Chapter 8). The main types of insurance advice not subject to FSA rules are travel insurance when sold along as part of a holiday package, and extended warranties when sold in conjunction with the goods covered.

The FSA rules governing non-investment insurance advice include the following requirements:

- **type of advice**. Before concluding a contract with you, advisers must tell you whether their advice is based on the products of a single provider (tied advice), a limited number of providers (multi-tied advice), or a fair analysis of the market (which, although this need not cover the whole market, basically counts as independent advice). Advisers must also tell you if any provider has a significant stake in the adviser's firm (since this might influence the advice given). Information about the type of advice does not have to be given at the time if you are just shopping around for quick quotes

* **suitable advice**. The adviser should ensure that any policy recommended is suitable for you given your demands and needs. The adviser should seek relevant information from you including, for example, the risks you want to insure against and any existing cover you already have. The adviser must explain to you your duty to disclose all 'material facts' (any factors that might influence an insurer's decision to insure you or the terms on which it might offer cover). In assessing suitability, the adviser must take into account the possible impact on you of any exclusions, excesses, limitations and conditions in the policy.

Occupational pension scheme advice

In general, to find out about an occupational pension scheme offered through your job, you should talk to the pensions administrator★ at work or the pension scheme trustees★. They can give you information about the scheme but are unlikely to give advice.

If you are considering transferring pension rights you have built up in an occupational scheme to another pension arrangement, you might seek advice from an independent financial adviser★ (see page 19) or, if a large sum is involved, a consulting actuary★. Consulting actuaries are regulated by their professional body (for example, the Institute of Actuaries★) and are required to give you independent advice.

General financial advice

An adviser might recommend you take out a variety of different financial products, for example, some insurance and some investments. The adviser must comply with the advice rules outlined above for each type of product. Confusingly, an adviser might be independent for investment advice but, say, multi-tied when giving mortgage advice. And, where an adviser is tied to certain companies for one product, he or she might be tied to different companies for another product. You therefore need to check the type of advice that can be offered for each type of product.

Information or advice?

Take care not to confuse information with advice. Advisers regulated by the FSA must make clear to you at the outset whether they offer an advice service or only information. Some products, such as stakeholder pensions (see Chapter 12) are deemed to be straightforward enough to be sold without advice. You may instead be given or guided through 'stakeholder decision trees' designed to help you make your own choice, but this does not count as advice. If you buy without taking advice, you lose some of the protection available to consumers in the event of something going wrong (see Chapter 3).

Basic advice

From April 2005, a new suite of stakeholder products is due to become available (see Chapter 17). Most of these can be sold through a new 'basic advice' regime. A basic adviser uses filter questions and a ready-prepared script to check whether a stakeholder product is suitable for you based on limited information about you. The adviser can offer you any or all of the different stakeholder products (e.g. child trust fund, medium-term investment product, stakeholder pension) but, for each one can offer only the product from a single provider. This could be a different provider for each product. The firm the adviser works for must be authorised. The adviser must be competent but does not need to hold a financial advice qualification. You have the protection of the Financial Ombudsman Service (see Chapter 3).

How advisers are paid

Advisers who are employed by a product provider are normally paid a salary but might also receive bonuses or commission according to the amount they sell.

Tied and multi-tied agents usually receive commission from the provider each time they sell a product from that provider. Different providers pay different amounts of commission. How much each one pays on each product to each agent is a commercial decision.

Where to go for advice

Financial product	Type of advice you want	Main type of adviser	How to find this type of adviser
Savings	Tied	Product provider (bank, building society, National Savings & Investments)	Go direct to provider
	Independent	Independent financial adviser (but only as part of more general advice)	IFA Promotion* Institute of Financial Planning* Personal Finance Society*
Packaged investments (eg personal pensions [1] and unit trusts) or General financial advice	Tied or multi-tied	Product provider/distributor [2] or its appointed representative [3]	Product provider/distributor Banks, building societies *Yellow Pages* Internet search engine
	Independent	Independent financial adviser	IFA Promotion* Institute of Financial Planning* Personal Finance Society*
Other investments	Independent	Stockbroker	Association of Private Client Investment Managers (APCIMS)* London Stock Exchange*
Mortgages	Tied or multi-tied	Product provider/distributor [2] or its appointed representative [3]	Product provider/distributor Banks, building societies *Yellow Pages* Internet search engine
	Independent	Independent broker	[4]
Equity release schemes	Tied or multi-tied	Product provider/distributor [2] or its appointed representative [3]	Safe Home Income Plans*
	Independent	Independent financial adviser	IFA Promotion* Institute of Financial Planning* Personal Finance Society*

General insurance	Tied or multi-tied	Product provider/distributor [2] or its appointed representative [3]	Product provider/distributor Banks, building societies *Yellow Pages* Internet search engine
	Independent	Insurance broker	British Insurance Brokers Association*
Term insurance or health insurance	Tied or multi-tied	Product provider/distributor [2] or its appointed representative [3]	Product provider/distributor Banks, building societies *Yellow Pages* Internet search engine
	Independent	Insurance broker Independent financial adviser	British Insurance Brokers Association* IFA Promotion* Institute of Financial Planning* Personal Finance Society*
Occupational pension schemes	Tied or multi-tied	**For details of your own scheme or a new employer's scheme:** scheme officials **For transfers to a personal pension:** product provider/distributor [2] or its appointed representative [3]	Pension scheme administrator* Pension scheme trustees* Product provider/distributor Banks Building societies
	Independent	Independent financial adviser Consulting actuary	IFA Promotion* Institute of Financial Planning* Personal Finance Society* Association of Consulting Actuaries* Society of Pension Consultants*

[1] From spring 2005 employers will be able to give you advice about a personal pension or stakeholder scheme at work provided the employer pays into the scheme on your behalf and does not itself derive commercial benefit from the scheme. Employers do not need to be authorised to give this advice.
[2] A provider might offer just its own products. Alternatively, it may have adopted the products of other provider(s) into its range and so be able to offer you a wider choice. Some firms, called 'distributors', do not have their own products at all but offer those from a selection of providers.
[3] An appointed representative is a firm which acts as an agent of another firm (called the 'principal'), such as a provider. The representative sells/advises on some or all of the products available from the principal. Appointed representatives come in many forms. For example, many banks and building societies are appointed representatives selling the mortgages, insurance and investments of another firm; estate agents often act as appointed representatives for mortgage lenders; travel agents may be appointed representatives for travel insurers; shops and lenders may be appointed representatives for insurers offering loan payment protection insurance, and so on. See Chapter 3 for more information about appointed representatives.
[4] At the time of writing, there is no central directory you can contact to be sent a list of independent mortgage brokers. Organisations that can help you find an independent financial adviser (eg IFA Promotion*, the Institute of Financial Planning*, or Personal Finance Society*) can tell you whether an adviser's service includes independent mortgage advice. For other mortgage advisers, use *Yellow Pages* and Internet search engines but check that the adviser is independent before doing business.

25

Commissions may be in the form of a lump sum ('initial commission') at the time of sale, smaller amounts (called 'renewal commission' or 'trail commission') paid each month or year that the product remains in force, or a mixture of the two. You indirectly pay the commission through the charges built into the product. The table below shows some examples of typical commission payments.

Independent advisers may be paid either by commission, in the same way as tied and multi-tied agents or by a fee paid direct by you to the adviser.

Mortgage advisers and, from mid-2005, investment advisers who call themselves 'independent' must let you pay by fee if you want to. This might be the only way to pay or you might have the option of commission instead. See Chapter 1 for the pros and cons of each way to pay.

Examples of typical commission payments

Type of product	Commission rate	Example
Unit trust individual savings account (ISA)	3% initial plus 0.5% renewal	You invest £7,000. The adviser gets 3% × £7,000 = £210 at the time you invest. If the value of your investment did not change, he would also get 0.5% × £7,000 = £35 each year; but he will get more if your investment grows.
With-profits bond	6.75% initial	You invest £10,000. The adviser gets 6.75% × £10,000 = £675 at the time you invest.
Repayment mortgage	0.35% of the advance	You borrow £50,000. The adviser gets 0.35% × £50,000 = £175
Equity release scheme	3% of amount raised	You raise £30,000, the adviser gets 3% × £30,000 = £900
Income protection insurance	140% of the first year's premiums	You pay £30 a month, adviser gets 140% × £30 × 12 = £504

Sources: *Moneyfacts Investments Life & Pensions, Moneyfacts*

Commission rebates

Many advisers are willing to forgo part of their commission in order to attract your custom. The amount forgone – called the 'commission rebate' – is usually used to increase the amount invested in the product you are buying or enhance in some other way the benefits you'll get from the product. Occasionally, you receive a rebate as a cash lump sum. Some advisers (often called discount brokers) specialise in discount business and offer commission rebates as standard. With others, it's a matter for negotiation.

Do not be shy of asking about commission rebates. Nowadays most providers offer a 'commission menu' so that the adviser can choose either, say, a high commission or a lower one coupled with enhanced benefits for the client. Moreover, the market for financial advice is very competitive, and you have a lot of consumer power – so use it.

To negotiate a rebate, follow these steps:

- Ask what commission the adviser stands to get if you invest in or buy the recommended product.
- If you have seen the commission payable on similar products and know this particular commission looks high, or if you know the deal a discount business could get for you, use this information as a basis for deciding on the rough amount of commission rebate you are seeking. From mid-2005, investment advisers must on first contact give you a document entitled 'A guide to the cost of our services'. This includes comparative information about the commission other advisers receive – see Chapter 3.
- Ask what rebate the adviser is willing to consider or what enhanced terms he or she can get for you.
- Be prepared to haggle.
- If you cannot get the commission rebate you think is reasonable, be prepared to take your custom elsewhere.

Negotiate a rebate

If you pay for advice on a commission basis, the commission earned could be more than the real cost of advice you receive. So a proportion of the commission could be given back to you. Here's an example of how much you could save:

A couple each invest £7,000 in a stocks-and-shares ISA
Amount invested: £7,000 × 2 = £14,000
Upfront charge at 5%: 0.05 × £14,000 = £700
The adviser receives commission of 3%: 0.03 × £14,000 = £420
If the adviser agrees to take 1% instead of 3%, the commission is: 0.01 × £14,000 = £140
The total cost drops from 5% to 3%, saving you £420 – £140 = £280.

Which? November 2001

Could you be your own financial adviser?

Because you know your circumstances intimately, you are in the best position to identify your financial aims. However, you could fail to recognise aims which you should be weaving into your financial structure, unless you take a dispassionate and systematic look at your finances. Chapter 4 will help you do this.

Be aware that there is seldom just one solution which is definitely the best. Usually, there is a range of options of broadly equal merit. Even so, recognising those options as the suitable ones for you does require:

- a good knowledge of the financial system
- a good knowledge of the broad types of product available
- an understanding of how these broad products can be matched to your needs and situation
- good information about the specific products on the market and how to compare them.

Chapters 5–18 will introduce you to tools, techniques and information sources. At one time it was very hard to access and use these as readily and effectively as an experienced, well-equipped professional. However, in recent years, life has become much easier for the d-i-y adviser. If you have access to the Internet, you can find an enormous amount of information covering, for example:

- **company and product details** on individual company websites and IFA sites; with many, you can even transact your business over the Internet
- **general financial guidance** on independent websites, including regulators' sites such as that of the FSA★, or the sites of trade bodies, such as the Association of British Insurers (ABI)★, Investment Management Association (IMA)★ or the British Bankers' Association (BBA)★
- **personal finance websites★** – for example, FT Your Money, MoneyeXtra and Money Supermarket – that have a wealth of general information as well as tools to help you make decisions and organise your finances, and search facilities to help you find the best deals
- **calculators** both at company and personal finance sites, which crunch the numbers for you, helping you to work out how much

to save, what your mortgage might cost, and so on. Some, like the *Which?*★ online mortgage calculator, also take you through a series of questions to narrow the choice and produce a selection of mortgages with the features you have specified

- **comparative information** that lists the main features of products from different companies in a standard way so that you can readily make comparisons to help you shop around. You'll find this information on some personal finance sites and specialist sites like Moneyfacts★. The FSA★ publishes its own comparative tables. At the time of writing, these cover unit trust and oeic ISAs, personal pensions, stakeholder pensions, pension annuities, investment bonds, savings endowments, mortgage endowments and mortgages

- **online information booklets** produced by government departments, the FSA★, trade organisations, complaints bodies and so on

- **background information** on, for example, Budget changes, government press releases, legal information and so on.

Much of this information is also available to non-Internet users by phone or post. Bear in mind that, increasingly, you can get on to the Internet at public libraries, cybercafés and all sorts of other public places.

To sum up, good financial advice is the successful marrying of financial tools to personal details. At one extreme, you can simply hand your personal details to an adviser and leave him or her to do the rest. But at the other extreme, you can take over finding the financial tools and become, in effect, your own adviser. However, there is a halfway house which has a lot to recommend it. You can learn the broad principles of financial planning and block in your own 'financial skeleton' before you seek advice. Your adviser and you will then be able to work together efficiently in partnership to choose the appropriate covering for your financial bones. This will save both of you time – and save you money, if you are using a fee-based adviser. You will also be well armed to spot rogue advisers and protect yourself against deliberate or careless mis-selling.

In practice, you are likely to find that, some of the time, your own counsel is adequate. But in new or complex areas, such as pension planning or inheritance tax, it is well worth supplementing your own research with the opinion of advisers. In some provinces of financial planning, you should be especially wary of doing without professional advice; for example, if you have a farm or run your own business, are involved in family trusts or have investments abroad. Bear in mind that the more specialist your financial affairs are, the more specialist the advice you will require. Check carefully to ensure that the advisers you select have the expertise you need.

Chapter 3

Protection when you buy

Buying financial products or services usually involves trusting strangers to look after your money, so you want to be sure that the firms you deal with are honest, soundly run and are giving you straightforward, reliable information about their wares. The UK system of financial regulation aims to ensure this is the case.

The Financial Services and Markets Act 2000 makes it illegal to carry on most types of financial business in the UK without being either authorised by the financial regulator or specifically exempt from regulation. This applies whether a firm provides products, arranges deals involving them, gives advice about them, and so on. The regulator is the Financial Services Authority (FSA)★.

How you are protected

FSA regulation applies to most financial products and services, as shown in the table overleaf. The main exceptions are:

- **borrowing** Mortgages to buy a home lived in by you or your family and which are a 'first charge' on the home are mostly regulated by the FSA. ('First charge' means, if the home were sold, this loan would have to be paid off out of the proceeds first before any other loan.) However, most other types of borrowing, including buy-to-let mortgages, are governed by the rules set out in the Consumer Credit Act 1974 and come within the remit of the Office of Fair Trading and, at grass-roots level, local Trading Standards Offices

- **home reversion schemes** These are due to be regulated by the FSA from a future date which is unlikely to be before 2006. Some

How you are protected

	Type of financial product										
	Most mortgages	Other borrowing	Lifetime mortgages	Home reversion schemes	National Savings & Investments (NS&I)	Other savings	Most investments including investment-type life insurance	Personal pensions	Occupational pensions	Long-term care insurance	Other non-investment insurance
Regulator (see below for abbreviations)	FSA	OFT	FSA		HMT	FSA	FSA	FSA	PR	FSA	FSA
Checks to ensure firm is solvent, honestly and prudently run and that key people are 'fit and proper'	✓	[2]	✓	[1]	[3]	[5]	✓	✓	[4]	✓	✓
Rules governing the way a firm deals with its customers	✓	✓	✓	[2]	[5]	[5]	✓	✓	✓	✓	✓
You must be provided with information in a standard format about the service a firm provides and what the service costs	✓	✗	✓	[1]	[5]	✗	✓	✓	✗	✓	✗
You must be provided with information about the products in which you are interested in a standard format to help you compare one product with another	✓	✗	✓	✗	✗	✗	✓	✓	✗	✓	✗
Usually you have a cooling off period during which you can change your mind and cancel a deal without penalty	✗	[6]	✓	[2]	✗	[7]	✓	✓	✗	✓	✓
Complaints procedures	✓	[2]	✓	[2]	✓	✓	✓	✓	✓	✓	✓
Compensation scheme	[8]	✗	[8]	✗	[3]	✓	✓	✓	[9]	✓	✓

FSA = Financial Services Authority; OFT = Office of Fair Trading; HMT = HM Treasury; PR = Pensions Regulator (from April 2005. Occupational Pensions Regulatory Authority before then).
[1] No statutory regulation. Firms who have chosen to join are subject to voluntary regulation by Safe Home Income Plans (SHIP).
[2] Yes, if the firm is a bank, building society or insurance company. Otherwise no statutory requirement.
[3] The government is directly responsible for running of NS&I. It could draw on taxpayers money to make good any loss
[4] More rigorous rules being introduced during 2005.
[5] Most providers have voluntarily agreed to abide by the Banking Code. Copy available from the provider on request.
[6] Yes, if you sign a credit agreement other than at the lender's premises.
[7] Generally no, but yes in the case of cash ISAs.
[8] Generally no, but yes in the case of advice about these products.
[9] Compensation schemes apply in some circumstances.

providers have joined a voluntary scheme of regulation run by a trade body called Safe Home Income Plans (SHIP)★

* **National Savings & Investments (NS&I)** NS&I is an agency which offers and runs savings products on behalf of the government. Rules governing these are set out in Acts of Parliament and regulations made under the Acts
* **occupational pension schemes** These are covered by a completely separate system of regulation. For details of the compensation arrangements that might apply if things go wrong, see page 47. For details of some other aspects, see Chapter 12.

When you are protected

You are protected by the FSA rules provided you deal with an 'authorised' firm directly or the agent of an authorised firm.

If you deal with a firm which is not authorised, you are not protected. Therefore, it is very important to check that a firm is authorised before you start to do business with it. To check authorisation, consult the FSA Register★.

Checking the FSA Register

You can check a firm's entry on the FSA Register★ either online or by phone. If you use the online service, follow the links to 'Firm and Person Check'. You use the Firm Check service to check whether a firm is authorised and the Person Check Service to check whether a named person (for example, an adviser you have previously used) is active and working for an authorised firm. The table overleaf explains how the Register can help you decide whether to do business with a firm.

As well as telling you whether a firm is authorised, the Register tells you the sort of business the firm is allowed to carry out (in each firm's entry under 'Permissions'). It is important to check the 'Permissions' because, for example, many firms of advisers are not allowed to handle clients' money (in which case you should, for example, write cheques direct to providers).

Mortgage advisers were newly required to become authorised by the FSA from 31 October 2004. Some firms which failed to meet this deadline have been given 'interim authorisation' for up to a year. This means they can legally trade and must abide by FSA

What the FSA Register tells you

Firm's authorisation status shown on the Register	What does it mean?	Is it OK to do business with this firm?
Authorised	The firm is authorised by the FSA	**Yes.** If something goes wrong, the Financial Ombudsman Service can deal with your complaint and you might qualify for redress from the Financial Services Compensation Scheme
Exempt - appointed representative	The firm is not authorised but it works as an agent for another firm which is authorised (called the 'principal') – see page 34	**Yes.** You have exactly the same protection as if you were dealing directly with the principal. Check on the Register to find out who the principal is
Exempt - professional firm	The firm is not authorised. Its financial business is incidental to its mainstream work (for example, as a solicitor or accountant) and its Designated Professional Body* regulates its activities including its financial business	**Yes.** But, if something goes wrong, you use the professional body's complaints and compensation arrangements not those of the FSA
EEA authorised	The firm is authorised not by the FSA but by an equivalent regulator abroad	**Yes.** But, if something goes wrong, you use the overseas regulator's complaints and compensation arrangements not those of the FSA
No longer authorised	The firm is not authorised and it is illegal for it to be doing business in the UK	**No.** You have no protection if anything goes wrong
Not on the Register – interim authorised	The firm is awaiting a final decision on whether or not it qualifies for authorisation	**Probably.** But, if something goes wrong, you are not covered by compensation arrangements
Not on the Register – any other reason	The firm is not authorised and it is illegal for it to be doing business in the UK	**No.** You have no protection if anything goes wrong

rules (see Chapter 2). If anything goes wrong, you can use the Financial Ombudsman Service (see page 44) but you are not covered by the Financial Services Compensation Scheme (see page 46). Interim authorised firms are not on the FSA Register but must tell you that this is their status. Interim authorisation also applies to some non-investment insurance advisers for a variety of reasons following their entry to FSA regulation from 14 January 2005 onwards.

Appointed representatives

Many firms are not themselves authorised by the FSA and are instead 'appointed representatives' working for an authorised firm. The firm they work for is called their 'principal'.

Appointed representatives come in all shapes and sizes. Many banks and building societies are appointed representatives. Insurance agents, travel agents selling holiday insurance, estate agents arranging mortgages, and shops arranging loan protection insurance are all appointed representatives. Many large businesses arrange for one part of the organisation to be authorised and for various subsidiaries to act as its appointed representatives. Appointed representatives may be tied (able to sell just one provider's products), multi-tied (able to sell products from several providers) or independent (able to sell any product on the market) – see box on page 36.

An appointed representative can have only one principal for each of the following types of business: investments, mortgages and lifetime mortgages. For example, a firm might be the representative of one provider for investments and another different provider for mortgages. The principal for each type of business is responsible for the conduct of its appointed representatives. If you have any problem with the appointed representative, you can complain to the principal and you have all the same protection and rights as if you were doing business directly with the principal.

In the case of non-investment insurance, a firm can simultane-ously be an appointed representative for more than one principal. Where this happens, the principals must elect one of their number to act as 'lead principal'. That will be the firm you deal with if you have a problem with the appointed representative.

Tied, multi-tied and independent representatives
Appointed representatives may be tied, multi-tied or independent:

- **tied** The appointed representative works for a single provider that offers only its own products
- **multi-tied** The representative works for:
  - a single provider that has adopted the products of other providers into its range
  - a 'distributor' firm – in other words a principal that has no products of its own but offers a range of products from several providers
  - several different providers; this is possible only in the case of non-investment insurance
- **independent** The principal may itself be an independent firm. Alternatively, the principal might be an 'independent network'. This is an umbrella firm for financial advisers that sorts out the authorisation requirements and often also offers centralised services, such as research and back-office administration, leaving its appointed representatives to get on with the main business of giving advice.

To check the status of an adviser, ask for the Initial Disclosure Document (see opposite).

Important information
The FSA requires some firms to give customers information about themselves and their products in a standard format. These documents tell you important information in a clear way without marketing hype, and can help you when you are shopping around for a good deal. You can pick out these documents from all the other literature you get because they carry the FSA's key facts logo (see page 38). If you read nothing else, at least read the documents bearing this logo.

Standardised information about a firm

With some financial products, the FSA requires firms to give you information in a set format so that you can more easily see what sort of service you are being offered, know what the service will cost and compare what's on offer from different firms.

Initial disclosure document (IOD)

If you go to a firm dealing with mortgages regulated by the FSA, lifetime mortgages or, by mid-2005, packaged investments (see page 18) or long-term care insurance, on first contact the firm must give you an Initial Disclosure Document (IDD).

The IDD tells you about the service you will get from the firm, including:

- which provider(s) the firm deals with; for example, the whole market if the firm is independent, or named provider(s) in the case of a tied or multi-tied agent
- whether or not you will be given advice
- what you will have to pay for any advice
- what to do if you have a complaint
- whether the firm is covered by the Financial Services Compensation Scheme.

Non-investment insurance firms don't have to give you an IDD unless the insurance is being supplied in conjunction with a mortgage or investment. But the firm must still give you similar information before any contract is concluded (or soon afterwards if you have bought over the phone).

A guide to the cost of our services

By mid-2005, if you seek advice about packaged investments (see page 18) or long-term care insurance, along with the IDD (see above), you must be given a document called 'A guide to the cost of our services' (also called 'the menu'). Using a standard format, this sets out your options for paying for the advice (fee, commission of a choice) and how much the advice might cost.

If the firm charges a fee, the document will set out the fee rate that you will be charged. If the firm is paid by commission, the document must include a table showing the maximum commission the firm will get for selling different types of product. The table must also include the average commission paid across the market as a whole so you have some idea of whether this firm will be paid less, more or in line with other advisers.

The document helps you compare the cost of advice from different sources when you are shopping around for an adviser. The average commission rates are useful if you intend to try negotiating a commission rebate (see page 27).

Standardised information about products

Key facts document

When you enquire about a packaged investment or long-term care insurance, you will be given a key facts document (KFD). (In some cases, you may instead be given a 'key features document' – this is a forerunner of the KFD, showing broadly the same information, but in a different format. Key features documents are being phased out and replaced by KFDs.)

The KFD summarises important information about a specific product including, for example, who the product is aimed at and what needs it addresses, your commitment (for example, whether you must invest on a regular basis), the risks inherent in the product (such as whether the value of the investment can fall and whether you might lose some of your money if you cash in early), choices you might have to make (such as in which fund to invest your money) and where to get more information.

The KFD includes a key facts example. This is personalised to you and shows how the charges for the investment might affect the return you get over a span of years based on set assumptions – see page 40. You can use these figures to compare the cost of the product with other similar products.

If you have a particular target – for example, building up a certain amount of pension by retirement or building up a lump sum to pay off a mortgage at the end of its term – the key facts example will also show how much you might get back at the end of the target period, again based on set assumptions. This is just an estimate but helps you to work out whether you are saving enough to meet your target.

In the case of pensions, the estimate of what you might get is also shown in today's money – see below. This helps you to make allowance for the way inflation eats into the buying power of your money over the years. To counter the effect of inflation, you'll need to save extra.

What is 'today's money'?

If you are saving or investing to pay for future spending, you need to allow for the effect of inflation because rising prices reduce the buying power of your money.

For example, suppose you currently spend £100 on your weekly groceries. If prices rose over the next ten years by 2.5 per cent a year, you would need £128 to buy the same basket of groceries. If you still had just £100 to spend, you would be able to buy only the equivalent of £78 of groceries at today's prices. So £100 in ten years' time would be worth just £78 in today's money.

Key facts illustration

When you enquire about a specific mortgage or lifetime mortgage, you will be given a key facts illustration (KFI) describing the important features of the mortgage in a set format. Typically, as you shop around, you might collect KFIs for several mortgages, and these documents will help you compare one with another to see which offers the best value and best meets your needs.

The KFI for a mortgage includes a summary of the information you provided and on which the KFI is based (for example, the amount you want to borrow and over what period), the type of mortgage (for example, repayment or interest-only), the overall cost of the mortgage – see page 42, the monthly payments, risks inherent in the mortgage (such as the monthly payments rising if interest rates change), charges, insurance you are required to take out, and so on.

The KFI for a lifetime mortgage includes a summary of the information you have supplied (such as your age and the amount you wish to borrow), description of the mortgage (for example, the type of interest), charges, if applicable the amount of income you'll receive after deducting any mortgage repayments and charges, the risks involved and important things to consider (for example, what

Key facts example for an investment showing the effect of charges

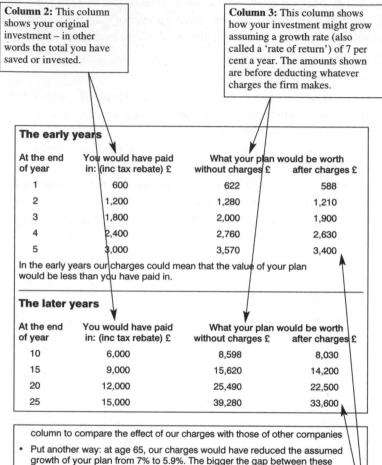

Column 2: This column shows your original investment – in other words the total you have saved or invested.

Column 3: This column shows how your investment might grow assuming a growth rate (also called a 'rate of return') of 7 per cent a year. The amounts shown are before deducting whatever charges the firm makes.

The early years

At the end of year	You would have paid in: (inc tax rebate) £	What your plan would be worth without charges £	after charges £
1	600	622	588
2	1,200	1,280	1,210
3	1,800	2,000	1,900
4	2,400	2,760	2,630
5	3,000	3,570	3,400

In the early years our charges could mean that the value of your plan would be less than you have paid in.

The later years

At the end of year	You would have paid in: (inc tax rebate) £	What your plan would be worth without charges £	after charges £
10	6,000	8,598	8,030
15	9,000	15,620	14,200
20	12,000	25,490	22,500
25	15,000	39,280	33,600

column to compare the effect of our charges with those of other companies

- Put another way: at age 65, our charges would have reduced the assumed growth of your plan from 7% to 5.9%. The bigger the gap between these two rates, the more expensive the plan.

Reduction in yield (RIY): This shows the fall in your yearly return because of the charges. The bigger the fall, the more expensive the product. You can use this figure to compare the cost of one product with another. In the example here, charges cut the return from 7 per cent to 5.9 per cent, so charges take 1.1 per cent. Another plan that reduced the yield to say 6.2 per cent (a fall of 0.8 per cent) would be cheaper.

Column 4: This column shows the actual return (also called the 'yield') you might get once the provider's charges have been deducted. The higher the figure, the better the return. If the figure is less than the amount in column 2, you'd get back less than you had invested. You can compare this column with the same column for another similar product to see which looks cheapest.

Key facts example for a pension showing the effect of inflation

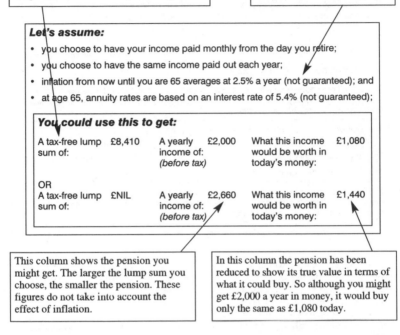

This example shows what you might get back from a personal pension at a chosen retirement age of 65. The fund has built to £33,600 and you can choose to take part as a lump sum. The rest must be taken as pension.

No-one knows what will actually happen between now and reaching age 65, so the figures shown are estimates based on the assumptions listed.

Let's assume:

• you choose to have your income paid monthly from the day you retire;

• you choose to have the same income paid out each year;

• inflation from now until you are 65 averages at 2.5% a year (not guaranteed); and

• at age 65, annuity rates are based on an interest rate of 5.4% (not guaranteed);

You could use this to get:

| A tax-free lump sum of: | £8,410 | A yearly income of: (before tax) | £2,000 | What this income would be worth in today's money: | £1,080 |
| OR A tax-free lump sum of: | £NIL | A yearly income of: (before tax) | £2,660 | What this income would be worth in today's money: | £1,440 |

This column shows the pension you might get. The larger the lump sum you choose, the smaller the pension. These figures do not take into account the effect of inflation.

In this column the pension has been reduced to show its true value in terms of what it could buy. So although you might get £2,000 a year in money, it would buy only the same as £1,080 today.

happens if you move home, what happens if you marry, the obligation on you to maintain your home, warning that inflation will erode the value of your income over time, the impact, if any, of changing interest rates), statement of the amount you owe and when (for example, taking into account any interest which is 'rolled up' to be repaid along with the original sum borrowed), and so on.

Information about non-investment insurance

In good time before you take out non-investment insurance (such as some types of health insurance, house and car insurance, and so on), you must be given certain information, including a policy summary and statement of price. In addition, orally your attention must be drawn to any significant or unusual terms in the contract.

Key facts illustration for a mortgage showing the overall cost of a mortgage

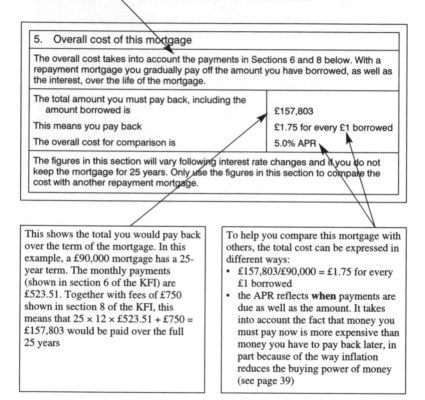

This part of the KFI tells you about the cost of the particular mortgage covered by the KFI. It can be used to help you compare one mortgage with another. The figures include interest, capital repayments and certain charges, such as arrangement fees, valuation fee and legal costs, but they do not include the cost of any charges or what you would have to save each month to pay off an interest-only loan at the end of its term.

5. Overall cost of this mortgage

The overall cost takes into account the payments in Sections 6 and 8 below. With a repayment mortgage you gradually pay off the amount you have borrowed, as well as the interest, over the life of the mortgage.

The total amount you must pay back, including the amount borrowed is	£157,803
This means you pay back	£1.75 for every £1 borrowed
The overall cost for comparison is	5.0% APR

The figures in this section will vary following interest rate changes and if you do not keep the mortgage for 25 years. Only use the figures in this section to compare the cost with another repayment mortgage.

This shows the total you would pay back over the term of the mortgage. In this example, a £90,000 mortgage has a 25-year term. The monthly payments (shown in section 6 of the KFI) are £523.51. Together with fees of £750 shown in section 8 of the KFI, this means that 25 × 12 × £523.51 + £750 = £157,803 would be paid over the full 25 years

To help you compare this mortgage with others, the total cost can be expressed in different ways:
- £157,803/£90,000 = £1.75 for every £1 borrowed
- the APR reflects **when** payments are due as well as the amount. It takes into account the fact that money you must pay now is more expensive than money you have to pay back later, in part because of the way inflation reduces the buying power of money (see page 39)

The policy summary is a key document detailing the main features of the policy, contact details, your cancellation rights, what to do if you have a complaint, and so on. It must carry the key facts logo. The summary must either be a separate document or, if included in other literature, clearly separated out as key information. If the insurer or agent producing the summary prefers, it can instead give you this information in a full-blown key facts document – which you can easily recognise because it will carry the key facts logo (see page 36).

Cooling-off periods

With many financial products, you have a cooling-off period during which you can change your mind and back out of the deal without penalty. This can be a useful breather in which to reconsider whether you really need this product and whether it is the best deal for you. The literature you are sent after entering into the deal will include a notice telling you if you have a cooling-off period and how long it is. The table below summarises the minimum period you usually get.

Time to change your mind

Type of product	Usual cooling-off period	Comment
Life insurance and pensions	14 days	Whether or not you receive advice
Unit trusts and open-ended investment companies (oeics)	14 days (or may be reduced to 7 days if within an individual savings account (ISA))	Only if you have received advice. Otherwise no cooling-off period
Other stocks-and-shares ISAs	7 days	Only if you have received advice. Otherwise no cooling-off period
Cash ISAs	14 days	
Other investments	Usually none	
Mortgages and lifetime mortgages	Usually none	But 7 days for any tied product if it was not included in the offer document
Term life insurance, critical illness cover	30 days	
Other non-investment insurance	14 days	

What to do if you have a complaint
Complain to the firm

If you are not happy with the service from, or conduct of, a financial firm, you should first complain to the firm or the branch of it with which you were dealing. If you are not happy with the response, take your complaint higher within the firm, for example to the managing director or head office. If you still do not receive a satisfactory response, the company is obliged to tell you how to take your complaint further.

All firms within the FSA's jurisdiction are required to:

* have a formal complaints system
* publish details about the system and send these to consumers as soon as a complaint is made
* publicise the availability of the system and membership of the ombudsman scheme (see below)
* give a substantive response to a complaint within eight weeks. The response might agree with your complaint, disagree or say that more time is needed to investigate the matter fully. If it disagrees, you can take your case to the ombudsman scheme. The firm should set out its final decision in writing (sometimes called a 'letter of deadlock') together with details of how you can contact the ombudsman.

The FSA Register★ and any IDD (see page 37) contain details of who you should contact within a firm if you have a complaint.

Independent complaints bodies

The Financial Ombudsman Service (FOS)★ is a one-stop shop for most complaints about financial products and is the largest ombudsman scheme in the world. If a firm has failed to resolve a complaint to your satisfaction, you can usually ask the FOS to look at it provided the firm is a member of the scheme.

Firms authorised by the FSA must belong to the FOS. Other firms have voluntarily agreed to join. At the time of writing, National Savings & Investments (NS&I) was in the process of joining the FOS (but until it does so is covered by the NS&I Independent Adjudicator★). From April 2006, most complaints about borrowing and credit are also due to come within the remit of the FOS. Until then, complaints about loans can be dealt with by the Finance and Leasing Association (FLA) Arbitration Scheme★ provided the firm is a member of the FLA.

The main complaints the FOS cannot deal with are those against occupational pension schemes. If the scheme is unable to settle the matter, it should be referred to the Pensions Advisory Service★

(OPAS). If OPAS can't resolve the dispute you can take it to the Pensions Ombudsman*.

All the complaints schemes mentioned in this section are free for you to use. If you are unhappy with a decision made by the FOS, you can take your case to court (see below). Decisions of the Pensions Ombudsman or an arbitrator are binding on you as well as the firm.

Using the FOS is free, though if you act improperly or unreasonably or cause unreasonable delays during the dispute resolution process, the ombudsman can direct that you pay something towards its costs. You can never be asked to pay anything towards the costs of the firm with which you have the dispute.

You usually have six months from receiving a firm's substantive response to your complaint within which you can take your case to the FOS. If you delay longer than this, expect your complaint to be turned away (though the FOS does have discretion to waive the time limit). Make your complaint on the form provided by the FOS.

The scheme is designed to be easy to use and you should not need the help of a solicitor. If you do use one, you'll have to pay your legal costs yourself and cannot claim them back even if the ombudsman decides the case in your favour.

Initially, the FOS tries to help you and the firm reach agreement through a process of conciliation. If this fails, the FOS can make a decision that the firm must accept.

The FOS can call for whatever evidence it needs to determine a dispute. Usually, its research into a case is paper-based, but it can call on you to give oral evidence. Its decision might involve ordering the firm to return money or assets, reinstate policies and pay compensation. The maximum award binding on the firm is £100,000. The FOS can direct a higher award, but the firm can't be forced to pay any excess over the £100,000 limit. Unlike the firm, you are not bound by the ombudsman's decision and can take your case to court if you want.

Going to court

As an alternative to using an ombudsman or arbitration scheme, or if you are unhappy with a decision by the FOS, you could sue the firm which has caused your loss by taking it to court. However, this is more expensive than using an ombudsman or arbitration scheme, often takes a lot longer, and you risk having to pay your opponent's costs or damages. An ombudsman scheme also has the advantage that it can make decisions and awards on the basis of what is fair and reasonable rather than just the strict legal position. (Arbitration schemes are more formal and work in a similar way to the courts, making decisions based on the strict legal case.)

If you do go to court, the case is likely to be dealt with more quickly and cheaply if you are able to use the small claims track (also called the 'small claims court'). You can do this if the amount you are claiming is no more than:

* £5,000 in England and Wales
* £2,000 in Northern Ireland
* £750 in Scotland.

To find out more, contact your local County Court* (or, in Scotland, the Sheriff's Court*).

Compensation

A complaints scheme or court may find in your favour, but will the firm be in a position to pay up? Many financial firms are required to have professional indemnity insurance, which might ultimately provide the compensation. The problem comes when the firm has gone out of business and does not have enough assets or insurance to pay compensation.

Provided the firm is authorised by the FSA (see page 33), you might be able to obtain redress from the Financial Services Compensation Scheme (FSCS)*.

The FSCS can pay compensation in cases where you have lost money due to an authorised firm's fraud or negligence and the firm has ceased trading. The maximum compensation you can get depends on the type of financial product involved – see table opposite. For more information, contact the FSCS*.

Separate compensation arrangements apply to occupational pension schemes:

* **Pensions Compensation Scheme** This may step in where any type of occupational scheme has been targeted by dishonesty, the employer has gone out of business and the assets in the pension

Summary of the Financial Services Compensation Scheme

Type of financial product	Amount of your loss covered by compensation	Maximum compensation
Deposits (e.g. bank and building society accounts)	100% of the first £2,000 90% of the next £33,000	£31,700
Investments (e.g. unit trusts, shares)	100% of the first £30,000 90% of the next £20,000	£48,000
Long-term insurance (e.g. life insurance)	100% of the first £2,000 At least 90% of the remainder (including future benefits already declared)	Unlimited
General insurance (e.g. car insurance, home insurance)	*Compulsory insurance* (e.g. third-party motor insurance, employer's liability insurance): 100% of claim *Non-compulsory insurance* 100% of first £2,000 90% of remainder	Unlimited Unlimited
Mortgages and lifetime mortgages (but only advice about and arranging them)	100% of the first £30,000 90% of the next £20,000	£48,000

scheme fall more than 10 per cent short of the amount needed to pay members' pensions and benefits. Compensation is claimed by the scheme trustees and distributed to members according to statutory rules which give the highest priority to people already receiving pensions. The scheme is funded through levies on occupational pension schemes

- **Pension Protection Fund (PPF)** This is a new scheme expected to start in April 2005. It may pay out where an employer goes out of business and its defined benefit scheme (see Chapter 12) has too few assets to fully meet the pension and benefit claims of members. Unlike the existing compensation scheme, there need not have been any dishonesty to trigger a payment from this fund. Again, claims are made by the scheme trustees and distributed according to statutory rules. The PPF will be funded by levies on participating schemes

- **Financial Assistance Scheme** The government has set up this scheme to help members of defined benefit schemes who had already lost pension rights before the PPF started up. FAS will replace up to 80 per cent of the lost pension of workers close to retirement but as yet it is unclear how much other workers might get.

Buying without advice

If you decide to buy financial products without taking financial advice, you lose some of the protection you would otherwise have under the FSA rules:

- **cooling-off period** In some cases (see page 43), you do not have a breathing space within which to change your mind
- **complaints (see page 43) and compensation (see page 46)** If the product turns out to be unsuitable for you – for example, it includes risks you are unhappy taking – you cannot complain that you were poorly advised or claim compensation for any resulting loss. The decision to take out the product was yours and you have only yourself to blame. However, you are still covered by the complaints and compensation procedures regarding other aspects of the product – for example, failure to provide you with necessary information, bad administration, and so on.

Self-defence

Although the financial system is designed to protect consumers, it cannot shield you from every eventuality. It pays to protect yourself as well. Follow these ten steps when you buy financial products:

1. Think twice before buying without advice – you lose some of the legal protection (see above).
2. Go only to authorised advisers. Check that an adviser is authorised by consulting the FSA Register★.
3. Know your adviser. Is the adviser tied, multi-tied or independent? If tied or multi-tied, are you especially interested in the products of that company, or do you particularly value the

convenience, say, of using that provider? Consider getting advice from an independent adviser who can look at the full range of companies' products.

4. How can the adviser help you? Is the adviser authorised for the type of investment business you are interested in? Does the adviser have expertise in the financial areas you need help with?

5. Be prepared. Be clear about your financial objectives and the priority you attach to them – see Chapter 4. To comply with the 'know your customer' rule, an adviser or salesperson must find out a lot about you. Make sure you have the information to hand.

6. Be informed. Know what literature to expect, read it all – especially documents labelled 'key facts'. Ask questions if there are gaps in your knowledge.

7. Be sceptical. If a deal sounds too good to be true, then it is probably suspect. High returns always go hand in hand with high risk. Don't take terms like 'free' and 'guaranteed' at face value – check exactly what is on offer. And always remember that any guarantee is only as good as the company making it. Query the appropriateness of a deal if the adviser stands to get an unusually large commission.

8. Never be pressurised into making a deal on the spot. Take your time and make sure that the product on offer fits in with your financial plans. Discounts and special offers are poor compensation for bad, hasty decisions.

9. Most independent advisers are not authorised to handle their clients' money. The firm's entry on the FSA Register* will say if they are. If not, never hand money over to the adviser. Instead, make payments to the company or companies you are investing in or buying from. If the adviser looks after investments on behalf of clients, check exactly what safeguards there are to protect the clients. If you are not happy with them, insist on looking after your own investments.

10. Always get, and keep in a safe place, receipts, documents, records of interviews and telephone conversations, and so on. If anything does go wrong, it is essential that you have this information.

Chapter 4

Choosing your financial goals

It is very easy to respond in an *ad hoc* fashion to needs and opportunities as they arise without thinking about how they contribute to your overall finances. The key to financial planning is to have a comprehensive overview of your circumstances, your needs, your wants, and the priority you attach to each of your financial objectives. This gives a framework on which to base your decisions.

To build your framework, work through the following stages:

- identify and prioritise your financial goals
- assess what resources you have available to commit towards meeting those goals
- if necessary, revise your goals in the light of available resources
- consider the personal factors which will influence how you meet your goals.

This will give you a strong, coherent structure on which to build. You can then go on to identify the appropriate financial tools for meeting your targets, given your priorities, resources and personal factors. The final step – deciding which particular companies' products to choose – is perhaps the hardest for the d-i-y financial planner. You need to keep a close eye on the various financial markets, being aware of new product launches, changes to existing products, special promotions, and the impact of external events, such as changes in the law or economic crises, on the various types of product. This used to be very laborious and time-consuming and *Which?* used to suggest that, at this stage, it might be sensible to seek professional help. However, the Internet is fast changing all that. Most product providers now have a website. You can rapidly get product information from these and, if you want to, make your purchase over the Net too. There are also many websites – including Switch with *Which?*★ and the FSA's★ site – that compare products from different providers, letting you easily pick out those with the features you need.

Finally, be aware that your financial framework and the choice of products to meet your needs should be reviewed regularly. Certain events in life – such as marriage, separation or divorce, having children, promotion at work, receiving an inheritance, being made redundant, reaching retirement – clearly signal that it is time for a review. Even apart from these events, there are changes over time to the economic and social climate and to the opportunities available, so it makes sense to review your financial plan every year or so. The review is also a time to assess how well on track you are for your longer-term objectives and to decide whether you need to make any adjustments, such as increasing the amount you are saving.

The whole process of drawing up your financial framework and fitting a financial plan around it is summarised in the chart overleaf.

Identifying and prioritising your goals

Your framework should adapt to the changing phases of your life. To some extent, these phases vary from person to person, but it is possible to map out a typical sequence – see the chart on page 53. You personally might not pass through all these phases, but some will certainly apply.

Each phase is characterised by a different set of opportunities and demands which will tend to determine the financial priorities you choose. Possible priorities are outlined in the descriptions that follow. These are not set in stone, and what is right for one person may be quite wrong for another. Their aim is to set you thinking about your own phase of life and your own financial goals.

To the goals dictated by the life phase you need to add your own personal hopes and ambitions: for example, maybe you want to retire when you are 50, in which case pension planning will need to be a much higher priority in the early phases of life than is shown in the outlines below; or you might want to take a year off work to sail around the world, which would probably influence your savings targets.

Your objectives and the way you prioritise them should reflect not just what you would *like* to achieve financially, but also what

How to build your financial plan

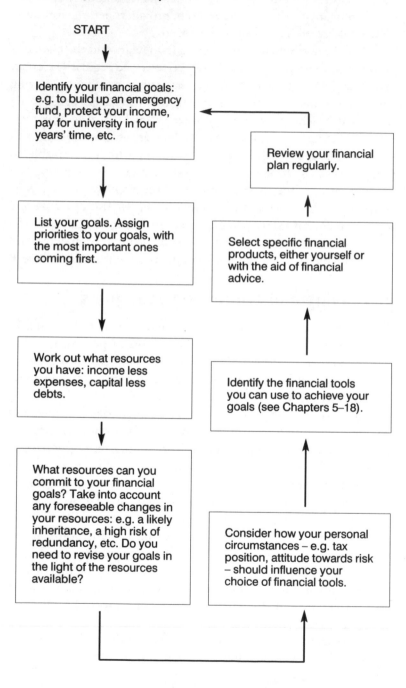

START

Identify your financial goals:
e.g. to build up an emergency
fund, protect your income,
pay for university in four
years' time, etc.

List your goals. Assign
priorities to your goals, with
the most important ones
coming first.

Work out what resources
you have: income less
expenses, capital less
debts.

What resources can you
commit to your financial
goals? Take into account
any foreseeable changes in
your resources: e.g. a likely
inheritance, a high risk of
redundancy, etc. Do you
need to revise your goals in
the light of the resources
available?

Review your financial
plan regularly.

Select specific financial
products, either yourself or
with the aid of financial
advice.

Identify the financial tools
you can use to achieve your
goals (see Chapters 5–18).

Consider how your personal
circumstances – e.g. tax
position, attitude towards risk
– should influence your
choice of financial tools.

you *need* to do given your family commitments, what the state provides, and so on. For example, though you might prefer not to dwell on the risks of life, if you have dependants you should consider how they would cope if you were no longer there. Similarly, it is very easy to ignore pension planning until it is too late to build up the level of income you would ideally like to enjoy when you retire.

Typical phases of life

Freedom of youth

This is the early phase of life, when you cease to rely on your parents and, all being well, start to earn your own living. Typically, no one is dependent on you, and your main priority is having a roof over your head. Quite possibly, rented accommodation fits in with your desire for mobility. Other commitments are likely to be few, but might include, say, paying off loans taken out during student days (though see Chapter 10 for suggestions on how a student loan can be part of your financial planning). The net result is likely to be a surplus of income over necessary expenditure. The temptation of youth is probably to spend the excess, but there are some bones you can build into your skeleton even now. In a realistic order of priority, these are:

- an emergency fund to draw on if you face unexpected expenses
- protecting your income in the event of your falling ill
- pension planning: it takes a lot of investment to build up an adequate pension, so the earlier you start the better
- short-term saving, for example for a car, holidays, and so on
- medium- to long-term non-pension saving for eventual house purchase plus other, non-specific reasons.

Typical phases of life

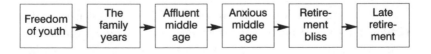

The family years

At some stage, most people find a partner whom they either live with or marry. This immediately creates a changed situation. Even if your partner is financially independent, you are likely to develop some joint commitments. These may be major items, such as sharing the costs of buying and running a home. In this case, you have to consider what would be the financial impact on your partner if, say, you fell ill or died, and similarly what the impact on you would be if your partner became ill or died. For those with children, the shared commitments are even more demanding and complex, requiring financial forethought and planning. Children are likely to exert greater pressures on your resources than will occur at any other stage of your life. If you or your partner stop working or cut back your work in order to care for the children, these resources will be further depleted.

In this situation, it is essential to decide what your financial priorities are. They are likely to take on this sort of shape:

- emergency fund
- protecting your own and your partner's income in the event of illness, at least to the extent that joint expenses would be covered
- life insurance on your own and your partner's life
- borrowing to buy a home
- planning for education, for example school fees if you opt for private-sector schooling, or the cost of maintaining your child(ren) at university
- pension planning: ideally, this should have higher priority but this might not be possible if funds are tight
- short-term saving for family events, for example presents, holidays, and so on
- medium- to long-term saving, if you have surplus funds.

Many couples separate or divorce, and, if children are involved, the financial pressures can become particularly severe. Often the same overall resources must be stretched to finance two households, extra childcare costs, solicitors' bills, and so on. Although money may be tighter, the overall needs and priorities associated with the family years are likely to be much the same as shown above. In particular, bear in mind that if you are relying on maintenance from a former husband or wife for part of your income, you probably still have a need for life insurance which would pay out if he or she were to die. Don't overlook pension planning both when negotiating the divorce settlement and afterwards, since often it will be appropriate to transfer some pension rights from one spouse to another.

Affluent middle age

When eventually the financial demands of a family subside, you may enter a phase of relative wealth. This would be a good time to anticipate future events. But if you choose simply to concentrate on the present, increased spending and personal ambitions are likely to dominate your priorities after basic needs have been met. Typically, your priorities might look like this:

• emergency fund
• protecting income against illness
• life insurance if you have a partner or other dependants
• fun targets – more holidays, hobbies, a second home and so on
• pension planning
• other saving.

Anxious middle age

Unfortunately, the relaxed feeling of early middle age tends to give way as you enter your fifties. Realisation grows that retirement is just around the corner, and perhaps you should be doing more to prepare for it. Pension planning should now move up your priorities and, for the first time, your thoughts might turn to the health problems of old age. At this phase of life, you might also find elderly parents becoming more dependent on you, though, equally, your resources might be boosted through inheritance.

The following profile of priorities is possible:

• emergency fund
• protecting income against illness
• life insurance if you have a partner or other dependants
• pension planning
• long-term care planning, if you are not confident of adequate state provision
• serious investment.

Retirement bliss

By the time retirement arrives, your earlier planning should be bearing fruit. With luck, this should be another relaxed phase of life. But it pays to have a weather eye on the future, making sure that your income will be sustained as retirement progresses and that you will be able to cope with increased costs due to health problems. At retirement, you are likely to receive a lump sum which you may want, at least partly, to invest rather than spend.

Priorities could be:

- an emergency fund
- continuing income if you or your partner were to die
- replacing perks that went with your job, for example a car, medical insurance, and spending on capital items expected to see you through retirement
- fun targets, for example increased travel, new hobbies, indulging grandchildren
- investment for income either now or later on (which also usually includes investing partly for growth in order to maintain the future buying power of the income)
- long-term care planning, if you are not confident that the state will provide
- inheritance planning – taking steps to reduce a potential inheritance tax bill at your death.

Late retirement

The last phase of life. Your priorities now depend very much on how well your earlier financial planning succeeded. For some, a shortage of income might be the top concern; for others, how to pass on their assets. Very loosely, then, priorities might be:

- an emergency fund
- continuing income if you or your partner were to die
- investing for income/boosting income
- paying for care if the health of you or your partner fails
- inheritance planning.

The impact of other factors on your goals

As well as responding to your life phase and personal ambitions, you will also have needs that arise because of the risk of outside shocks upsetting your financial plans. These shocks range from near-certain events, such as changes in interest rates and periodic changes to the tax system, to others that might not come to pass at all, such as being made redundant. Whether or not you respond to the threat of these shocks depends on how likely you think they are to happen to you and the severity of the impact they would have. You can gather statistics about the probability of certain events happening – how likely you are to have a fatal heart attack at age 40, how likely you are to be off work sick, how likely you are to live to a hundred, and so on. These may help to frame your perception, but different people will come to a different conclusion about the risks they think they personally face, coloured by their own temperament (optimistic or not) and circumstances (for example, a family history of illness). Likewise, the impact of a shock on your finances will vary from person to person depending on the resources you have, the expenses you have, how important it is to you to protect a particular lifestyle, and so on.

Your perception of the risks posed by outside shocks will tend to vary according to the general economic climate. For example, in a recession people tend to save more because they perceive a higher risk of becoming unemployed and want the means to keep going financially if their main income is lost. Inflation can have a complex influence on financial planning.

In the early stages of high inflation, people often save more to cope with rising prices but, if inflation persists, they may save less as they become aware that the value of their savings is being eroded. In a climate of low inflation, the headline rates of return from investments may seem very low. Even though the real return – in other words the amount they get over and above inflation – might still be reasonable, people may decide to take higher risks as they seek higher headline returns.

Assessing your resources

If you had unlimited resources, you could meet all your financial goals without problem and would have little need for financial planning. For most of us, life is not so straightforward. Usually, it is impossible to achieve instantly all we would wish; hard choices have to be made and goals have to be approached step by step.

The second stage in your planning has to be a frank assessment of what resources you have, what claims there are on them, to what extent resources are already being used to meet your goals and what surplus (if any) is available to further your plans. There are two parts to assessing your resources:

- **drawing up a budget** This means writing down your income from all sources and listing all your spending. It's usually easiest to do this for a period of a month. Include any quarterly or yearly amounts by dividing by three or 12 as appropriate. Subtract your spending from your income to see what income (if any) you have left over to set towards your targets. If your spending comes to more than your income, this is not sustainable over the long term, so your top priority should normally be getting them at least back into balance. Consider what spending you can cut or ways you could boost your income
- **taking stock of existing financial products** List the savings, insurance and other financial products you already have. Are they already targeting your financial needs? Are they the right products given your needs? Consider how you could reallocate existing products to meet your goals and whether you should cancel products that no longer meet your needs.

Once you have completed this stage, you should have a reasonably clear idea of what resources – both assets and money set aside out of income – are currently available for meeting your targets. Also consider how your resources might change in the foreseeable future, since this could influence your choice of financial tools, for example borrowing (that is, committing future resources to current spending), or insurances with the option to increase payments later on.

Revising your goals

At this point, you might come to the conclusion that your goals are too ambitious in the light of the resources you have available. Something will have to give. You have several choices:

- boost your resources: for example by taking on extra work to increase your income

- alter one or more goals: for example if you had pencilled in a tour of India for next year, defer the trip for a year or two; if you had planned to retire at 55, consider retiring at 60 instead
- abandon one or more goals at least temporarily. If you have prioritised the targets realistically, the ones you abandon should be those to which you have given the lowest priority.

Alternatively, you might find that you have more resources than you had anticipated. This opens the way to increasing the scale of one or more goals, accelerating the timescale over which you plan to meet the targets or adding further targets to your plan. Once again, if you have allocated your priorities correctly, any new goals should be added after existing goals and would be the first to go if resources became tighter.

As you can see from the chart below, your financial goals are like a ladder, with your most fundamental priorities at the base and less

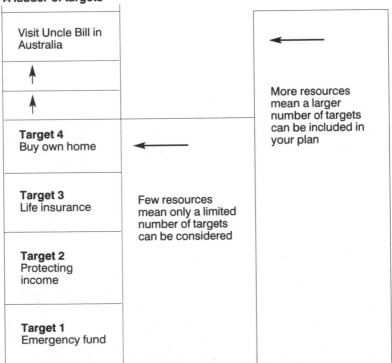

A ladder of targets

Visit Uncle Bill in Australia	
↑	More resources mean a larger number of targets can be included in your plan
↑	
Target 4 Buy own home	
Target 3 Life insurance	Few resources mean only a limited number of targets can be considered
Target 2 Protecting income	
Target 1 Emergency fund	

important objectives on the higher rungs. The more resources you have, the higher up the ladder you can climb. A temporary fall in resources would mean retreating down the ladder a little; a windfall inheritance or unexpected pay rise would let you climb a bit higher.

Personal factors

In practice, measuring up your goals against available resources can be done only in a broad-brush fashion, if you have not thought about what financial tools could be used. After all, you need to know how quickly an investment might grow, or how much it might cost to buy a particular type of insurance. But before you can pick the financial tools, you need to consider the personal factors that will tend to make some more appropriate than others. There are five key factors: tax, your attitude towards risk, your ethics or religion, your timescale for investment and your state of health.

Your tax position

It is essential that you consider the impact of tax on your financial planning, especially when choosing investments, because the way the proceeds are taxed will have a big impact on the return you get. Throughout Chapters 5–18, your attention is drawn to the tax treatment of the various financial tools, and guidance is given on how this should influence your planning.

The main taxes that concern you will be income tax and capital gains tax (see below). Inheritance tax, which may be due on what you leave when you die and on some lifetime gifts, is also important. Chapter 15 provides a brief introduction. For more information, see *The Which? Guide to Giving and Inheriting* published by Which? Books★.

These taxes are all administered by the Inland Revenue★ which produces a wide range of explanatory booklets, some of which are mentioned in this book.

The tax system is reviewed each spring in the annual Budget and other changes are often announced in the autumn Pre-Budget Report. These are usually broadcast live and full details are available from HM Treasury★. Summaries are published in the next day's newspapers, in personal finance magazines★ and on many personal finance websites★. Make sure you keep abreast of these changes as they will often have a major impact on your financial planning.

Income tax

Income tax is charged on most types of income, including earnings as an employee, profits from self-employment, interest and dividends from most investments, pensions, and so on. It is charged at one of three main rates – the starting, basic and higher rates. In the 2004–5 tax year, these are 10 per cent on the first £2,020 of income, 22 per cent on the next £29,380 and 40 per cent on anything over £31,400. However, you do not pay tax on all your income because:

- some types of income are specifically tax-free, for example the return from National Savings & Investments (NS&I) certificates and interest from a cash individual savings account (ISA)
- certain expenses qualify for income tax relief, for example donations to charity under gift aid or Give As You Earn, and amounts you pay into a pension scheme or plan
- you get an allowance which lets you have your first slice of income tax-free. You might get other allowances too.

The main tax allowances for 2004–5 are shown in the table on page 62. The personal allowance is deducted from your income before tax is worked out and so gives you tax relief up to your top rate of tax. The personal allowance is higher if you are aged 65 or over, and higher again if you are aged 75 or over.

If you are a married man and you or your wife were born before 6 April 1935, you can get married couple's allowance. (This allowance was abolished for younger couples from April 2000 onwards.) This allowance gives tax relief at a rate of 10 per cent as a reduction in your tax bill.

People aged 65 or over lose some of their allowances if their income exceeds a certain limit (£18,900 in 2004–5). They lose £1 of allowance for every £2 by which their income exceeds the income limit. The personal allowance is reduced before any married couple's allowance. However, the allowances are never reduced below a certain level. You stop losing your allowances when:

- **your personal allowance** has been reduced to the amount someone under age 65 gets – in other words, £4,745 in 2004–5
- **your married couple's allowance** has been reduced to £2,210 in 2004–5.

Main income tax allowances in 2004–5

Allowance	Amount	Saves you up to this much tax if you pay tax at:		
		Starting rate	Basic rate	Higher rate
Personal allowance – under age 65	£4,745	£202.00[1]	£1,043.90	£1,898.00
Personal allowance – 65 to 74	£6,830	£202.00[1]	£1,502.60	£2,732.00
Personal allowance – 75 and over	£6,950	£202.00[1]	£1,529.00	£2,780.00
Blind person's allowance	£1,560	£151.00	£343.20	£624.00
Married couple's allowance – age 68 to 74	£5,725	£202.00[1]	£572.50	£221.00
Married couple's allowance – 75 and over	£5,795	£202.00[1]	£579.50	£221.00

[1]Income too low to use whole allowance.
[2]Income too high to get age-related addition, so allowance is restricted to £2,210.

The table opposite shows the range of income for which someone over 65 will be losing age allowance. If your income is within this range, in effect your top rate of tax is 33 per cent, rather than just the basic rate of 22 per cent. Therefore, choosing tax-free income will often be particularly worthwhile for you.

Example: age allowance

In 2004–5, Jack is 72 and his wife is 76. Because of his age, Jack qualifies for a higher personal allowance of £6,830. But Jack's income is £19,500. This is £600 above the limit at which age allowance starts to be lost. Therefore, his age allowance is reduced by £600 ÷ 2 = £300, to £6,530.

Jack also qualifies for married couple's allowance. He gets the higher rate of £5,795 because his wife is over age 74. Jack's income is not so high that this allowance has to be reduced.

Capital gains tax

Capital gains tax (CGT) is charged on profits you make from selling or disposing of assets, such as investments, second homes, antiques, and so on. Chargeable gains are added to your taxable income for a

Range of income where you are losing age allowance in 2004–5

Your status[1]	Income range
Single person or wife aged 65 to 74	£18,900 to £23,070
Single person or wife aged 75 or over	£18,900 to £23,310
Married man under 65, wife 70 to 74	£18,900 to £25,930
Married man under 65, wife 75 or over	£18,900 to £26,070
Married man aged 65 to 69, wife under 70	£18,900 to £23,070
Married man aged 65 to 69, wife 70 to 74	£18,900 to £30,100
Married man 65 to 74, wife 75 or over	£18,900 to £30,240
Married man 70 to 74, wife under 75	£18,900 to £30,100
Married man 75 or over, wife any age	£18,900 to £30,480

[1]Ages refer to age reached during the tax year.

given tax year and, in 2004–5, CGT is levied at 10 per cent on any part of the gain falling within the starting-rate band, 20 per cent on any part within the basic-rate band, and 40 per cent on any part falling within the higher-rate band. However, some or all of your capital gains escape tax because:

- gains on some assets are tax-free: for example, your main home
- some transactions are tax-free: for example, gifts of assets to your husband or wife
- expenses associated with buying and selling the asset can be deducted before tax is worked out
- gains due purely to inflation up to March 1998 are not taxed
- losses on other assets can usually be deducted
- gains built up from April 1998 onwards may be reduced by 'taper relief' if you have held the asset for long enough
- the first slice of otherwise taxable gains each year (£8,200 in 2004–5) is tax-free.

Your attitude towards risk

Everyone's temperament is different. Some people give high priority to security and predictability. Others are relaxed with, or even crave, a high degree of uncertainty. The degree of uncertainty – or risk – with which you are comfortable will shape your financial planning and the financial tools you select, especially in relation to saving and investing.

Your attitude towards risk is not simply a reflection of temperament. It depends also on such factors as:

- **your income** If you have little cash to spare, you might quite rightly be reluctant to take risks with it; the more 'surplus' income you have, the more adventurous you can afford to be financially
- **your age** In later years, especially after retirement, it may be difficult or impossible to replace any money you lose, which will tend to make you cautious; when you are young and earning, you can usually make good your losses
- **your responsibilities** If, for example, you have a young family dependent on you, it might be unacceptable to risk their financial security; with only yourself to consider, the consequences of a gamble going wrong may not seem as important.

Starting out

The goals

Jason is 27 and works as a research chemist. He's been in full-time work sin 1991 but joined his present company only in 1998. He's single and living shared rented accommodation. He is considering buying his own house b there have been redundancies at work recently, so he has some concerns abc job security. Jason is also thinking about a career break to travel or work abro for a few years. Finally, Jason wants to make sure he'll eventually have a go pension.

The resources

Jason has an after-tax income of £1,200 a month. He pays £255 a month in re and £100 on other bills. Food and household expenses account for £200. T other big expense for Jason is running a car. Repaying a car loan costs him £12c month. Tax, insurance and petrol come to £100. Jason usually has £30 to £50 month outstanding on his credit card. He estimates that leisure spending com to about £100 a month. This leaves spare cash of around £200 to £300 a mon which he currently puts in a savings account. Having recently paid the deposit c his car, Jason has just £500 in that account. His only other assets are £4,0c worth of shares which he'll receive in four years' time from a previous employer share option scheme. Jason joined his current employer's pension scheme

---

Throughout, this book highlights the areas where risk is a key element in your choice of financial tools and suggests ways in which you can attempt to match risk to your own attitude.

Your ethics or religion

Some people are not willing or able to consider the full range of products available because of their ethical stance or religious beliefs. For example, many people do not want their money to be supporting companies involved in alcohol, gambling, tobacco or the arms trade or damage the environment. Others wish actively to support companies that promote fair trade with the developing world or have good employment practices. This may be a personal ethical choice or stem from religious beliefs, such as Methodism or Islam. For help finding ethical products, see Ethical saving and investing* in the Addresses section.

---

99 and contributes £80 a month. He'll get a pension of one-sixtieth of his final lary for each year he's in the scheme.

e financial plan

Save £100 a month out of surplus income to build up an emergency fund of at least £3,000 in an instant-access cash ISA.

Jason's savings account offers a poor rate of interest. Shop around for a better one.

Compare the cost of a mortgage with the current rent. If – as is likely – a mortgage would cost no more, Jason should buy a home sooner rather than later. In the meantime, he should save towards the cost of house purchase using a savings account or the cash ISA.

Jason should check what protection he has through work if he is off sick for a prolonged period. If the cover looks inadequate, he should consider taking out income protection insurance.

Jason should put any remaining spare cash in a unit trust, OEIC or investment trust savings plan, investing through an ISA for tax-efficiency.

The employer's pension scheme is a good one. Making more pension payments is not a high priority for now.

Which? January 2000

Your timescale for investment

This factor is in many cases intrinsic to your financial goals. For example, if you are saving for a holiday or to pay for a wedding, you generally have a set date in mind by which you need the proceeds of your investment. Some financial tools are completely inappropriate for such financial targets, either because they tie up your money for too long a period or because their capital value fluctuates and you cannot be sure of getting back the amount you need at a precise point in time. On the other hand, some financial aims are either long-term or open-ended and give you scope to choose from a much wider range of investments.

Your health

Health is a factor you need to consider when you take out many types of insurance and when you buy some types of annuity (a form of investment which is basically an educated gamble on how long you will live). Poor health can push up the cost of many insurances or even bar you from having them. The chapters that follow discuss the health factor wherever appropriate.

Chapter 5

Saving for emergencies

The most fundamental step in financial planning is ensuring that you have some cushion to fall back on in an emergency. This is not simply crisis management – mending a leaking roof, sudden car repairs, bailing out children stuck abroad penniless. It can also be an 'opportunity fund', letting you take advantage of special offers and events that arise unexpectedly.

Two decisions should be made about your emergency fund:

- How much do you need?
- Where should you keep it?

How much emergency fund?

This depends on your circumstances, lifestyle and the type of emergencies you might have to cope with. If you are self-employed, for example, you might need quite a large buffer to cover short-term falls in receipts or a brief period of illness not covered by your income protection insurance (see Chapter 7).

If your income would not be protected at all in the event of illness, you may be concerned to build up a sizeable emergency fund, though you should weigh up whether it would be better to divert some of those funds into appropriate insurance.

If you have a large family, the probability of a crisis arising may be higher simply because, with more people involved, there's more risk of something going wrong. If you live in an older property, there may be a higher risk of unforeseen repairs being required.

You need to examine your situation and decide what size of emergency cushion feels right for you. Whatever you decide now should be reviewed periodically as your circumstances change: for example, if unemployment threatens, you may want to build up extra reserves, or as your children become independent, a smaller buffer may be enough. As a very rough guide, for most people an emergency fund of between £1,000 and £5,000 is usually adequate.

Where to keep your fund

Conventional wisdom is that an emergency fund should be kept where you have instant access to it in times of need. Of course, you could meet that requirement by simply stuffing fivers under the mattress, but in reality an emergency fund:

- should be kept in a secure place. There should be no risk at all of losing the money put into your fund. This means that you shouldn't store it at home where it would be vulnerable to theft, nor invest it in assets which may fall in value.
- should not be idle. It should be earning you some return.

The best place for an emergency fund is in some form of deposit account run either by a building society, bank or National Savings & Investments (NS&I) (see Chapter 16). An instant access account is an obvious choice, and you might consider accounts which let you make withdrawals through cash machines so that you can cope with emergencies outside banking hours. Postal, phone-based and Internet accounts often offer the best rates of interest.

If you have instant access to credit – for example, you have a high spending limit on your credit card which you usually do not fully use – you could consider putting at least part of your emergency fund in an account which requires a short period of notice (up to a month, say) if, in exchange, you will get a better rate of interest.

Similarly, although between £1,000 and £5,000 might be enough as an emergency fund, you might consider adding it to other lower-risk savings if this would give you a large enough lump sum to cross an interest-rate threshold on a tiered account and so earn a better return.

If you do not need your whole ISA allowance for investing in share-based investments, it makes sense to put your emergency

> **Tip**
> You do not need *instant* access to an emergency fund if you can rely on credit in an emergency. This may allow you to invest for a better return.

fund within a mini-cash ISA wrapper – that way, the interest it earns will be tax-free. You may need to do this gradually over two or three years, if your fund is larger than the annual ISA allowance. See Chapter 11 for information about ISAs.

If you have a mortgage, you might instead consider an all-in-one mortgage account as a possible home for your emergency fund – see page 290. The 'return' will generally be considerably higher than you could get on an instant access account and should also beat notice accounts.

The chart overleaf summarises your choices for an emergency fund.

Emergency fund if your income is low

If you are on a low income, it might be hard to set any money aside as an emergency fund. But don't underestimate your need for such a fund. Without some rainy-day money to fall back on, you risk falling into debt every time a domestic crisis strikes – say, the washing machine breaks down or your car fails an MOT. If you are claiming means-tested state benefits (such as income support, income-based jobseeker's allowance or pension credit), you might be able to get a loan from the social fund, but you can't bank on that. So it is worth trying to build up at least some emergency savings – say, £100 or £200.

Consider an instant access bank or building society account for your emergency fund. With only a small sum to save, the amount of interest you will earn will be low and access to your money will be the highest priority. Therefore, an account with a cash card or one where you can pay in and draw out at a convenient branch might be more suitable than a postal or phone-based account.

Another option could be the Savings Gateway. This is a government savings scheme for people of working age on a low

Choosing a home for your emergency fund

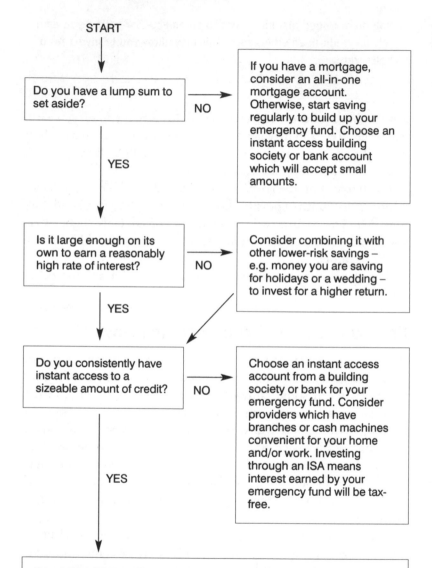

START

Do you have a lump sum to set aside?

NO → If you have a mortgage, consider an all-in-one mortgage account. Otherwise, start saving regularly to build up your emergency fund. Choose an instant access building society or bank account which will accept small amounts.

YES

Is it large enough on its own to earn a reasonably high rate of interest?

NO → Consider combining it with other lower-risk savings – e.g. money you are saving for holidays or a wedding – to invest for a higher return.

YES

Do you consistently have instant access to a sizeable amount of credit?

NO → Choose an instant access account from a building society or bank for your emergency fund. Consider providers which have branches or cash machines convenient for your home and/or work. Investing through an ISA means interest earned by your emergency fund will be tax-free.

YES

Consider relying on the credit for an immediate response to an emergency. Pay off the credit by drawing on an emergency fund invested for higher interest, for example in a notice account (with a notice period of up to one month) with a building society or bank, or a National Savings investment account. Investing through an ISA means interest earned by your emergency fund will be tax-free.

income. At the time of writing, the government had piloted the scheme and was expected to announce that it would soon be available nationwide – possibly from April 2005. In the pilot, over an 18-month period savers could choose to pay between £1 and £25 a month into a Savings Gateway account, up to a maximum of £375 in total. The savings did not earn interest as such, but for every £1 the saver paid in the government matched this by £1, so doubling the amount built up. The government bonus was added at the end of the 18 months. In the meantime, the saver could withdraw his or her own money at any time provided at least £1 was left in the account and withdrawals did not reduce the government bonus.

If a nationwide scheme is implemented, the Savings Gateway could be a good way to build up your emergency fund. At the end of 18 months, you might then shop around and switch to an instant access bank or building society account.

Ethical emergency fund

Michelle has savings and some other financial products, but none of her financial decisions so far has been made with ethical considerations in mind. Michelle wanted to change this, so *Which?* appointed two independent financial advisers (IFAs) who specialise in ethical finance*. The advisers asked Michelle about her financial circumstances and her ethical priorities before recommending financial products.

Michelle's savings account is with a high-street bank, however the IFAs suggested she steer clear of the main high-street banks for ethical reasons. These banks have commercial lending arms, so can lend your money to any company they choose, which could include those involved in the arms trade or animal testing, for example. The exception is Co-operative Bank (and its online bank, Smile), which is well-known for its ethical stance. Co-op refuses to invest in companies involved in activities such as animal testing and genetic modification, and seeks to support companies and organisations involved in activities such as recycling and fair trade. Mutual organisations, such as building societies and credit unions, are usually a safer bet than most banks as they tend to lend only to individuals. Some building societies do lend to companies, though, so it's a good idea to ask about lending policies before you open an account. The IFAs also felt Michelle could be making more of her savings financially. With a mini cash ISA from a building society she could invest up to £3,000 a year tax-free. To find out more about banks' and building societies' ethical policies, consult the Ethical Investment Research Service (EIRIS)* ethical banking supplement. *Ethical Consumer* magazine* also reports on banks' and building societies' ethical records.

Which? March 2003

Chapter 6

Protecting your family

A top priority if you have dependants is to ensure that they are protected financially if you were to die. The main way to meet this goal is to take out life insurance.

Bear in mind that not only the loss of a breadwinner's salary could cause financial hardship: if you are caring for children, your spouse or partner might need to pay for professional childcare and/or babysitters if you were to die. Similarly, you should take into account any extra costs of running the house, maintaining the garden, and so on. A government survey found that, nationwide, housework – which even today is still done mainly by women – takes up more hours each day than paid work. If all the cooking, cleaning, childcare, gardening, and so on had to be paid for at the market rates for each activity, they would be worth some £340 billion – about half of the whole national income.

If you have identified that you need some life insurance (see chart overleaf), the next step is to work out how much. You might require a lump sum, for example to pay off the mortgage, as well as replacement income, which could be provided either by income-paying life insurance (known as family income benefit) or by insurance which pays out a lump sum which you could invest to produce the required income. This is discussed further on page 85. To find out the basic cash and income your family would need in the event of your death, work through the Calculator (see page 75). If you are married or live with a partner, you should each work through the Calculator separately. The notes following the Calculator will help you to fill it in.

Who needs life insurance?

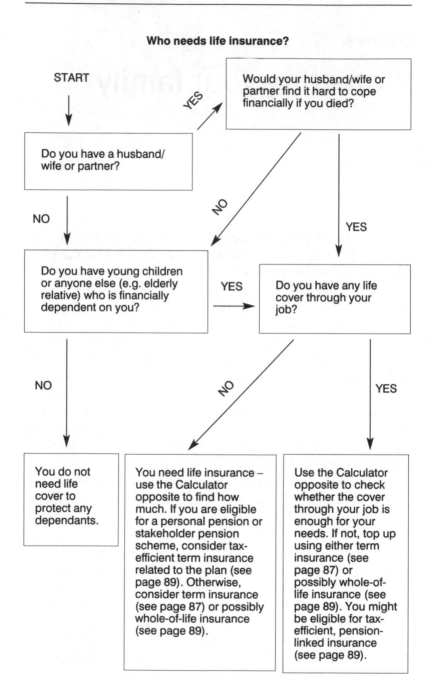

START

Do you have a husband/ wife or partner?

YES → Would your husband/wife or partner find it hard to cope financially if you died?

NO ↓

NO → Do you have young children or anyone else (e.g. elderly relative) who is financially dependent on you?

YES → Do you have any life cover through your job?

NO ↓

You do not need life cover to protect any dependants.

NO → You need life insurance – use the Calculator opposite to find how much. If you are eligible for a personal pension or stakeholder pension scheme, consider tax-efficient term insurance related to the plan (see page 89). Otherwise, consider term insurance (see page 87) or possibly whole-of-life insurance (see page 89).

YES → Use the Calculator opposite to check whether the cover through your job is enough for your needs. If not, top up using either term insurance (see page 87) or possibly whole-of-life insurance (see page 89). You might be eligible for tax-efficient, pension-linked insurance (see page 89).

Life insurance calculator

Part 1: Cash required and cash available   £

Funeral expenses	a	
Emergency fund to cover household expenses for, say, two months	b	
Repayment of mortgage	c	
Repayment of other loans	d	
Inheritance tax	e	
Bequests in will to people other than dependants	f	
Other lump-sum expenses	g	
TOTAL CASH NEEDED =a+b+c+d+e+f+g	A	
Payout from existing insurance to cover mortgage	h	
Lump-sum payout from any other existing insurance policies	i	
Savings and investments which would be cashed in	j	
Capital raised from sale of assets	k	
Bereavement payment from state	l	
Other lump sums available	m	
TOTAL CASH AVAILABLE = h+i+j+k+l+m	B	
NET LUMP SUM NEEDED Work out A – B. If the answer is zero or less, set C equal to zero Otherwise C = A – B	C	

Part 2: Change in income and expenses   £/month

I: Reduction in income

Your earnings after tax and other deductions	n
Your pension	o
Your state benefits	p
Your spouse's/partner's earnings if he or she would give up work or work fewer hours	q
Income from investments which would be sold	r
Other income lost	s
TOTAL REDUCTION IN INCOME =n+o+p+q+r+s	D

II: Increase in income

Widowed parent's allowance or bereavement allowance from the state	t
Other state benefits	u
Other pensions	v
Income from any existing life insurance policies	w
Earnings if your spouse/partner would start work or work longer hours	x
Other	y
TOTAL INCREASE IN INCOME = t+u+v+w+x+y	E

III: Reduction in expenses

Mortgage and other loan repayments paid off	z
Living expenses saved	aa
Life insurance premiums and pension contributions	bb
Other	cc
TOTAL REDUCTION IN EXPENSES = z+aa+bb+cc	F

	£/month
IV: Increase in expenses	
Cost of childcare	dd
Cost of home help/odd-job person/gardener, etc.	ee
Cost of replacing fringe benefits of job, e.g. running a car, private medical insurance premiums	ff
Other	gg
TOTAL INCREASE IN EXPENSES = dd+ee+ff+gg	G

Part 3: Amount of cover required	£
Work out D + G − E − F. If the answer is zero or less, set H equal to zero. Otherwise H = D + G − E − F	H
Extra income needed each year = H × 12	I
Estimated lump-sum insurance needed to produce income I (see the table on page 86)	J
TOTAL LUMP-SUM INSURANCE REQUIRED = C+J	K

Part 1: Cash required and cash available

Funeral expenses (a)

Death is a costly affair. Among other items, there could be the funeral director's fees to pay, including the cost of a coffin and hearse, minister's fees, charges for the crematorium and/or burial plot, gravediggers' fees, flowers, and so on. Marking a grave with a headstone is another optional but expensive item to consider. As a rough guide, expect the total bill to be around £2,000. This is normally paid out of the estate you leave, but during your lifetime you do have the option of taking out a pre-paid funeral plan (see page 92). And in some cases, the state might help (see page 83).

Emergency fund (b)

Following death, there is usually a period of confusion and coming to terms with the new situation. Your family is likely to need a financial breathing space in which to sort out long-term money affairs. There might also be delays in distributing your possessions and turning them into cash if necessary. An emergency fund will tide your dependants over during this period. It need not be provided by life insurance. It could, for example, be money which you have in a joint account with your spouse or partner. Since there could be a delay before a life insurance policy pays out, it is a good idea to have at least part of the emergency fund in an instantly available form (see Chapter 5).

Repayment of mortgage (c)

If you have a mortgage, you might also have some life cover which will automatically pay off the mortgage in the event of your death (see Chapter 9). In this case, any value you put under 'c' will be balanced by the same amount under 'h' below. With a repayment mortgage or ISA mortgage (which are not necessarily sold in a package with insurance), you might not have matching life cover. You will have to decide whether you would want to pay off the mortgage.

Repayment of other loans (d)

This covers things like the debt outstanding on your credit card(s). If you have taken out credit insurance to pay off, for example, a bank or car loan in the event of death, then the amount of loans covered by insurance will be balanced by an identical amount under 'i' below.

Inheritance tax (e)

Chapter 15 considers whether there is likely to be any inheritance tax to pay on your estate (your assets less your debts) when you die. If your estate is worth less than £263,000 (in 2004–5) or you leave everything to your husband or wife, there will be no tax to pay. From a future date yet to be announced, it is expected there will be no tax on whatever you leave to a same-sex partner where you have registered your partnership under new civil partnership rules.

Bequests to people other than dependants (f)

Your will, or the rules of intestacy if you did not make a will, may require some of your assets to be given away. See Chapter 15 for more information.

Other lump-sum expenses (g)

These might include, for example, buying a car to replace a company car which you had through your job (but not the expenses of running it – see 'ff' on page 85).

Payout from existing insurance to cover mortgage (h)

This could be an endowment policy to repay an endowment mortgage or a mortgage protection policy to pay off a repayment or ISA mortgage. See Chapter 9.

Lump-sum payout from any other existing insurance policies (i)

This would include insurance taken out with a loan other than a mortgage. It would also include any other life insurance which you already have either through your work or policies you have taken out yourself.

Savings and investments which would be cashed in (j)

These could range from cash in a bank account to a portfolio of shares. If the investment had been producing an income, the effect of cashing it in will have to be taken into account at 'r' below.

Capital raised from the sale of other assets (k)

This could be the sale of valuable possessions, such as a car, boat, jewellery, and so on. You might consider trading down to a smaller home and so releasing some capital, but bear in mind that there could be a long delay before you manage to sell.

Bereavement payment from the state (l)

Bereavement payment is a tax-free lump sum from the state (£2,000 in 2004–5) paid to a widow or widower provided the deceased husband or wife had paid enough National Insurance contributions (see page 83). From a date yet to be announced (expected to be in late-2005), same-sex partners who have registered their relationship as a civil partnership may also qualify for bereavement payment in the same way as married people.

Other lump sums (m)

If your income and capital are very low, you might qualify for an emergency payment from the Social Fund. Other possible sources of help are gifts or loans from relatives.

Part 2: Change in income and expenses

Your earnings after tax and other deductions (n)

This is the amount of take-home pay which your household would lose if you are working. If you are an employee, enter your monthly pay after deducting income tax, National Insurance, contributions to an employer's pension scheme and any other deductions. If you run your own business, it is the amount of money which you draw out of your business for personal use.

Your pension (o)

Put here the amount of any pensions which would cease to be paid if you were to die. This could be state pension, pension from an employer's scheme or from a personal plan. If your spouse or other dependants would receive another pension, for example bereavement allowance from the state or a widow(er)'s pension from a pension scheme, enter this at 't' or 'v' below.

Your state benefits (p)

If you receive any state benefits, for example jobseeker's allowance or incapacity benefit, enter here the amount which would be lost. If your spouse or other dependants would receive other benefits instead, enter these at 'u' below.

Your spouse's/partner's earnings (q)

You are most likely to enter an amount here if you have children. Would your spouse or partner have to cut back on or stop work to look after them?

Income from investments which would be sold (r)

If you entered an amount under 'j' above, then put here any income which would be lost as a result.

Other income lost (s)

This might include, say, maintenance payments from a former spouse.

Bereavement benefits from the state (t)

A widow or widower under state pension age at the time of the husband's or wife's death might qualify for widowed parent's allowance or bereavement allowance (see below) if the deceased person had paid enough National Insurance contributions (see page 83). From a date yet to be announced (expected to be late-2005), same-sex partners who have registered their relationship may also qualify for these benefits in the same way as married people.

Widowed parent's allowance

This is payable where your spouse is caring for a child or children (and entitled to claim child benefit) or expecting your unborn child. The allowance is made up of:

- a basic amount (£82.05 a week in 2005–6); plus
- half of any state additional pension you had built up (and in some cases more than half of additional pension built up before April 2002). See Chapter 12 for information about state pensions.

Your husband or wife might also qualify for an increase in child tax credit or become newly eligible to claim it – see Chapter 10.

Widowed parent's allowance is taxable. The allowance stops when your spouse ceases to be entitled to receive child benefit or, if earlier, reaches state pension age, or remarries.

Bereavement allowance

If your widow or widower is not caring for children, he or she can obtain bereavement allowance provided he or she is over the age of 45 at the time of your death. But the allowance is paid only for a maximum of 52 weeks. The amount paid is age-related and, at 2004–5 rates, is at least £23.88 a week. The allowance is taxable.

Bereavement after state pension age

If husband and wife are both over state pension age at the time of the death, the surviving spouse can use the late spouse's contribution record to claim or boost a state pension. The maximum payable is the full basic pension for a single person (£79.60 in 2004–5) plus half the late spouse's additional pension (or in some cases a higher proportion of any pre-2002 additional pension). From a date to be announced (expected to be late-2005), same-sex partners who have registered their relationship as a civil partnership will be treated in the same way.

A widow over state pension age whose husband was under that age at death can also claim or boost a state pension in much the same way by using her late husband's National Insurance record. But this will not apply to widowers or same-sex civil partners until 2010.

Other state benefits (u)

A surviving husband, wife or partner caring for children might qualify for child tax credit – or an increased amount if the family had already been getting this benefit – see Chapter 10.

If the surviving spouse or partner would be on a low income, they might qualify for other means-tested benefits, such as working tax credit, income support or pension credit (see 'More information' on page 95).

Other pensions (v)

Enter here pensions your widow(er), partner and/or children would receive from occupational pension schemes which you belong to or personal pensions or stakeholder schemes you have. If these schemes or plans would pay out a lump sum, include it under 'i' or 'm' above.

Income from any existing life insurance policies (w)

If you already have life insurance which would pay out a regular income (that is, a family income benefit policy), record the monthly payout here.

Your spouse's/partner's earnings (x)

Would your spouse or partner take up a job, increase their hours or take up higher-paid work? Enter the likely increase.

Other (y)

Include here any other increases in income, such as rent from letting out a room in the family home. Enter the amount accordingly.

Help from the state for your widow or widower[1]

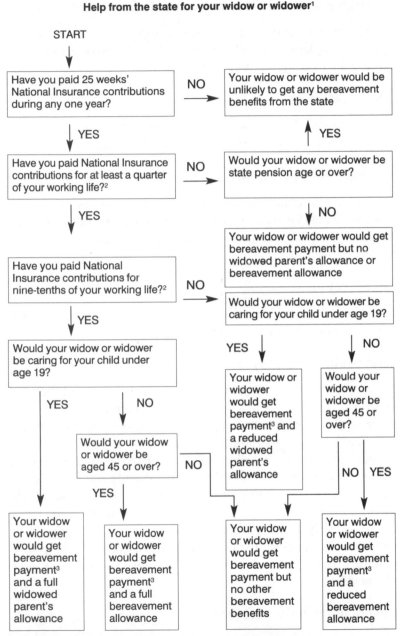

START

Have you paid 25 weeks' National Insurance contributions during any one year? — **NO** → Your widow or widower would be unlikely to get any bereavement benefits from the state

YES ↓ | ↑ **YES**

Have you paid National Insurance contributions for at least a quarter of your working life?[2] — **NO** → Would your widow or widower be state pension age or over?

YES ↓ | ↓ **NO**

Your widow or widower would get bereavement payment but no widowed parent's allowance or bereavement allowance

Have you paid National Insurance contributions for nine-tenths of your working life?[2] — **NO** → Would your widow or widower be caring for your child under age 19?

YES ↓ | **YES** ↓ / **NO** ↓

Would your widow or widower be caring for your child under age 19?

YES ↓ / **NO** ↓

Your widow or widower would get bereavement payment[3] and a reduced widowed parent's allowance

Would your widow or widower be aged 45 or over?

Would your widow or widower be aged 45 or over? — **NO** →

YES ↓ | **NO** | **YES**

Your widow or widower would get bereavement payment[3] and a full widowed parent's allowance

Your widow or widower would get bereavement payment[3] and a full bereavement allowance

Your widow or widower would get bereavement payment but no other bereavement benefits

Your widow or widower would get bereavement payment[3] and a reduced bereavement allowance

[1] From a date to be announced, expected to be late-2005, same-sex partners who have registered their relationship as a civil partnership will qualify in the same way.
[2] Working life is officially defined to start with the tax year in which you reach age 16.
[3] Provided your widow or widower is under state pension age at the time of your death.

Mortgage and other loan repayments (z)

If the mortgage and/or other loans would be repaid ('c' and 'd' above), your family would no longer have to make repayments. Record the monthly amount saved here.

Living expenses (aa)

There is likely to be some reduction in food bills, travelling expenses, entertainment, and so on. Enter the amount accordingly.

Life insurance premiums and pension contributions (bb)

If you are paying for life insurance or into a pension plan, these amounts would be saved. Don't include deductions from your pay, for example for 'superannuation', as these are already accounted for under 'n'.

Other (cc)

Any other reductions in expenses, for example maintenance payments which no longer have to be paid to a former spouse.

Cost of childcare (dd)

Record here any increase in the amount the family would pay for childcare. If both you and your spouse or partner work anyway, there might not be much change from the current position. But if you stay at home to look after the children, your spouse or partner would face a hefty bill for a nanny, childminder or nursery, unless you have relatives or friends who would be willing to help. Bear in mind too that if you are the main bread-winner, your spouse or partner might have to take up work (increasing the family income under 'x') but might incur childcare costs in order to do so. They might qualify for help with childcare costs from the state or through an employer (see Chapter 10).

Cost of home help, etc. (ee)

Would your dependants pay for other people to do jobs around the home which you had carried out?

Cost of replacing fringe benefits of your job (ff)

Your survivors might want to carry on enjoying some or all of the perks of your job. Replacing some fringe benefits, such as a company car, might mean paying out a lump sum and should be entered under 'g' above. But with others, regular expenditure might be required: for example, paying premiums for private medical insurance to cover hospital bills (see Chapter 8) or petrol and insurance for your car. Bear in mind, though, that any tax on such benefits will be saved.

Other (gg)

Enter here any other extra expenses not covered elsewhere.

Part 3: Amount of cover required

Do the sums shown in the Calculator. If amount 'I' is greater than zero, you need life insurance to provide the extra income shown. Either choose a family income benefit policy (see page 88) to provide the required amount, or lump-sum insurance which could be invested to provide the income. If you opt for the latter, consider who would manage the investments. The table overleaf gives a rough guide to the size of lump sum you might need.

Add the lump sum required to produce the income your dependants would need to the cash sum (if any) worked out at 'C'. This tells you the total amount of lump-sum life insurance you ideally require. The next section describes the types of policy you could choose.

Which type of insurance?

There are two broad types of life insurance: **protection-only ('term insurance')** and **investment-type**. If your main need is for protection, there are two schools of thought:

- The first recommends that you choose protection-only insurance, which is called 'term insurance'. In its simplest form, it pays out a specified amount if you die within a selected period of years. If you survive, it pays out nothing. It is the cheapest way overall of buying the cover you need. The numerous variations on this basic theme are described below.

Lump sum needed to provide each £1,000 of income each year

Period for which income is to be paid	Assuming invested lump sum grows by 4% a year and income stays the same each year	Assuming invested lump sum grows by 4% a year and income grows by 2% each year
5 years	£4,600	£4,800
10 years	£8,400	£9,200
15 years	£11,600	£13,100
20 years	£14,100	£16,700
25 years	£16,200	£20,000

- The second recommends that you choose a whole-of-life policy which is one form of investment-type policy. As the name suggests, this provides cover for as long as you live. Since the policy must eventually pay out, it builds up an investment value which you can cash in by surrendering the policy. But it takes many years for a surrender value to build up and, in general, whole-of-life policies are an expensive buy if your main need is protection. However, a variation called a 'maximum protection policy' lets you buy a high level of cover at a premium which is initially very low. This type of policy is discussed in more detail on page 89.

You should definitely avoid taking out an endowment policy if your primary need is protection. Endowment policies are investment-type life insurance which pay out if you die within a specified period (the endowment period) and also pay out if you survive. On the face of it this may seem appealing – something to gain whether you die or not – but such policies are an expensive way of buying life cover. Endowment policies can have a role to play in your financial planning, and this is considered in Chapters 9, 11 and 13, but they are not a good tool for straightforward protection of your dependants.

Variations on the term insurance theme

Level term insurance

The standard policy pays out a set lump sum on death. You choose what level of cover you need and the period for which you require it – for example, until the children have finished their education. The lump sum is paid out tax-free if you die within that term.

The premiums you pay are set at the time you take out the policy and depend largely on the level of cover, the term you choose, your age at the start and your state of health. You will normally be charged more – or even refused cover – if your work, hobbies or lifestyle are deemed to be particularly risky. Some insurance companies reserve the right to increase the premiums – often substantially – if they experience unusually high levels of claims against their term insurance policies. This is a device which was adopted in response to the problem of deaths through AIDS.

Increasing term insurance

This works much like the basic term insurance, except that the level of cover increases – and usually the premiums too – for example by 5 per cent a year or in line with inflation. It is worth considering this type of policy, especially if you are insuring for a long term, because increasing prices eat away at the value of a fixed level of cover as the years go by.

Increasable term insurance

This variant gives you the option to increase the level of cover either at set intervals – such as on each anniversary of taking out the policy – or when particular events occur – for example, marriage or the birth of a child. You pay extra in premiums for any increase in cover, but the premiums are worked out on the basis of your health at the time you first took out the original policy, even if your health has subsequently deteriorated.

Decreasing term insurance

With this variant, the amount of cover reduces year by year. The two main uses for this type of insurance are to repay loans, such as a mortgage (see Chapter 9), or to cover a potential inheritance tax bill on a lifetime gift (see Chapter 15).

> **Tip**
> Overall, term insurance is the cheapest way to buy large sums of life cover to protect your family. A maximum protection plan might be cheaper in the early years, but watch out for premium increases later on. Steer clear of other investment-type life insurance, such as endowment policies – they are an expensive way to buy life cover.

Renewable term insurance

This version allows you to extend the insurance term when it comes to an end. The premium you then pay is based on your health at the time you took out the original policy, even if your health has subsequently deteriorated. This can be a useful variation for dealing with the unexpected, for example a child who stays in full-time education for longer than you had expected.

It is also a good option if you cannot, at present, afford the level of cover you need for the period you want. Instead, you could take out the cover you need but for a shorter period. At the end of the period, you could take up your option for a further period. Premiums would then be higher because you would be older, but there would be no additional charge even if you had developed health problems.

Convertible term insurance

With this type of term insurance, you have the option at specified dates to convert your protection-only policy into an investment-type insurance policy based on your health at the time you took out the original term insurance. This option is of limited use.

Family income benefit insurance

Instead of paying out a single lump sum, this type of term insurance pays out a series of regular tax-free lump sums which you can use as income. The income starts to be paid at the time of death and continues until the end of the policy term. Since the policy pays out less overall the longer you survive, this is generally the cheapest form of term insurance and can be a good choice for families. A useful variation allows the regular income to increase over time to counteract the effects of inflation.

Pension-linked term insurance

If you are eligible to have a personal pension or stakeholder pension scheme (see Chapter 12), you are also eligible to take out pension-linked term insurance. The advantage of taking out term insurance in this way is that you get tax relief at your highest rate on the premiums you pay for the insurance.

The drawback is that currently it might reduce the amount you can save for retirement, though from 2006 this is unlikely to be a problem (see Chapter 12). If you are taking out the term insurance now, you can use up to 10 per cent of the amount you are paying into the personal pension or stakeholder scheme to pay for life cover.

Although you get tax relief, pension-linked term insurance is not always competitively priced, so you should still shop around and compare with ordinary term insurance.

If you are in an occupational pension scheme, you will often get some life cover through the scheme. Usually, this is limited to four times your salary. If your scheme offers less than the maximum cover, you may be able to increase it by paying additional voluntary contributions (AVCs) (see Chapter 12) either to an in-house AVC scheme or a free-standing scheme. In either case, what you pay qualifies for tax relief at your highest rate.

Maximum protection policies

Over the years, *Which?* has generally advised that you keep your protection and investment arrangements quite separate, independently choosing the best options to meet each need. However, there is one type of investment-type life insurance which does need to be considered within the context of protection: flexible whole-of-life policies which give the option of choosing maximum protection.

These are unit-linked policies (see Chapter 18). The premiums you pay go into an investment fund which is divided up into units. The value of your policy depends on how the price of these units moves and that, in turn, depends on the value of the underlying investments in the fund. You decide how much life cover you want within limits:

Tips

- If you cannot afford the amount of life insurance cover you need, you do not necessarily have to insure for less. Consider taking out the full cover but for a shorter time, using renewable term insurance, which guarantees that you can take out a further policy at the end of the original term when perhaps you can afford to pay more.
- If you are eligible for a personal pension or stakeholder pension scheme, you can get tax relief on what you pay for term insurance. Don't assume that pension-linked term insurance will always be the cheapest cover; compare it with the premiums payable for ordinary term insurance too.

- **minimum cover** Most of your premiums remain in the investment fund and hopefully build up a good cash-in value to give you a return on your investment. Alternatively, you might use the fund which has built up to pay for insurance later on: for example, to cover a potential inheritance tax bill (see Chapter 15).
- **maximum cover** Your units in the investment are cashed in each month to pay for the life cover. At this highest level of cover, and assuming a given return on the investment fund, it is expected that cover can be maintained at the same premium for, say, five or ten years. After that, it is likely that premiums would have to rise to maintain the same level of cover.

The policy is reviewed regularly, usually after the first ten years and after that every five years. At the review, the balance of premiums, investment fund and cover are checked. If your current premiums and fund are insufficient to maintain the chosen level of cover, either the premiums must increase or you must reduce your cover.

A maximum protection policy can be cheaper than term insurance in the early years and is, therefore, an option to consider if you need a lot of cover now for the lowest possible premium. But you must bear in mind that, at the policy review, your premiums are likely to rise or the cover reduce.

Other things to consider

Joint life policies

Instead of you and your spouse or partner taking out separate insurance policies, you could take out a joint life policy. A 'first death' policy covers both your lives and pays out once on the death of the first of you to die. A 'last survivor' policy pays out once on the death of the second of you to die. For protecting dependants, the 'first death' option is usually the more appropriate. A joint life policy will be suitable only if you both need to insure for the same amount. For example, a joint life policy may be ideal for paying off a mortgage in the event of one of you dying, but less suitable as a means of replacing lost income since the income needs will vary depending on which of you has died.

Writing life insurance in trust

If the proceeds of a life policy are paid to your estate on death, there can be a long delay before the money becomes available to your dependants and there could be inheritance tax to pay on the proceeds (see Chapter 15). Writing an insurance policy in trust avoids these problems by ensuring that the policy pays out direct to your dependants, bypassing your estate altogether. Many insurance companies give you the option of writing a policy in trust at no extra charge and have standard forms for doing this.

Life-of-another policies

So far, this chapter has considered life insurance policies you take out based on your own life, which pay out either to your estate or indirectly to someone else via a trust. An alternative is a policy which pays out direct to someone else if you die. This is called a life-of-another policy. For example, your husband, wife or partner takes out life insurance based on your life. If you die, the policy pays out direct to him or her, so there is no need to write the policy in trust.

With all types of life insurance, at the time the policy is taken out you must have an insurable interest in the life of the person covered. This means that you must stand to lose financially if he or she were to die. You are assumed automatically to have an unlimited insurable interest in your own life and in that of your husband or wife. From a

> **Tip**
>
> In the vast majority of cases, it makes sense to have your life insurance policy written in trust. Make a point of asking the insurer's advice about arranging your policy this way.

date yet to be announced (likely to be late-2005), same-sex partners who have registered their relationship as a civil partnership will also be assumed to have an unlimited interest in each other's lives. When it comes to other people, your insurable interest is limited to the amount that you would lose if they died. Therefore, a life-of-another policy cannot be taken out on someone with whom you have no financial connection. The main disadvantage of a life-of-another policy is if your relationship breaks down: your former spouse or partner owns the policy and has the absolute right to the proceeds if you were to die, so you may need to take out your own policy to ensure that any children would be financially provided for. On the other hand, where a relationship has already broken down, a life-of-another policy taken out by a parent with care of the children on the life of the absent parent can be useful as a way of protecting the family against the loss of maintenance payments in the event of the absent parent dying.

Waiver of premium

Both term insurance and whole-of-life policies may include 'waiver of premium'. This lets you suspend your premiums for a certain period in specified circumstances: for example if you are unable to work because of illness. You need to check the policy wording carefully to see precisely what conditions apply. Not all policies offer the waiver. With those that do, the waiver is sometimes automatically included and sometimes an optional extra. As an option, it could increase your premiums by around 6 per cent, say. Waiver of premium is a relatively cheap and straightforward way of making sure that your life cover would continue even if your finances were temporarily straitened.

Prepaid funeral plans

Even the simplest funeral is not cheap, and the idea of paying for your own funeral *in advance* is catching on in the UK. The advantages of a prepaid funeral are that you can choose the type of funeral you want and you don't have to feel a burden to relatives by leaving them to pick up the tab. Also, it's easier to shop around for the best deal when you are planning ahead. Very few people feel inclined to shop around different funeral directors immediately following a death in the family.

Typically, a prepaid plan works like this. You choose a funeral and pay for it at today's prices – either by handing over a lump sum or by making instalments spread over, say, five years. The idea is that the plan will pay for your funeral whatever the increase in funeral costs between now and then.

In practice, you can't always rely on all the funeral costs being met. You need to check the small print carefully to see just which costs are guaranteed to be paid and which are not. Also check what is included as part of the funeral. For example, a simple funeral might not include a church service – your estate or relatives would have to pay extra if this was to be part of your funeral. So be wary if you are attracted to a prepaid funeral plan. If a plan does not guarantee to cover all the costs, it might be better simply to earmark some of your savings or investments to cover eventual funeral expenses.

The money you pay for the plan is invested. It builds up a fund which the funeral director uses eventually to finance your funeral.

This raises concerns about what happens to the money you pay in. For example, in 1993, £35,000 disappeared from a prepaid scheme in Huddersfield and 30 elderly people's funeral arrangements were jeopardised. Fortunately, another company stepped in to help.

On the back of this and similar incidents, prepaid funerals plans were brought within the scope of the Financial Services and Markets Act 2000 (see Chapter 3). The Financial Services Authority (FSA)★ has the powers, if necessary, to make rules governing the way such plans are run. However, FSA regulation does not apply to plans where the money you pay in is used to buy a whole-of-life insurance policy (which is already within the scope of the FSA's regulations) or the money is held in a trust fund that meets certain conditions. In a trust fund, the money should be safe from misuse by the funeral director and from the director's creditors if the firm goes bust.

The funeral industry has set up its own self-regulatory body called the Funeral Planning Authority (FPA)★ to ensure that its members meet the conditions which exempt plans from FSA regulation. FPA

Expensive funeral

Brendan took out a funeral expenses life insurance plan in 1990 when he was 69. It is designed to pay out £1,808 for a monthly premium of £16.95. However, he realised that by March 1999, he had paid more than the policy will ever pay out. He asked the company what he should do. It said he could surrender the policy and receive £422.36 now; stop paying the premiums but keep the policy – it would then pay out the paid-up value of just £578.96 when he dies; or keep up the premiums to ensure his family receives the full £1,808. Whatever he does, Brendan will lose money.

Which? January 1999

---

members observe a code of conduct which includes requirements to provide adequate information about what is covered in a contract, charges and so on. Members must have proper complaints procedures. Consumers also have access to the FPA's conciliation service and independent arbitration. If a member goes out of business, there is a commitment that the FPA will try to arrange for other members to take over the contract. Membership of the FPA is voluntary, so make sure any firm you deal with does belong to this organisation.

Do not confuse prepaid plans with funeral expenses insurance. The latter is life insurance which on death pays out an amount which is intended to be enough to cover your funeral costs. However, the insurance is not linked to any particular funeral and there is no guarantee that it will be enough to cover the costs. Funeral expenses insurance is often poor value – because you are usually elderly when you start the plan, the premiums are high, and if you live a long time, you can end up paying more for the plan than it will pay out.

Prepaid funeral plans are sold through funeral directors and often advertised in magazines aimed at older people. If you do take out a prepaid funeral plan, don't forget to let your relatives know about it – otherwise they may arrange and pay for a funeral elsewhere, in which case your plan will be wasted. When choosing a prepaid funeral plan, be sure to ask: whether the firm belongs to the FPA; whether the proceeds are paid into a trust fund and who administers it; whether all disbursements are covered, regardless of inflation (and if this applies equally to burial and cremation); whether all incidental expenses are covered; what happens if you choose to pay by instalments and die before completion; and whether you can choose your funeral director without restriction.

More information

To find out more about most of the state benefits for which your dependants might qualify, see the relevant leaflets published by the Department for Work and Pensions (DWP)★. Leaflets are available from Jobcentre Plus★, The Pension Service★, many public libraries and some post offices.

Child benefit and tax credits are administered by the Inland Revenue★ – from where you can obtain explanatory leaflets and claim forms.

To find out which insurance companies offer the best-value protection insurance, see the regular surveys published by Moneyfacts★, and surveys in *Which?*★ and specialist personal finance

Leaflets about state benefits you might claim following a death

DWP leaflets

NP45	A guide to bereavement benefits
GL14	Widowed?
CA09	National Insurance contributions for widows or widowers
D49	What to do after a death in England and Wales
D49S	What to do after a death in Scotland
IS20	A guide to income support
RR2	A guide to housing benefit and council tax benefit
GL16	Help with your rent
GL17	Help with your council tax
GL18	Help from the social fund
GL23	Social security benefit rates
SB16	A guide to the social fund
SERPSL1	Inheritance of SERPS: Important information for married people

Inland Revenue leaflets

CH2	Child benefit claim form and notes
WTC2	Child tax credit and working tax credit – a guide

For information on what to do after a death in Northern Ireland, see the website *www.ssani.gov.uk*

magazines. Having narrowed down your choice to a few companies, contact those companies direct and ask them to send you literature about the policies you are interested in and to give you a quotation of how much you'll have to pay for the cover you want. (Some may refer you to an independent adviser.)

Got it covered

Andrea, 38, and Steven, 40, have two children, aged six and three. Andrea works part-time and her employer provides her with life cover of four times her salary. Steven, who is self-employed, has no life cover but pays into a personal pension. Both salaries are needed to cover the family's costs.

If Steven died ... Because Steven is the higher earner and has no life cover, the family would be particularly vulnerable if anything happened to him. Andrea would receive the fund that has built up in his personal pension but that's all. Andrea needs a regular income while the children are growing up. She would like to keep working but would want to be flexible about her hours, particularly while the children are very young. If Steven's income was lost, Andrea thinks she would need about £2,500 extra each month. However, she also needs to think about retirement. She is a member of her pension scheme at work, but if she continues to work part-time and reduces her hours further, this might not produce enough pension to live on so it might need topping up. A family income benefit policy on Steven's life which pays out an income of £30,000 a year for 18 years would provide Andrea with the income she needs until their youngest child is 21. A level term insurance policy for £50,000 would give her a nest egg for retirement and emergencies.

If Andrea died ... If Andrea's income was lost, Steven estimates he would need about £1,000 a month to cover extra childcare costs and to allow him to reduce his hours slightly to have more time with the children. He would have a lump sum of about £60,000 paid from Andrea's employers, so Steven does not need further capital. He needs a buffer to top up his earnings until the children are independent. A family income benefit policy on Andrea's life paying an income of £12,000 a year for 18 years would meet his needs.

Which? November 2000

Chapter 7

Protecting your income

It is estimated that you are 20 times more likely to be off work for six months because of sickness or injury than you are to die before reaching retirement. Few people question the need for life insurance to protect their dependants if they were to die, but only one working person in ten has any specific long-term financial protection if they are unable to work because of sickness. But few people would find it easy to cope with the financial impact of a prolonged illness. So why is this area of financial planning so often neglected? There are three main reasons:

- a mistaken belief that the state and employers will provide. A survey by Norwich Union Healthcare found that a quarter of the UK workforce believes they would receive their full salary from their employer or be supported by the state if they fell ill
- the high cost and complexity of insurance to protect your income.

What help can you expect if you fall ill?

The table on page 101 summarises the main types of health crisis that might damage your income. The two middle columns tell you broadly what help you might get from the state and from your employer. The final column suggests ways in which you can provide for yourself. The various ways of doing this are described more fully starting on page 104.

Protection from the state

Most people assume that the state provides a safety net to catch anyone who is unable to earn a living and has no other income to rely on. After all, is that not why we pay National Insurance? But you

---

Warning

Do not rely on the state to provide you with a reasonable income if you were unable to work for a long period due to illness or disability. You have to pass strict medical tests to qualify for incapacity benefit, and even then the average long-term payment was only £83 a week in 2004. The government has announced plans to cut state support even further.

---

might be surprised at how little the state would provide if you could not work because of a long-term illness or disability. The core help you can expect if you are off work sick for any length of time is incapacity benefit; the main rules for this are described below. In the case of disability, you might qualify for other state benefits – see page 102.

For the first 28 weeks

No benefits are payable for the first three days of illness. After that, most employees qualify for Statutory Sick Pay (SSP) which is paid by your employer – see page 104.

If you are self-employed or you are an employee who does not get SSP, and provided you have paid enough National Insurance contributions (see the chart on page 103), you can claim the lower rate of short-term incapacity benefit. In 2005–6 this is a tax-free £57.65 a week. There is no extra if you have children but you can claim child tax credit (see Chapter 10). You can claim an increase for your husband, wife or partner, but only if:

- they are caring for dependent children of the family (an increase of £35.65 a week in 2005–6), or
- your spouse or partner is aged 60 or over (an increase of £43.95 a week in 2005–6), and
- if working, your spouse or partner earns no more than the amount of the increase.

During this first stage, you can qualify for incapacity benefit because you are unable to do your normal job – you will need sick notes from your doctor. However, you may be required to attend a 'work-focused interview', the purpose of which is to identify work you could do and to help you draw up a plan for training, getting a job or starting a business if appropriate. If you refuse to attend the interview, your benefit may be cut or lost completely. From week 29 onwards, you must pass a strict medical test called the 'personal capability assessment'. It looks at your ability to perform certain functions, such as standing, seeing and reaching. You'll have to be found incapable of doing *any* work, not simply your normal job, in order to continue getting benefit. The personal capability assessment also focuses on what work you could undertake, despite your illness or disability.

From week 29 to week 52
Provided they satisfy the medical assessment, both employees and the self-employed switch to higher-rate short-term incapacity benefit (£68.20 a week in 2005–6). Although the amount is higher, it is now taxable. If applicable, you continue to get an increase for your partner but this is now taxable. If you have a family, you may qualify for child tax credit (see Chapter 10).

After a year
You switch to long-term incapacity benefit (£76.45 a week in 2005–6). If you are terminally ill or you are very severely disabled, you can get this rate of incapacity benefit from the twenty-ninth week onwards.

There is also an increase if you are under age 45 at the start of the illness. If you are under 35, you get an extra £16.05 a week in 2005–6. Between the ages of 35 and 44, you get less – £8.05 a week in 2005–6.

If you have children, you still get extra for your husband, wife or partner caring for your children, though this is paid at a higher rate than previously (£45.70 a week in 2005–6) provided he or she earns no more than £56.20 a week. This is taxable. You continue to claim child tax credit if you have dependent children (see Chapter 10).

Long-term incapacity benefit is not payable if you are over state pension age, but you will usually qualify for state retirement pension instead (see Chapter 12).

Reductions in incapacity benefit
Any incapacity benefit you qualify for will be reduced if you have income from pension schemes (which could be personal pensions, stakeholder schemes or occupational schemes) or income protection insurance (either your own policy or cover provided by an employer) and this income exceeds a given threshold. In 2005–6, the threshold is £85 a week (unchanged since its introduction in 2001). For every £1 of such income above £85 a week, you will lose 50p of benefit.

Do you need to protect your income in case of illness?

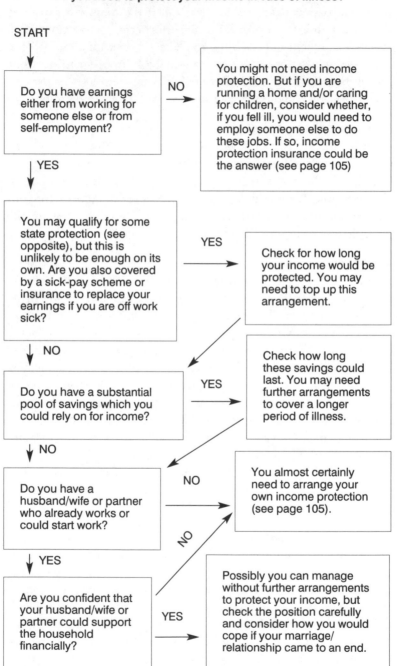

START

Do you have earnings either from working for someone else or from self-employment?

NO →

You might not need income protection. But if you are running a home and/or caring for children, consider whether, if you fell ill, you would need to employ someone else to do these jobs. If so, income protection insurance could be the answer (see page 105)

↓ YES

You may qualify for some state protection (see opposite), but this is unlikely to be enough on its own. Are you also covered by a sick-pay scheme or insurance to replace your earnings if you are off work sick?

YES →

Check for how long your income would be protected. You may need to top up this arrangement.

↓ NO

Do you have a substantial pool of savings which you could rely on for income?

YES →

Check how long these savings could last. You may need further arrangements to cover a longer period of illness.

↓ NO

Do you have a husband/wife or partner who already works or could start work?

NO →

You almost certainly need to arrange your own income protection (see page 105).

↓ YES

Are you confident that your husband/wife or partner could support the household financially?

NO ↗

YES →

Possibly you can manage without further arrangements to protect your income, but check the position carefully and consider how you would cope if your marriage/relationship came to an end.

How your income might be protected if you fall ill

What can go wrong	Help from the state [1]	Help from your employer	Possible private health insurances
You are off work sick for between 4 days and 28 weeks	• Incapacity benefit (lower rate) if you don't qualify for Statutory Sick Pay • Child tax credit if you have dependent children	• Statutory Sick Pay (unless your earnings are very low) *or* • Employer's own sick pay, if more generous than statutory scheme	• Sickness and accident insurance • Income protection insurance
You are off work sick for more than 28 weeks	• Incapacity benefit (higher rate/long-term rate) but you must pass a strict medical assessment • Disability benefits • Child tax credit if you have dependent children	• Sick pay if your employer runs a long-term scheme • Pension through early retirement on ill-health grounds	• Sickness and accident insurance – unlikely to extend beyond two years • Income protection insurance • Personal pension or stakeholder pension scheme – benefits can be paid from any age if you retire because ill, but the pension could be very low, especially if you are young
You have an accident which seriously maims you	• Benefits as above if you cannot work • Industrial injuries benefit if accident is work-related and you are an employee	• Protection as above if you cannot work • Lump sum if your employer has taken out accident insurance for employees	• Insurances as above if you are unable to work • Accident insurance • Critical illness insurance – some policies
You are diagnosed with a life-threatening illness	• Benefits as above if you cannot work	• Protection as above if you cannot work • Retirement pension might be replaced by a lump sum if you are not expected to live long	• Critical illness insurance

[1] In addition to the benefits listed, you might also qualify for income support, housing benefit and council tax benefit if your income is very low.

Other help from the state

Various benefits are available if you are deemed to be long-term disabled. For example, you might get disability living allowance if you need help with your personal care or have mobility problems. Where an injury was due to an accident at work or you suffer from an industrial disease, you might get industrial injuries disablement benefit.

Whether or not you get illness- or disability-related benefits, if your income is low, you might qualify for means-tested benefits to top up your income. If you are available for work, this will usually be non-contributory jobseeker's allowance. If you are not able to work, you might be able to claim income support. You might also qualify for help paying rent and council tax. You will not normally be able to get means-tested benefits if you have savings of more than £8,000. The benefit you get will be scaled down if your savings are less than this but still more than £3,000. Higher capital limits apply to people over age 60 and people living in residential and nursing homes.

If you have a disability but work at least 16 hours a week, you may be able to claim working tax credit including a disability element (see page 155).

How much help from the state?

Precisely what benefits you will qualify for and how much help you get will depend on your particular circumstances. See below for an example of how much a single-earner family with two children might get.

Example: how much state help?

Joe is self-employed and was earning £28,000 a year after tax, but has been off work for over a year with back problems. His wife Delia does not go out to work but looks after their two children, aged 2 and 3. In 2004–5, Joe is getting long-term incapacity benefit for himself of £74.15 a week plus an increase for Delia of £44.35, making a total of £118.50 a week or £6,162 a year. After tax, this is reduced to £6,020. The couple also claim child tax credit (see Chapter 10) made up of two individual elements (2 x £1,625 = £3,250) and the family element of £545. In total, the couple's income is £9,815 a year, in other words just a third of their previous income.

Who can get incapacity benefit?

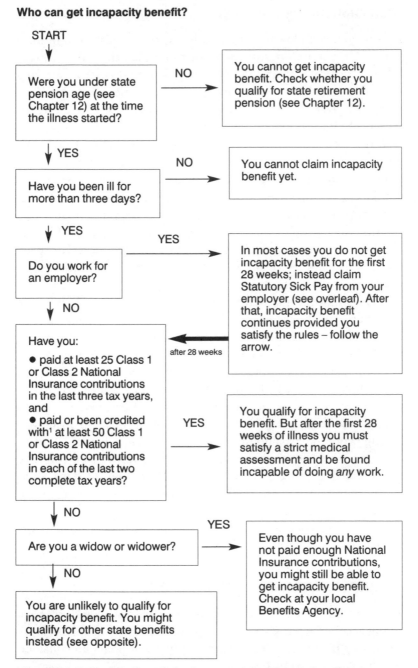

START

Were you under state pension age (see Chapter 12) at the time the illness started?

NO → You cannot get incapacity benefit. Check whether you qualify for state retirement pension (see Chapter 12).

YES

Have you been ill for more than three days?

NO → You cannot claim incapacity benefit yet.

YES

Do you work for an employer?

YES → In most cases you do not get incapacity benefit for the first 28 weeks; instead claim Statutory Sick Pay from your employer (see overleaf). After that, incapacity benefit continues provided you satisfy the rules – follow the arrow.

NO

Have you:

- paid at least 25 Class 1 or Class 2 National Insurance contributions in the last three tax years, and
- paid or been credited with[1] at least 50 Class 1 or Class 2 National Insurance contributions in each of the last two complete tax years?

after 28 weeks

YES → You qualify for incapacity benefit. But after the first 28 weeks of illness you must satisfy a strict medical assessment and be found incapable of doing *any* work.

NO

Are you a widow or widower?

YES → Even though you have not paid enough National Insurance contributions, you might still be able to get incapacity benefit. Check at your local Benefits Agency.

NO

You are unlikely to qualify for incapacity benefit. You might qualify for other state benefits instead (see opposite).

[1] You may have been credited with contributions if you were out of work because of, say, illness or unemployment.

Protection through your job

By law, your employer must usually pay you at least a minimum amount if you are off work sick for more than three days; this is called Statutory Sick Pay (SSP). In 2005–6, SSP is set at £68.20 a week. It is taxable just like ordinary pay, so income tax and National Insurance may be deducted from it if you also have some other income. SSP is payable for up to 28 weeks.

If you earn less than the 'lower earnings limit' – a figure set by the government each year, equal to £82 a week in 2005–6 – your employer does not have to pay you SSP. A few other groups of employees are not covered by the scheme, including workers over state pension age, anyone on a contract lasting less than three months and people working for overseas employers. If your employer does not pay you SSP, he or she must give you a claim pack SSP1. This includes a claim form for incapacity benefit, which you might be able to get instead.

Your employer may run a sick-pay scheme which is more generous than the minimum SSP: for example, maintaining your full pay for several months and then perhaps half-pay for a few more. Some employers take out insurance to provide income for sick employees over a longer period; this is called 'group income protection insurance'. The insurance works in a similar way to the private insurance you can arrange for yourself (see below), except the income it pays out is taxable. Income protection insurance through your job usually counts as a tax-free fringe benefit.

If you are unlikely to be able to return to work at all, you may qualify for early retirement on the grounds of ill health. This could trigger an immediate pension from your employer's pension scheme if it runs one – see Chapter 11.

Check your contract of employment to see what arrangements apply to you.

Arranging your own protection

The main way in which you can make sure that you would still have enough to live on if you could not work because of illness is by taking out insurance. There are three types of policy to consider, which are described below.

Warning

Whenever you apply for insurance, you are under a duty to disclose all 'material facts', in other words information that might affect an insurer's decision to cover you or the premium that will be charged. This is especially important with health insurances, where a subsequent claim may be refused if you have failed to disclose information about symptoms or treatment you have had for a health problem you already had before applying for cover (called a 'pre-existing condition').

Income protection insurance

Income protection insurance (IPI) replaces part of your income if you are unable to work because of illness or disability.

Income from IPI that you pay for yourself (rather than provided by your employer – see opposite) is tax-free. Insurers limit the amount of income you can cover. Typically, the maximum income you are allowed to replace is 50 to 65 per cent of your income before tax (your gross salary if you are an employee or your taxable profits if you are self-employed). Usually this limit includes replacement income from all IPI policies, pension schemes and so on. Often it also includes benefits you are entitled to claim from the state. You won't be able to claim more than the permitted maximum, so it's important to work out the limit which applies to you and make sure you don't pay extra for cover you wouldn't be able to have.

The replacement income is normally paid until retirement or until you recover, whichever comes first. But some budget policies limit the maximum payout period to, say, two or five years. This makes the plans cheaper, but would leave you unprotected if you suffered a prolonged illness or permanent disability.

There's no doubt that IPI is expensive, but there are various steps you can take to cut the cost.

You choose how soon after the onset of an illness you want the policy to start paying out. This is called the 'waiting period' or 'deferred period' and can normally be 4, 13, 26, 52 or even 104 weeks. Choosing a longer waiting period reduces the premiums you pay. You can fit the waiting period to your other resources, for example a sick-pay scheme at work, or savings.

When choosing the amount of income you want the policy to provide, you do not have to opt for the maximum allowed under the policy rules. You can choose a lower amount. Work out what level of spending you need to cover.

The payout can be at a flat rate. Alternatively, you can opt for an increasing income – worth considering, since otherwise inflation will erode the value of the income. There are two aspects to this: first, you want to know that the amount you would start to get if you made a claim is being increased each year; secondly, once an income is being paid, you want to be sure that it will be increased. The drawback is that the premium increases each year along with the cover.

Watch out for the definition of 'inability to work' used by the policy. There are three possibilities:

- inability to do your own job
- inability to do a job for which you are suited by training and experience
- inability to do any job.

The last definition is the broadest, reducing the likelihood of your having a valid claim, so you should expect to pay less for a policy using this definition. The first definition is the narrowest and usually the most expensive. Some policies change the definition after, say, two years of claiming. For example, you might be covered for the first two years if you can't do your normal job, but then payouts cease unless you are so ill or disabled that you can't do any job.

Premiums are set on one of three bases. Most common and generally cheapest are *reviewable premiums*. These are set for an initial period – usually five years – after which they can be increased if the insurance company finds that claims by its policyholders are higher than it had expected. But any increase in premiums as a result of a review will apply to *all* policyholders as a group, not just to selected individuals.

Renewable policies have a fixed term, typically five years, after which you can take out a further fixed-term policy but based on your age at renewal and, with some companies, a reassessment of your health and other factors at that time.

The most expensive policies have *guaranteed premiums*, which are set for the full duration of the policy and do not increase (except with increases in cover).

How premiums are set at the start of the policy depends on a wide range of factors:

- **your sex** Usually, women have to pay substantially more (for example, around half as much again) as men for the same cover. This is because, as a group, they tend to make more claims and for longer periods.
- **your age** at the time you first take out the policy. IPI is more expensive the older you are, because older people tend to have more health problems.
- **your job** Some jobs carry bigger risks to health than others. For example, your premiums will be lower if you have a relatively 'safe' job, such as a bank manager, civil servant, computer programmer, or secretary, than if you are a manual worker or driver, say. Some workers, for example bar staff and divers, might find it hard to get cover at all. Some plans offer cover to housewives and househusbands, deeming the value of their work to be equivalent to earnings of, say, £10,000 a year. The insurance providers set their job categories according to their own experience of claims. A job treated as high risk by one insurer might be assigned a lower risk by another, so it is definitely worth shopping around.
- **your state of health** Expect to pay higher premiums or be refused cover altogether if you already have health problems. However, with most policies, once you have been accepted for cover you will not be turned down or have your premiums loaded because you *subsequently* claim on the policy. But while all IPI insurers refuse claims related to AIDS or HIV, a few will not continue your cover at all if, having taken out a policy, you are subsequently diagnosed as HIV-positive.
- **your hobbies** Expect additional premiums or restrictions on cover if you enjoy flying, racing or other sports which insurers consider dangerous.
- **your lifestyle** Smokers are often charged more, you'll usually have to give details of how much alcohol you drink regularly, and insurance companies want to find out whether there's a risk of your contracting HIV.
- **the chosen level of payout** The higher the income you choose, the higher the premiums.

- **the waiting period** The sooner you want the payout to start, the higher the premiums.
- **other policy options** For example, you pay more for increasing policies than ones paying out a level benefit.

Income protection policies can either be pure insurance, in which case your monthly premiums go directly to buy the cover you've selected, or they can be investment-linked. With the latter, your monthly payments are invested and the cost of the insurance is paid from your investment fund. Your plan is reviewed, typically, every five years. If the investments have grown by a target rate or more, cover continues at the standard price (and you might receive a cash sum when the policy comes to an end). But if the investments have not grown as well as expected, your premiums are increased or the cover might finish earlier than you had originally intended.

Payment protection insurance

Payment protection insurance is designed to make the interest payments on a loan if you are unable to work because of illness. It helps you cope with that particular expense but is no substitute for income protection insurance (see opposite).

Payment protection insurance is a type of sickness and accident insurance (see opposite) and often will also pay out if you become unemployed. The payouts, which are tax-free, are for a limited period – usually a maximum of one or two years. Often it is not worth taking out this cover because:

- it is costly relative to the size of payout
- unless the loan is secured on your home (see below), keeping up the repayments is unlikely to be a top priority if your income suddenly dropped
- these policies are riddled with exclusions so you need to check carefully that a particular policy would pay out in your case given your health and employment details.

Be on your guard against taking out this insurance unwittingly. Lenders often automatically include it in a loan quote even though taking out the cover is optional. Check quotes carefully and, if you don't want cover, ask for a quote without the insurance.

Where a loan is secured on your home, you could lose your home if you failed to keep up the payments. This applies to mortgages (see

Chapter 9) and any other loan secured against your home. In this situation it may be worth taking out loan payment protection insurance (called 'mortgage payment protection insurance' if you take it out to cover a mortgage) but you'll still need to check the small print carefully to make sure the policy would pay out given your circumstances. For more about mortgage payment protection insurance, see Chapter 9.

Sickness and accident insurance

Accident insurance pays out a tax-free lump sum if you suffer a specified injury or die: for example, you might get £5,000 for the loss of a finger or a big toe, £10,000 for the loss of hearing, £100,000 for permanent disability. Although this type of insurance is very cheap – sometimes it is even offered free as an enticement to you to take up some other financial product – the probability of your suffering the particular injuries which are covered is very low. On the whole, accident insurance on its own is not worth buying.

However, accident insurance is often included with other insurances, such as travel policies and car insurance. It is also sometimes combined with sickness insurance. The sickness insurance element of the policy typically pays out a limited income (but might not cover the first few weeks of illness) for a maximum of two years, if you cannot work because of illness or an accident. The income is tax-free. Unlike IPI, there is no ongoing cover with sickness insurance; you simply take out the policy for a year at a time. At renewal, the premiums can be increased or cover refused if you have built up a record of claims or suffered a deterioration in your health. For this reason and because of the limited period for which the benefits are payable, sickness insurance is a poor substitute for IPI.

Critical illness insurance

Critical illness cover (CIC) pays out a sizeable tax-free lump sum if you are diagnosed with a specified life-threatening condition or have to undergo certain types of surgery. Over the last ten years or so, CIC has become increasingly popular due to its relative cheapness and seeming simplicity.

CIC policies are often sold as part of a mortgage package and are also sold as stand-alone policies. CIC is also commonly combined with life insurance, with some policies paying out either on diagnosis of a specific illness or on death, and others paying out in both events.

When you first take out the policy, you may be able to opt for 'buy-back CIC' or 'buy-back life insurance' which lets you take out further CIC or life cover, often at a nominal cost, after you have claimed on a CIC policy. This is certainly worth considering. Survival rates from a critical illness are often good and it is usually impossible to get new cover in the years immediately following such an illness. Typically, buy-back CIC covers the major three critical illnesses – heart attack, stroke and cancer – from which you are most likely to recover but also risk a further attack.

There is often a waiting period between diagnosis and payout: for example, 28 days or even as long as six months or a year for certain conditions, such as total permanent disability. However, if the diagnosis is clear-cut, the insurer might be prepared to waive the waiting period.

The maximum payout varies from policy to policy, with £500,000 or £1 million being common, though cover for higher amounts might be available on request. Where the policy is linked to your mortgage, the lump sum is obviously designed to pay off the mortgage but, with other policies, there are no restrictions on how you use the money. For example, you might use it in the same way as an income protection policy to cover living expenses while you are off work, but equally you could pay for private medical treatment, buy the services of a carer, adapt your home, put it towards retraining for a less stressful career, help your dependants or even take a holiday.

Nearly all policies cover seven core conditions: cancer, heart attack, stroke, kidney failure, coronary artery bypass, multiple sclerosis and major organ transplant. Insurers who are members of the Association of British Insurers (ABI) – and most are – agree to use standard definitions of both these core conditions and many of the additional conditions that policies typically cover, such as blindness, motor neurone disease, Parkinson's disease and third degree burns. The ABI reviews these definitions usually once every three years.

Although CIC seems on the surface to be a fairly straightforward type of insurance, medical advances make it increasingly complex. Health conditions that a few years ago were unequivocally 'critical' may no longer be life-threatening or disabling. This is leading to more complicated definitions of medical conditions, making it much harder to understand what is and is not covered by a CIC policy.

Beware of policy exclusions: for example, some policies do not cover Alzheimer's or Parkinson's disease if it is first diagnosed after the age of 60, which is very likely to be the case. Also, do not be overly impressed by long lists of ailments; often another policy will cover the same conditions but under one of its broader headings. For example, in recent years some insurers have added Creutzfeldt Jakob Disease (CJD) as a specified condition, but this would almost certainly be covered under another section, such as coma, terminal illness or total permanent disability.

Cancer, heart attacks, stroke, total permanent disability and multiple sclerosis account for nine-tenths of all claims, with cancer topping the list by a wide margin (54 per cent of all claims). Government statistics show that about one person in three develops cancer and around a fifth of the population have a cardiovascular disease, ranging from angina and high blood pressure through to heart attacks and stroke. Overall, nearly two-thirds of the population suffer a critical illness at some stage in their lives. In the past they would often have died, but survival rates are now reasonably good. For example, 40 per cent of cancer sufferers survive for five years or longer, and over half of heart attack victims are alive ten years later.

CIC is substantially cheaper than IPI, which makes it look a tempting substitute. However, although a large lump sum from a critical illness policy could be used to provide a replacement income for an extended period, the range of conditions it covers is by definition limited. If you are unable to work because of, say, a back injury or stress (both common conditions), a critical illness policy will not be any help.

Warning

Some policies combine CIC with life insurance but pay out just once – either on diagnosis of a life-threatening condition or on death, whichever happens first.

Be wary of these policies. They make sense if you intend to use the payout to, say, pay off your mortgage. But, if you would use the payout to cover care costs while you were ill but also want to protect your family if you die, this type of policy is not suitable unless it includes a life cover buy-back (see page 109). Without a buy-back, using the payout during your lifetime would leave your survivors unprotected in the event of your death.

Don't underestimate homework

Melanie, 28, and Peter, 31, have recently had their first baby, which started them thinking about their finances. In particular they were worried about what would happen if either one of them died or couldn't work. *Which?* drafted in the help of two independent financial advisers to give them advice.

Peter is a children's worker and Melanie is a full-time mother. The couple have a monthly income of £1,350 but, because of some fairly strict budgeting, still manage to save £100 each month and have around £150 left over.

As well as life insurance – a real priority – the advisers look at income protection. Neither of the experts recommend critical illness cover – it isn't as helpful as income protection and should be seen as an extra rather than an alternative.

The risk of being off work for six months is considerably higher than the risk of dying before the age of 60. As Peter is the only earner, it's important that the family could cope financially if he couldn't work. But forking out for income protection insurance is unnecessary. Because his income is reasonably low, the total amount of state benefits he could claim would actually be greater than the maximum amount he could insure himself for. That's because insurers don't want claimants to be better off sick than when working. The maximum benefit Peter could get under a policy would be around £200 tax-free a week. The couple will need to review the situation if Peter's salary increases and/or the benefits he could claim change.

They also need to think about what would happen if Melanie became too ill to look after the baby. They might need to pay for childcare or help around the house. It could be worth taking out insurance to cover these expenses, as Melanie would not be entitled to state benefits or sick pay. Most income protection policies allow you to take out houseperson's cover. You're usually limited to a maximum yearly benefit of around £15,000. The family could expect to pay between £20 and £25 a month for a policy that would start to pay out after six months of illness. The cost would be higher if they wanted the policy to start paying out earlier.

Which? September 2002

More information

To find out more about the state benefits you might qualify for if you are ill, contact Jobcentre Plus★ or, if you are over pension age, The Pension Service★.

See the table below for a list of useful leaflets about state benefits. Most are published by the Department of Work and Pensions (DWP)★, but tax credit leaflets are produced by and available from the Inland Revenue★.

Free leaflets about the main state benefits if you are ill or disabled

Leaflet number	Title
DWP leaflets	
SD1	Sick or disabled
SD2	Sick and unable to work?
SD3	Long-term ill or disabled?
IB1	A guide to incapacity benefit
IB214	Incapacity benefit: the personal capability assessment
GL23	Social security benefit rates
Inland Revenue leaflet	
WTC2	Child tax credit and working tax credit – a guide

Check your contract of employment or talk to your Human Resources department to find out what arrangements your employer has for paying sick employees.

Magazines such as *Money Management*★ publish regular surveys of income protection policies and critical illness insurance. Having identified suitable policies, you can contact most companies direct. However, because of the complex nature of income protection insurance and the many factors influencing premiums, this is an area where it is probably worth visiting an independent financial adviser. A good adviser will have access to a database of most or all of the policies available and can arrange quotations of those which would be most suitable for you.

Chapter 8

Insuring against illness and dental bills

Unlike most of the other areas described in this book, insuring against illness does not meet an *essential* need – after all, the National Health Service (NHS) provides cradle to grave care, doesn't it? Well, up to a point. The promise of a huge increase in funding for the NHS over the period to 2008 has not stemmed a steady increase in the number of people willing to 'go private'. Their decision reflects actual or perceived shortcomings in NHS provision.

Over 1 million surgical procedures every year are carried out privately. A survey by *Which?* found that the most common reasons for choosing private treatment are:

- to see a consultant more rapidly
- to avoid NHS waiting lists for operations, and
- to choose a convenient time to be treated.

Private treatment is not cheap and one way to cover the cost is to plan ahead by taking out private medical insurance (PMI). PMI covers some 6.7 million people with nearly three-quarters getting cover through work.

When it comes to dental check-ups and treatment, you may have little choice but to go private, since dentists in some areas will no longer accept NHS patients at all. Dental insurance is one of several options which can help you avoid large, unexpected bills – see page 124.

Who needs private hospital treatment?

Traditionally, the NHS provides cradle-to-grave care largely free at the point of use. Like any service which is free to users, there is a built-in tendency for demand to mushroom. Resources are limited, so some form of rationing or queuing is inevitable. Various government measures aim to cut hospital waiting lists – for example, mobile surgery units, contracting private hospitals to undertake NHS treatment and even sending NHS patients to hospitals abroad. But the government target of a maximum wait of 18 weeks from GP referral to treatment can still seem a long and worrying time and it does not include any period spent waiting for scans and tests prior to diagnosis which can add many months to the time between first seeking medical help and getting treatment.

Clearly, waiting months for treatment is likely to be unpleasant, especially if you are in pain. But in some cases it can be a financial disaster as well. For example, if you run your own business, you simply may not be able to afford to be off work for months pending treatment. The same thinking is behind the increase in the number of employers offering cover for private treatment as a fringe benefit to employees.

More controversially, going private might sometimes give you access to better treatment. For example, a case in the news in April 2000 involved a woman suffering from breast cancer. Her consultant explained that one drug existed which would almost certainly cure her while a second was good but less reliable. Because the first drug was considered too expensive, the district health authority would not allow it to be prescribed on the NHS. However, the drug, which had been in use for many years, was available to patients who could pay for private treatment.

Going private lets you choose a time to go into hospital which is convenient for you, given your family, work and other commitments. You can expect quality treatment because you will be seen by a consultant rather than a more junior doctor, as is often the case on the NHS. Going private also lets you enjoy hotel-style facilities, such as your own room, TV and private bathroom.

On the minus side, most private hospitals do not have on-site emergency facilities, so even if you opt for the private route you will still be treated on the NHS in a crisis. This means you might have to be moved to another hospital if your condition became critical.

Who needs medical insurance?

A major drawback of private treatment is its high cost (see the table on page 118). However, it is estimated that only four out of every

100 procedures cost more than £5,000. So one option is to set aside some of your savings and simply pay for private treatment as and when you need it (called the 'self-pay' option). The most common operations done on a self-pay basis are hip replacements, cataract removal and knee replacements, reflecting the fact that older people make up a high proportion of self-payers. Shopping around for a hospital is often worthwhile. Some hospitals run special deals, such as a fixed price for selected operations, particularly at times of the year when demand for beds tends to be lower. There are even specialist advisers – Health Care Navigator★ and Go Private★ – which for an annual fee take customers through the process of getting private treatment at an affordable price.

Given that medical insurance is costly, especially as you get older, the self-pay route may be a good option for many people. But it is not without drawbacks. The first is that a need for treatment might arise soon after you had started saving and before you had built up a large enough fund. The second is that, however much you saved, there would always be an outside chance that you would need very costly treatment – for example, a series of operations – that would require more than you had set aside. You could resign yourself to falling back on the NHS if your savings are not enough.

Or you could take out a loan to cover the shortfall. Many private hospitals offer their own loan arrangements. Alternatively, you can plan ahead by taking out appropriate insurance.

The most direct way to insure yourself is to take out private medical insurance (PMI) – see opposite. In the past, this was an alternative to using the NHS or paying yourself for private treatment. But, increasingly these days, you can use PMI in conjunction with the self-pay option largely due to the growing use of PMI policies with a large 'excess' (see page 121).

Hospital cash plans (see page 122) are sometimes erroneously viewed as an alternative to PMI. While these cash plans in no way fully fund private treatment, they can help you to meet the cost in part or cover some of the incidental costs of being in hospital.

The plans you make for coping financially with hospital treatment depend in part on how likely you feel it is that you would need such treatment. The table on page 118 shows the proportion of people in Britain receiving hospital treatment in a year. It shows that at younger ages women are slightly more likely than men to attend a hospital and that as you might expect hospital treatment tends to increase with age.

The chart on page 119 summarises who needs medical insurance.

Private medical insurance (PMI)

What is PMI?

PMI is insurance to cover the costs of receiving private hospital treatment. It has a long history, dating from pre-NHS days, when people paid into friendly societies which then helped members financially in times of need. Some PMI providers, such as BUPA, are still non-profit-distributing bodies. But many commercial insurance companies also offer PMI nowadays.

It is important to realise that no PMI policy covers every possible private treatment cost. PMI is designed to cover only 'acute illnesses', that is, conditions which can be cured or substantially alleviated by treatment. In particular, 'chronic illnesses', such as arthritis or multiple sclerosis, which would require long-term treatment, are excluded. However, treatment for an acute problem related to a long-term illness might be covered: for example, a hip replacement to ease pain and immobility caused by arthritis. Cover for mental conditions – which in one form or another affect one person in four in Britain – is generally very restricted or excluded altogether.

Other common exclusions are cosmetic surgery, treatment for alcoholism or drug abuse, treatment for infertility or normal pregnancy, and AIDS. Most standard policies also do not cover seeing a GP privately, routine check-ups and dental work (unless carried out in a hospital), although some of the more comprehensive policies do.

One other important exclusion is so-called 'pre-existing conditions', that is, health problems you already have at the time you apply for insurance. Most PMI providers are willing to 'underwrite' these conditions. That means that they look at the likelihood of such conditions causing a claim and either charge you a higher premium or put special rules into your policy, such as refusing to cover any treatment related to the condition. Some providers offer a 'moratorium' approach. How this typically works is that the PMI provider refuses to pay for any treatment relating to the condition until two full years have gone by without your needing treatment for it. After that, the health problem is covered just like any other.

Guide prices to some common private treatments

Treatment	Cost
Varicose vein treatment	£1,050–£1,850
Hernia	£1,050–£2,025
Cataract removal	£1,275–£2,560
Hip replacement	£5,500–£9,750
Heart bypass	£9,500–£12,500

Source: Health Care Navigator as published in *Which?* May 2002

Proportion of people receiving hospital treatment and time spent in hospital

Receiving treatment as:	Men aged:				Women aged:			
	16-44	45-64	65-74	75+	16-44	45-64	65-74	75+
Inpatient in 12-month period	5%	8%	15%	18%	9%	8%	8%	16%
Average number of nights as inpatient in 12-month period	5	7	7	11	4	7	7	14
Day patient in 12-month period	7%	8%	11%	12%	9%	8%	10%	10%
Average number of separate days as day patient in 12-month period	2	2	2	4	2	2	3	3
Outpatient or casualty patient in 3-month period	11%	15%	24%	26%	12%	16%	20%	25%

Source: National Statistics, *Living in Britain: Results from the 2002 General Household Survey*, The Stationery Office, 2004

Warning

If you have a health problem which is covered by an existing PMI policy, you should be very wary about switching to another policy because you would lose cover for that health problem.

What does PMI cover?

PMI covers the cost of treatment as an inpatient or daypatient in a private hospital or a private ward or pay bed in an NHS hospital. Outpatient treatment might also be included.

Top-of-the-range plans – sometimes called 'comprehensive' – cover treatment, whether as an inpatient or an outpatient, in most or all private hospitals and wards, and the full cost of treatment is paid by the insurance. These plans usually include extras such as complementary

Who needs medical insurance?

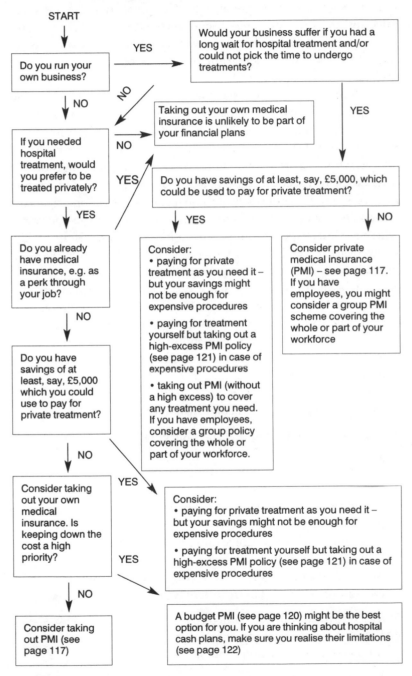

medicine (for example, osteopathy and chiropractic) and home nursing. Some add in the cost of seeing GPs privately and dentists' and opticians' charges. Cover may extend abroad. A top-of-the-range plan can easily cost you hundreds of pounds a month. Not surprisingly, then, there is a whole spectrum of policies offering less cover in exchange for lower premiums.

What might be dubbed 'standard plans' cover fewer extras than the top-notch plans, and outpatient treatment is often covered only if related to a spell as an inpatient. But a major way of keeping down cost is to restrict the range of hospitals you can use. A common way plans do this is to offer you a choice between three lists (or more) of hospitals. One list covers most or all private hospitals and wards, the next excludes the most costly of these (generally the more expensive London hospitals) and the third is limited to the hospitals and wards which are least expensive. If you use a hospital which is not on the selected list, there is no guarantee that the full cost will be met; instead, you get an 'out-of-band' benefit of a specified cash sum for each night in hospital. The more restricted the hospital list you choose, the lower your premiums. If you live outside London, you are unlikely to need the most comprehensive list. The important point to check is that the list you choose includes the private facil-ities that you would want to use – because they are convenient to your home, for example.

'Budget plans' keep down costs by limiting cover further still. This can be done in one or a combination of the following ways:

- capping the amount which the policy will pay out overall each year
- capping the amount which the policy will pay out for certain areas of cover: for example, surgeons' fees, outpatient costs
- excluding cover altogether for some treatments: for example, physiotherapy, outpatient care
- restricting you to a single and fairly limited list of private hospitals and wards
- 'six-week waiting plans'. These cover private treatment only if the waiting list for NHS treatment is longer than six weeks.

At least one insurer has contained cost by introducing a new type of PMI that covers treatment only for two specific, albeit relatively common conditions: heart problems and cancer.

High-excess PMI plans

The traditional breakdown between comprehensive, standard and budget plans is being broken through the emergence of a relatively new type of PMI: the 'high-excess plan'. Instead of cutting cover, these plans offer standard or comprehensive coverage but keep the cost down by requiring you to pay a large 'excess'. An excess is the first part of a claim which you agree to pay yourself. The insurance kicks in to pay any amount over and above the excess. The amount of excess and impact on price vary from one company to another but, for example, agreeing to pay the first £1,000 could cut the premium by around a quarter and a £2,000 excess could knock as much as 60 per cent off the price. You should check carefully the basis used to work out the excess. A few policies apply the excess to every claim, so if you claimed several times you would have to pay the excess several times over. Most policies apply the excess to each policy year, so even if you claimed twice in the year you would still only pay one excess – but you need to watch out where a claim straddles two policy years as you could then be charged two lots of the excess. At least one company charges just one excess a year but sets the clock ticking at the start of the claim, so you have a full 12 months within which to settle the claim or make further claims without a second excess being incurred. Also watch out if there are cash limits on the payout – check if the cash limits include any excess you pay (in which case, the policy may in fact pay out very little). It is better if the limits apply over and above any excess.

High-excess plans are a good idea if you have some savings which you are happy to use towards the cost of private treatment but you want to be protected against larger bills. Some experts suggest that budget PMI should be approached in the same way – in other words, be prepared to pay to fill in the gaps in cover, particularly the cost of initial private outpatient consultations.

What does PMI cost?

With PMI, you get very much what you pay for. If you want a comprehensive plan, you pay a high price or a high excess. If you want to pay less, you must accept restrictions or be prepared to meet part of the cost of treatment yourself.

Apart from the type of cover you choose, age is the other major influence on price. This reflects the fact that the older you are the more likely it is that you will need hospital treatment. Figures from the Association of British Insurers suggest that someone aged 65 will generally pay more than twice as much as someone aged 45 who will typically pay around a quarter more than someone aged 35. Some PMI insurers have also started to take your postcode into account on the basis that people in some areas tend to experience more health problems than people living in other districts.

Some companies offer numerous discounts on premiums under certain circumstances: for example, if you belong to a particular profession, have a certain credit card, belong to a particular motoring organisation, and so on. There is often a discount (5 per cent, say) if you agree to pay annually rather than monthly. A few plans have a no-claims discount, so that the next year's premium is reduced if you don't make any claims. One of the most effective ways to cut the cost is to choose a high-excess plan (see page 121) or agree a voluntary excess with other types of plan.

The cost of medical insurance can rise rapidly from one year to the next, reflecting overall claims experience and increases in the cost of private treatment.

Hospital cash plans

What is a hospital cash plan and what does it cover?

This pays out a tax-free cash sum for each day you are treated as an inpatient or daypatient in either an NHS or a private hospital. This type of insurance may be combined with a range of other cash benefits: cash payments if you need dental treatment or chiropody, for example, or become pregnant.

Hospital cash plans are not a substitute for PMI: the cash payments are typically small – for example, one leading plan pays from £10 up to £80 a night, depending on the premium level you choose – and they are not enough to cover the cost of private treatment. Usually, they are marketed as useful for covering the incidental costs of being in hospital: childcare or relatives travelling to visit you, for example. It is sometimes suggested that they are also useful as a way of replacing earnings lost because of being off work, but once again the low payments and the fact that the size of the sum paid out is totally unrelated to the income you may need to replace mean that such plans are a poor substitute for proper income protection insurance (see Chapter 7).

How worthwhile a hospital cash plan will be depends crucially on the amounts it pays out and the probability that the events which trigger the payments will occur. Particular points to note are as follows:

- There is often a waiting period before any benefits become available. Often this will be, say, six months, but it may be longer for some types of claim.
- Usually, claims connected with health problems you had before taking out the plan or before the expiry of the waiting period are not covered at all.
- You get a cash sum for each night you spend in hospital. According to a government survey, the 8 per cent of people who had been an inpatient one or more times during a 12-month period, on average spent eight nights in hospital during the course of the year.
- Plans sometimes cover a wide range of medical situations – for example, dental treatment, physiotherapy, staying in a convalescent home, having a baby, and so on. But payouts for some claims – for example, for dental treatment or getting a hearing aid – are restricted by an upper cash limit and may also be restricted to just half the actual cost you incur.
- Cover will often be for a whole family rather than just an individual, but bear in mind that children are unlikely to give rise to claims under some sections – for example, children receive free NHS dental treatment and sight tests and are far less likely than older people to need chiropody or hearing aids.

Research by *Which?* found that the average premium for a hospital cash plan in 1999 was £100, but the average amount claimed was only £75. But, of course, experience will differ from person to person.

All in all, cash plans are not a good tool for meeting specific financial targets, such as paying for private treatment or income protection. Nevertheless, they can provide handy lump sums from time to time and the outlay is relatively small. But carefully consider which benefits are likely to be relevant to you and check the small print for restrictions.

What a hospital cash plan costs

This depends on the level of benefits you choose but, in general, you could expect to pay from under £100 a year up to, say, £750 a

> **Warning**
>
> Hospital cash plans appear to be fairly cheap but can be poor value for money when you look at the restrictions and the low probability of claiming some of the benefits.

year for a family. At these higher levels, you might be able to afford a budget PMI policy instead.

Critical illness insurance

Critical illness cover (CIC) is described in Chapter 7. It pays out a tax-free lump sum if you are diagnosed with a life-threatening condition or you have to undergo certain specified types of surgery. Since there is no restriction on how you use the money, it could fund private treatment. However, you should not view CIC as an alternative to PMI. The latter pays out when you suffer an acute illness which can be cured or relieved by hospital treatment. CIC pays out mainly in the case of chronic or terminal illness. There is some potential overlap – for example, both policies might be triggered if you had a heart attack – but, on the whole, PMI and CIC are best viewed as complements of, rather than substitutes for, each other.

Dental insurance and dental plans

Who needs private dental treatment?

Around 7 or 8 million adults in the UK receive private dental treatment. You might choose to use a private rather than NHS dentist. Reasons vary but might include shorter waiting times, more convenient appointments and perhaps a wider range of treatments, including cosmetic dentistry. But many people are forced to go private because there is no NHS dentist in their local area.

In the UK, there are about 11,000 dental practices with an average of around 4,000 registered patients apiece. Roughly a quarter of registered patients are children and most of these are treated on the NHS. But, according to a survey by the Office of Fair Trading (OFT), over half of dental practices will not accept new adult patients on an NHS basis. This leaves residents in some areas with no choice but to go private.

What does private treatment cost?

Children, pregnant women and new mothers and people on a low income can qualify for free NHS dentistry. Most people have to pay 80 per cent of the cost of NHS treatment, but this comes to much less than the cost of private treatment as the examples in the table below show. The OFT survey also found big variations between different private dentists with the most expensive charging between four and 11 times as much as the NHS depending on the type of treatment.

Cost of NHS and private dental treatment compared

Type of treatment	What you pay under the NHS	Average cost if treated privately
Examination – existing patient	£5.32	£20.07
X-ray – one small film	£2.64	£6.31
Scale and polish	£8.36	£23.91
Amalgam filling – one surface	£5.64	£28.15
Root filling – molar	£71.10	£178.15
Extraction – single tooth	£6.55	£37.10
Whitening for 12 teeth	not available on NHS	£246.45

Source: OFT *Survey of dental practices*, March 2003.

Options for paying to go private

You could just pay for private treatment as and when you need it. This is fine if your dental health is generally good and you have either savings or access to borrowing to cover a big bill if unexpectedly you do need costly treatment. The alternatives are dental insurance or a dental plan.

Dental insurance

Dental insurance helps you cope with unexpected large bills and can also help you spread the cost of routine treatment depending on the level of cover you choose.

Generally there are three levels: emergency treatment only, emergencies and accidents, or comprehensive cover which covers routine treatment too. There may be a maximum payout, in which case you would have to pay the extra if a course of treatment cost more.

Insurance does not normally cover problems you already have, so you might need to pay for treatment to bring your teeth up to scratch becoming eligible to take out the insurance.

You pay a regular premium, either monthly or annually, and the amount you pay depends on the level of cover and with some policies varies with age.

Dental plans

Dental plans aim mainly to help you spread the cost of treatment.

With a capitation scheme, you pay a set amount each month which depends on an assessment of your dental health. The worse your teeth are, the more you pay. There is normally no further charge when you have check-ups or receive dental treatment, but there might be extra to pay if you need very expensive treatment.

With credit-based schemes, you get a special credit card which you use just for paying for dental treatment. It works like any other credit card – you make monthly repayments and are charged interest on any outstanding balance. But you usually get a maximum period – say, six months – over which to pay off the bill in full. Before choosing a credit-based scheme, check out whether you would pay less using your normal credit card.

More information

There are many variations on the PMI theme, so you need to check carefully what's on offer. Consult the regular surveys of private medical insurance in magazines such as *Which?*★ and *Money Management*★. The Association of British Insurers (ABI)★ can provide details of companies offering particular types of insurance. You can also gather this information from business directories kept in the reference sections of most public libraries. Several PMI providers have websites where you can get details of their products.

Your dentist can tell you if the practice is signed up to any dental plans and may be able to give you contact details for dental insurers. *Which?* publishes occasional surveys of dental plans and insurance. To find a practice accepting NHS patients, contact NHS Direct★ or use the search tool on the NHS website★.

Self-pay reduces delay

When Karen found a lump in her breast, it was all too horribly familiar. Her mother had had breast cancer and both of her sisters-in-law were receiving chemotherapy. On top of all this, the timing was terrible – she and her husband were due to go on holiday in just ten days' time.

Understandably, Karen wanted the lump diagnosed as soon as possible. Her GP referred her to the weekly breast clinic at her local hospital in the hope that she'd be treated as a priority case because of her family history. Karen was optimistic that she'd get an appointment for the following week and was very disappointed when she found out that the clinic was already fully booked.

Faced with the prospect of either spending her holiday miserable with worry or cancelling it altogether, Karen decided she couldn't face either option and contacted a local independent (i.e. private) hospital. She couldn't easily afford the £240 fee for a private consultation, but felt it was her only choice.

Karen saw a consultant that day and a simple biopsy revealed that the lump was actually a cyst. The results of a mammogram and ultrasound the following day confirmed there was nothing to worry about. Karen's relief was immense. In the end, she was given an NHS appointment four weeks after she had seen her GP.

Which? May 2002

Chapter 9

Buying a home

In one form or another, borrowing plays some part in most people's lives, whether it be a mortgage to buy a home or credit cards as a convenient way to shop. Borrowing enables you to bring forward the time at which a financial target can be met, and is worth considering if there is not enough time available to use the savings route or if the cost of borrowing is lower than the return you would get on saving.

Few people can afford to buy a home outright, and it would be totally impractical to save up the full cost of your home before you bought it; after all, you need somewhere to live in the meantime. Therefore, the usual practice is to take out a mortgage – a loan secured against the property you are buying. This practice has been encouraged by past governments through the giving of tax relief on the interest paid on a mortgage to buy your only or main home. However, this tax incentive was abolished from 6 April 2000 onwards (except for mortgages linked to some equity release schemes – see Chapter 13). Without any tax incentive, it usually makes sense to pay off your mortgage as soon as you can – in contrast to the position in earlier years. The removal of the incentive has had a dramatic impact on the types of mortgage which are suitable for most people. In particular, endowment mortgages (see page 132) – which were a popular choice in the past – should now have no place in the financial plan of most people choosing a mortgage for the first time. And, for many people, some form of flexible mortgage (see page 141) will often be a good choice.

There is a wide range of mortgages to choose from, though they fall into two main groups:

- **repayment mortgages,** where you gradually pay off the amount you have borrowed over the term of the loan, together with interest. Nowadays, nine out of ten first-time buyers and eight out of ten people moving house choose this type of mortgage
- **interest-only mortgages,** where you pay only the interest on the loan during its term. Usually, you simultaneously make other arrangements for paying back the capital at the end of the term. In the past, the most common type of interest-only mortgage was the endowment mortgage. Other variations are ISA (formerly PEP) mortgages – see page 136 – and pension mortgages – see page 138.

Repayment mortgage

This is the most straightforward type of mortgage. Your monthly payments pay off both interest and capital, which, provided you keep up the payments, ensures that the whole loan is paid off by the end of the term – see the table on page 137.

A further advantage of repayment mortgages is that they are very flexible and can easily be adapted if you run into temporary difficulties in making the repayments. For example, the most common mortgage term is 25 years at the outset, but, if you ran into problems, your lender might agree to extend the term. This would have the effect of reducing the monthly payments, making them more manageable. Another option might be to add arrears to the amount of the loan outstanding and then adjust the monthly payments, so that the arrears as well as the original loan are repaid by the end of the term.

The way these repayment mortgages are structured means that your payments in the early years are almost completely devoted to paying interest, and very little goes towards reducing the outstanding loan. Critics point out that a move in the early years of the mortgage leaves you back at square one with no reduction in the amount you need to borrow.

A point also to bear in mind is that, unlike some other types of mortgage, there is no built-in life cover to pay off the mortgage in the event of your death. If you have dependants, you will need to arrange separate life insurance, though this is easily done through a relatively cheap mortgage protection policy (a type of decreasing term insurance; see page 144).

Two factors stand out to make repayment mortgages a good choice for many people. The first is their low risk. If on a one-to-ten scale (one being the lowest risk and ten being the highest) you feel most comfortable with a risk of, say, four or less, a repayment mortgage would be most suitable for you. The second factor is their flexibility. In the current climate of unstable work patterns and no tax incentives for mortgages, it makes sense to have the flexibility both to cope with possible hiccups in your earnings and to pay off your mortgage early if you can. You can build in even more flexibility by opting for a specially designed flexible mortgage (see page 141).

Interest-only mortgages

These are the alternative to a repayment mortgage. You do not pay off the loan during the mortgage term. Instead, you pay just the interest and, in most cases, simultaneously pay into an investment to build up a lump sum which you will use to pay off the mortgage at the end of the term. The investment might be an endowment policy, ISAs (or, before April 1999, PEPs), a pension scheme, or indeed any other investment.

In effect, you are gambling that you can use the money you would otherwise have paid back to invest for a profit over and above the cost of borrowing that money. If your gamble pays off, you will either have an extra lump sum for your own use at the end of the mortgage term or you will have saved money during the mortgage term by paying out less each month than you would have paid for a repayment mortgage. If the gamble does not pay off, you either face a shortfall when you come to pay off your mortgage or you have to pay more over the mortgage term than you would have done with a repayment mortgage.

In the past, there were some good reasons why this gamble was likely to pay off. There are now some equally good reasons why the gamble may not work:

- **tax relief on your investment** Up to 1984, if you took out an endowment mortgage, you got tax relief (called 'life assurance premium relief') on the amount you paid into an endowment policy. This was abolished for new or altered policies from 1984. Now, only a pension mortgage (see page 138) offers you tax relief on the amount you pay each month in savings to repay the mortgage.

- **tax relief on the mortgage** The government used to give you tax relief on the interest payments, thus reducing the cost of to you of your mortgage. Tax relief was reduced and then abolished altogether from April 2000. This makes borrowing more expensive and reduces the likelihood that you will be able to invest the borrowed money at a profit.
- **inflation and investment returns**. People who had their mortgage in the 1970s and early 1980s benefited from high inflation, interest rates that were lower than inflation and high stock market returns. These conditions simultaneously reduced the real cost of borrowing and boosted the value of investments – ideal conditions for an interest-only mortgage. Today's economic climate is very different: inflation is low, interest rates are low but above inflation and stock market returns are modest. It seems less likely now that the return from investing will exceed the cost of a mortgage, so an interest-only mortgage does not look a good choice.

As you can see, although family and friends who had an endowment mortgage in the past might still tell you what a good deal they were, circumstances are very different now. Today an endowment mortgages is unlikely to be the best choice if you are looking for a new mortgage. However, if you already have an endowment mortgage taken out in past, you may be better off sticking with what you've got – see page 133.

The main types of interest-only mortgage are discussed in the next few sections and the main features are summarised in the table on page 137.

What distinguishes each type of interest-only mortgage is the type of investment used to repay the loan at the end of its term. Usually the investment is set up as part of a package with the mortgage. However, some lenders are prepared to make interest-only loans and leave entirely up to you how you will repay the capital at the end of the term. This might be suitable if, say, you expect to be able to sell the property at that time and repay the loan out of the proceeds, or you already have substantial investments which can be used eventually to repay the loan, or you run a business and anticipate using the proceeds of selling your interest in it. But, in 1997 it came to light that some people had been sold interest-only mortgages with no corresponding investment, thinking that they had taken out endowment mortgages. Make sure that you understand what type of mortgage you have and that, if there is no investment linked to it, you are comfortable with the situation.

Low-cost endowment mortgage

New endowment mortgages

An endowment mortgage comprises an interest-only mortgage linked to an endowment policy, which can work either on a with-profits or a unit-linked basis (see below for more about this). If the investment in the endowment policy grows at a reasonable rate, it is hoped that the policy will produce enough to pay off the loan at the end of the mortgage term and even leave you a bit of extra cash as well. But there is no guarantee that this will happen.

A useful aspect of linking your mortgage to an insurance policy, if you have dependants, is that the policy automatically gives you life cover, which would pay off the loan if you were to die during the term.

There are two major drawbacks with an endowment mortgage. As already mentioned, there is a very real possibility that the endowment policy will not grow enough to pay off the loan at the end of its term. This means the endowment mortgage can end up costing you more than a repayment mortgage and leave you with the problem of how to pay off any shortfall.

The second drawback is the very low cash-in value of the endowment policy if you stop paying the premiums in the early years. The costs associated with selling the policy (which include any commission paid to an adviser or salesperson) are intended to be spread over the full term of the policy. But if the policy stops early, these charges are set against the policy in full, even though the policy has had little time in which to build up much investment value. The result is that stopping the policy early can mean that you get back far less than you have paid in premiums, or even nothing at all. This makes endowment mortgages particularly inflexible if you run into problems keeping up the mortgage repayments. You may be able to alter the interest payments on the mortgage loan itself, but reducing or missing payments into the endowment policy might bring the policy to an end. A waiver of premium option (see page 92) might be at least a partial solution to this problem.

These drawbacks mean that endowment mortgages are not usually a good choice for anyone newly taking out a mortgage.

Existing endowment mortgages

Since there is no guarantee that the endowment policy will grow by enough to pay off the mortgage in full at the end of the term, it is essential that you check regularly to see if you are on track and, if not, take appropriate action.

In September 1999, the Association of British Insurers (ABI)* introduced a code of practice to ensure that endowment mortgage holders were given regular information about the progress of their endowment policy towards paying off the mortgage. Under that original code, it was envisaged that information would be needed only in the later years of the mortgage and then only at five-yearly intervals. The inadequacy of this approach became clear as the stock market started its long slide at the start of 2000 and, from July 2001, a new code came into force requiring endowment providers to send out review letters much more frequently:

- the first review should be no later than three years after the start of the endowment mortgage
- subsequent reviews should be sent to you at least every two years throughout the term of the endowment
- you can ask for more frequent reviews (but not more often than once every 12 months).

These reviews have since become known as 'reprojection letters'. They recalculate the return you might get from your endowment policy taking into account growth so far and standard growth assumptions and compare this with the mortgage loan to be paid off. The letters are colour coded. A 'red letter' signifies there is a high risk that the amount you'll get back from the endowment policy at the end of its term will fall short of the amount needed to repay your mortgage in full. An 'amber letter' indicates there is a significant risk of a shortfall. A 'green letter' means you are currently on track to repay your mortgage.

Stock-market performance affects any shortfall. So, you could have a green reprojection letter at one review but, if the stock market falls, get an amber or red letter next time. Similarly, if you have an amber letter at one review, a rise in the stock market might mean you get a green letter next time. But, if you get a red letter, there would normally have to be a very substantial rise in the stock market before you returned to green, so you should usually consider other action to put your mortgage back on track.

The most obvious action is to increase the amount you save each month. You may be able to do this by increasing the premium you pay into the endowment policy, although you don't have to do that. You could pay extra savings into another, quite separate investment – for example, an ISA. If you already have other savings and investments, you might simply choose to earmark some of these to meet the forecast shortfall.

Other options involve altering your mortgage by, for example, replacing part or all of the endowment loan with a repayment mortgage or repaying a lump sum early. But you need to check your situation carefully before going down any of these routes. Stopping the endowment policy or cashing it in may trigger charges including any market value reduction (see page 317) too. A better option might be to carry on with the endowment mortgage. If you are moving home or remortgaging (in other words, changing your mortgage without moving home), you could use your existing endowment policy to back the new mortgage loan. But, if you will be increasing the amount you borrow, consider a repayment mortgage for the extra amount.

If you took advice when you chose your endowment mortgage and you feel the advice was misleading – for example, you would not have been comfortable with stock market risk and the adviser did not check how you felt – you may be eligible for compensation if you have complained to the adviser or the Financial Ombudsman Service (see Chapter 3).

With-profits version of low-cost endowment mortgage
This is the traditional form of low-cost endowment mortgage. At the start of the mortgage, the endowment policy has a guaranteed value (payable at the end of the term or on earlier death), which is far smaller than the amount of your mortgage loan. But bonuses are added to this guaranteed sum. There are regular bonuses, usually credited each year, called 'reversionary bonuses', and normally a 'terminal bonus' added when the policy reaches the end of its term. Once added, the bonuses cannot normally be taken away (but can

be clawed back through a market value reduction if you cash in early – see page 317) and so the value of the policy grows and is intended by the end of the term to be worth at least as much as the amount of the mortgage loan. The aim of a with-profits policy is to produce steady growth protected from the thrills and spills of the stock market. Bonuses are smoothed, with money being kept back from good years to keep up bonus levels in the lean years. However, if the stock market turns in poor returns over a prolonged period, bonus levels will slide and the return from a low-cost endowment may then fall short of earlier expectations. This has been the experience in recent years, causing many people to be disappointed with the performance of their endowment policy, especially where they were misled into thinking when they took it out that the policy would definitely pay off the whole mortgage.

Despite this disappointment, provided you keep a with-profits policy going for its full term, it is a lower-risk investment than the direct exposure to the stock market that you would experience with, for example, a unit-linked policy. This makes with-profits investments compatible with people who would rate their attitude to risk at around five on a ten-point scale of risk. However, if you would be likely to cash in your policy early, due to the impact of a possible market value reduction (see page 317), the risk is greater – say, around six upwards. For more information about with-profits insurance, see Chapter 17.

Unit-linked version of low-cost endowment mortgage

With a unit-linked endowment mortgage, instead of the value of the policy depending on bonuses, it is linked directly to one or more funds of investments managed by the insurance company. The fund typically will be invested in shares, and you can often switch between the funds (see Chapter 18). The value of your policy will go up – and down – with the value of the underlying investments. Although share prices tend to grow over the long term, at any point in time stock markets can be riding high or in the doldrums. If share prices happen to be low at the time your mortgage comes to an end, the value of your policy will reflect this and might not be enough to pay off the loan. This makes the unit-linked version of endowment mortgages generally more risky than its with-profits cousin, and on a ten-point risk scale it scores around six upwards.

Even if you are happy with this level of risk, a unit-linked endowment mortgage is still unlikely to be the best choice, because an ISA mortgage will give you a very similar level of risk but has three important advantages:

- ISA mortgages benefit from favourable tax treatment; endowment mortgages do not
- the charges (even allowing for the cost of buying life insurance if you need it) for an ISA mortgage are usually much lower than the charges for an endowment mortgage
- there are usually no, or only low, surrender penalties if you cash in an ISA before the end of the mortgage term.

Given these differences, it is very difficult to justify choosing a unit-linked endowment mortgage nowadays. If you want a share-linked investment to pay off your interest-only mortgage, choose a broadly invested ISA.

Individual savings account (ISA) mortgage

With this type of interest-only mortgage, you pay into an individual savings account (ISA) to build up enough to pay off the mortgage at the end of its term. ISAs – which are described in Chapter 11 – are a tax-efficient way in which to invest in shares, unit trusts and many other investments: tax-efficient, because all growth from the underlying investments and some of the income is tax-free.

ISAs replaced personal equity plans (PEPs) from April 1999 onwards. From that date no new PEPs could be started but old PEPs can continue. You can earmark any PEPs you already hold, as well as any ISAs you now take out, to repay your mortgage.

You can use ISAs – and, since 6 April 2001, PEPs also – to invest in medium-risk investments such as corporate bonds, gilts and preference shares. But it is doubtful that these investments would produce a high enough return over the mortgage term to make this type of mortgage worthwhile, bearing in mind the relatively high cost of borrowing now that mortgage tax relief has been abolished. Therefore, if you choose an ISA mortgage it will almost certainly need to be invested predominantly in shares. Share-linked ISA mortgages are suitable only for people who place themselves at around six or more on the ten-point risk scale.

How different mortgages compare

	Repayment	Low-cost with-profit endowment	Unit-linked endowment	Pension	PEP/ISA
Guarantees to pay off loan	YES	NO	NO	NO	NO
May give you extra lump sum at maturity	NO	YES	YES	YES	YES
Tax advantages	NO	NO[1]	NO[1]	YES	YES
Life insurance built in	NO	YES	YES	NO[2]	NO
Monthly payments can be reduced easily	NO[3]	NO	NO	MAYBE	YES
Monthly payments can be increased easily	YES	NOT USUALLY	NOT USUALLY	YES	YES
Mortgage can be completely paid off whenever you choose without penalty[4]	YES	LOAN: YES POLICY: NO	LOAN: YES POLICY: NO	LOAN: YES PLAN: NO	YES

[1] Unless you are a higher-rate taxpayer. The proceeds of an endowment policy have already had tax deducted at the equivalent of the savings rate, but usually there is no higher-rate tax to pay.
[2] But can be added tax-efficiently.
[3] Unless the loan is designed as a 'flexible mortgage' (see page 141).
[4] With some loans, there is an early redemption charge if you pay off in the early years.

There is no built-in life cover with an ISA mortgage. If you have dependants, consider taking out term insurance – see Chapter 6.

Payments into an ISA are generally very flexible. This has the advantage that, if you run into temporary difficulties, it is easy to cut down or suspend payments into the ISA for a while. The flipside of this is that you need the self-discipline to ensure that you pay steadily into the ISA enough to build up the sum needed to repay the mortgage at the end of the day.

Since there are generally no penalties for altering the amount you save, or stopping or cashing in an ISA early, an ISA mortgage also gives you the flexibility to pay off your mortgage more quickly than originally planned.

Pension mortgage

A pension mortgage is the most tax-efficient mortgage of all, but is inflexible and does not suit everyone. You take out an interest-only loan and simultaneously pay into a personal pension (which can be a stakeholder pension scheme). The idea is that the tax-free lump sum payable at retirement – see page 237 – will be used to pay off the mortgage. This gives you a number of tax advantages:

- your payments into the pension plan qualify for tax relief at your top rate; no other type of mortgage has this advantage
- if you need life cover, you can use a term insurance policy linked to the pension plan, which means you get tax relief at the top rate on your premiums
- your investment in the pension plan builds up largely tax-free
- the lump sum used to pay off the mortgage is tax-free.

Against this, you must set the following disadvantages. First, if you no longer want to pay into the personal pension – because you decide to join a pension scheme at work, for example – you will have to find some other method of building up the sum needed to pay off your mortgage. Secondly, using a pension plan in this way reduces your scope for building up retirement income. Trying to use one financial tool to meet two targets is nearly always unwise and tends to cause a conflict.

Be particularly wary of taking out a pension mortgage if you are relatively young. If you are only, say, 25, but plan not to retire until age 65, do you really want a 40-year-term mortgage? Alternatively, will you really be happy to start taking at least some of your pension from age 55, say – long before your intended retirement age?

What sort of interest rate to choose

As well as choosing between the basic types of mortgage, there is a wealth of interest rate options too:

- **variable rate** The 'standard' option in the UK. The interest you pay rises and falls with interest rates generally in the economy, making it hard to know from one year to another what your payments will be. Interestingly, this is not the norm in some other countries, where the uncertainty of variable rates is considered too risky.

- **base rate tracker** A variable rate that moves up and down in line with changes in some reference interest rate, such as the Bank of England base rate.
- **fixed rate** You lock into a set interest rate for a fixed period of time, which could be just a year or two or as long as ten years. At the end of the term, you usually revert to the normal variable rate. Usually an arrangement fee has to be paid when you take out this type of mortgage, and there will be hefty penalties if you want to pay off the mortgage: for example, to switch to a cheaper lender. Generally avoid mortgages where the penalty period extends beyond the fixed-rate term (called a 'penalty overhang') because you may then be locked into an uncompetitive variable rate for a while. Choosing a fixed rate can be a speculative move – you choose a fixed rate if you expect interest rates generally to rise. If you are right, you will be quids in; if you are wrong and variable rates fall, you will have lost the gamble and be stuck with the higher fixed rate. But fixed rates also have the advantage that you know what your payments will be, which helps you to plan your budgeting.
- **discounted rates** Some mortgages, particularly those aimed at first-time buyers, have a lower rate of interest in the early years. This is useful if money is tight at present but you expect the situation to improve, for example as you work your way up the promotions ladder at work. But make sure that what is on offer is a genuine discount. Beware of deals where the interest saved in the early years is simply deferred and added to the outstanding loan – this is an expensive way to cut costs in the early years and can cause problems when you come to move house if the outstanding loan has become larger than the value of your home. As with fixed-rate deals, there are early redemption penalties if you pay off a discounted-rate mortgage in the early years, and usually the penalty period extends beyond the discount period. For example, even a discount for just one year may go hand in hand with redemption penalties in the first five years. This means that you may be locked into the lender's standard variable rate for some time.
- **capped rates** A capped rate varies in line with general interest rates but is subject to a limit: the rate is guaranteed not to rise above the interest rate cap. There might also be a floor below which the interest rate will not fall, even if general rates go lower;

Warning

Capped and discounted rates are usually linked to the lender's standard variable rate. Some lenders have tried introducing a new, lower standard variable rate for some customers while leaving existing capped- and discounted-rate borrowers linked to the old, higher variable rate. This meant the capped- and discounted-rate borrowers could be paying more for their mortgage than they would have done had the new variable rate also applied to them. Based on the particular terms of their mortgage contracts, some discounted- and capped-rate borrowers have successfully challenged the practice before the Financial Services Ombudsman. As a result, other borrowers in a similar situation might be entitled to claim compensation from their lender. If you think this might apply to you, contact your lender.

this is called an interest rate 'collar'. The deal runs for a fixed period of time, after which you revert to the normal variable rate. Capped rates give you some of the certainty of fixed rates, helping you to plan your budgets, without so much risk of being locked into a punishingly high rate. As with fixed-rate mortgages, expect to pay an arrangement fee for a capped mortgage and to face hefty early redemption penalties if you try to get out of a collared deal in the first few years.

- **cashback deals** With some standard variable-rate mortgages, you get a cash sum when you take out the mortgage. This can be a sizeable sum: for example, 5 or 6 per cent of the amount you are borrowing. You can use the cash however you like, so it can be handy to put towards the costs of moving, decorating your new home, and so on. Although a cashback is not strictly speaking an interest-rate option, it is useful to look at it here because one use for the cashback would be to invest it to give you a sum to call on if your mortgage rate rises. For example, if you borrowed £50,000 and the mortgage rate rose by 2 per cent over the first year of your mortgage, you could pay up to an extra £910 interest that year. This would be well covered by a 5 per cent cashback deal, giving you a £2,500 lump sum. After paying the extra interest you would still be in profit to the tune of £1,590. This looks a better option than, say, a one-year fixed-rate mortgage taken out at the same initial interest rate with an arrangement fee of £250, which would have saved you £910 – £250 = £660. This is a very simplified example; real life is more complex and your sums will need to take into account the difference in interest rates between deals and longer time periods than one year. With cashback deals, there is usually an early redemption penalty period of five years or so. If you pay part or all of the mortgage during that time, you generally have to pay back the cashback you received.

Some mortgage lenders let you mix-and-match different interest-rate options. For example, you could borrow part of your mortgage at a variable rate and part at a fixed rate. Compared with taking out the whole mortgage on a fixed-interest basis, you would gain some benefit if interest rates fall, though, conversely, you would suffer some increase if interest rates rose. Compared with taking out the whole mortgage at a variable rate, you would face a smaller increase in payments if interest rates rose but also a smaller decrease if interest rates fell. So mixing-and-matching is a way of hedging your bets.

Warning
Be very wary of taking out a mortgage which keeps interest payments low in the early years by deferring the interest and adding it to the outstanding loan. The amount you owe can grow alarmingly, increasing future costs and causing particular problems if the value of your property is falling.

Flexible mortgages

Many lenders now offer flexible mortgages. These are particularly suited to today's lifestyles, since jobs for life are now virtually unknown and your income may fluctuate widely during your working life, especially if you take career breaks to raise a family, say. Flexible mortgages offer some or all of three types of flexibility:

- **overpayments** You can pay off your mortgage more rapidly by making regular overpayments or by paying off ad hoc lump sums without incurring any redemption penalties. Flexible mortgages recalculate your outstanding mortgage balance on either a daily or a monthly basis, so your interest payments immediately adjust to any overpayment.

- **underpayments** You can reduce your regular mortgage payment or even take a complete payment holiday without being in default. There will be conditions attached to this option. For example, you might have to have built up a reserve of overpayments before being allowed to underpay. Also, underpaying increases your outstanding mortgage balance, and there will usually be a ceiling on the overall amount you can borrow (for example, 90 per cent of the value of your home).

- **further loans** You can withdraw extra lump sums from your mortgage account to be used for any purpose, without going through the formality of applying for a new loan. Once again, there are usually conditions. For example, you may have to have built up a reserve of overpayments against which you can borrow. And there will be a ceiling on the overall amount you can borrow through the original mortgage plus any subsequent loans.

Not all flexible mortgages offer all of these features, so you will have to shop around.

In response to the advent of flexible mortgages, many lenders have either stressed or improved the flexibility of their traditional mortgages. So before switching to a flexible mortgage, it could be worth checking what flexibility your existing lender can offer.

All-in-one mortgages

An increasing number of lenders offer all-in-one mortgages that combine a flexible loan with a current account and, in some cases, savings accounts and a credit card as well. In its simplest form, called a 'current account mortgage' (CAM), you pay your salary direct into the mortgage account where it immediately reduces your mortgage balance. You then draw against the account for your normal spending as you would with an ordinary current account. The mortgage balance and interest on it is calculated daily, so even money left in the account for only a short period of time has some impact on the cost of your mortgage. In the more sophisticated versions (called 'offset mortgages'), you have several accounts – one each for the mortgage, your current account, savings account and so on – running alongside each other. Each day the net balance for all the accounts is calculated and interest worked out on the overall total.

On the face of it, all-in-one mortgages are very efficient. Any positive balance in your current or savings account reduces your mortgage balance and so saves you interest. In effect then, your current account balance and savings are earning the mortgage rate of interest. Not only is that typically higher than the rates available on savings, but you are not charged any tax on the interest saved.

In effect, an offset mortgage puts you in a position where you are devoting the bulk of your savings to reducing your mortgage. This can save thousands of pounds off the cost of your mortgage and could mean you pay off the loan early. You still have the flexibility to divert your savings instead to other uses, in which case you give up some of the mortgage cost savings.

Of course, you don't need an offset mortgage to pay off your loan early. You could have an ordinary mortgage and a completely separate savings account. From time to time, you could use your savings to pay off a chunk of your mortgage. That too would save you thousands of pounds in mortgage costs and could mean paying off the loan early. But, unlike the all-in-one mortgage, your savings would not earn the mortgage rate of interest, you would have to pay tax on the savings interest and, having paid off part of the mortgage, it would be more difficult to change your mind and use your savings for some other purpose after all (because you would need to take out a new mortgage to 'get back' your savings).

The drawback of all-in-one mortgages is that the mortgage rate of interest is often higher than deals you could get elsewhere and, in particular, there are often no special deals, such as a low discounted rate for the first few years. If you have only a low balance in your current account and little in savings, the benefits you get from combining the accounts may be too small to outweigh the extra cost of the mortgage. And combining your finances in this way could be confusing, especially in the case of a CAM where you have just a single account for both your mortgage and current account. You need to be the sort of person who can efficiently keep track of their money.

If you are good with your finances, generally have a high current account balance, have reasonably high savings and you are a taxpayer (particularly a higher rate taxpayer), an all-in-one mortgage could be a good choice. But check the mortgage is reasonably priced and has all the features you want.

Mortgage packages

As if deciding the type of mortgage and the nature of the interest rate were not enough, mortgages often come packaged with other products, some of which may be worth having, others not.

Mortgage protection insurance

This is term insurance to pay off your mortgage if you die during the term. (It is not required with endowment mortgages, which have built-in life cover.) If anyone is financially dependent on you – your wife, husband, partner, children, elderly relative – this type of insurance is usually well worth having. However, if you have no dependants, there is no need for this cover and you might prefer to do without it (in which case your home would be sold on your death and the mortgage paid off out of the proceeds).

Be aware that a traditional mortgage protection policy may not be the most suitable type of life cover to protect a flexible mortgage. Mortgage protection policies are a type of decreasing term insurance (see Chapter 6) designed to track a mortgage balance that falls steadily over the years. Particularly if you use the flexibility to pay off your mortgage more slowly than a normal repayment loan, you could be underinsured. Consider taking out level term insurance instead.

Mortgage payment protection insurance

One of the biggest problems, if you lose your job or fall ill for a prolonged period, is how to pay the mortgage, because failing to keep up the payments could end in your losing your home. Until October 1995, if you became unemployed and your income and savings were low enough, you could qualify for income support to cover half your mortgage interest payments during the first 16 weeks and the full amount thereafter on up to £100,000 of loan. Since then, anyone under age 60 taking out a mortgage on or after 1 October 1995 is excluded from this safety net for the first nine months of claiming benefit. For existing borrowers, there is no cover at all for the first two months, and thereafter only half of the interest is covered for the next four months. To plug this gap, the government expects people taking out new mortgages simultaneously to take out mortgage payment protection insurance, which pays out if you are unable to work because of sickness, disability or unemployment. You can also take out this insurance to cover a mortgage you already have.

Mortgage payment protection insurance has been around for some time, though in the past it had limited appeal because of the many restrictions, often including a waiting period of, say, three months after taking out the policy before claims could be met, no cover for claims related to medical problems you had at the time you took out the policy, pregnancy, drugs or alcohol, HIV, and so on. Even more of a problem has been the list of people who are not normally welcomed by insurers for this type of policy, for example:

- part-time workers, meaning those who work fewer than 16 hours a week
- fixed contract workers
- people with no fixed income
- newly self-employed who haven't yet built up a track record
- people with risky jobs, for example divers
- people who already know that they are likely to lose their job.

Since the restriction on state support, insurers have been experimenting with less restrictive policies. However, you should take special care to read the terms of this type of policy to ensure that it provides cover which is suitable for you. The premium you are charged is linked to the size of your mortgage. It might also cover associated payments, for example, the cost of buildings insurance. According to the Council of Mortgage Lenders, the typical cost is around £5 a month for each £100 of your monthly mortgage payment.

Whether or not you need mortgage payment protection insurance depends on what arrangements are already in place to protect your income in case of illness (see Chapter 7) or unemployment. In general, it is probably a wise precaution to take out this cover. A few lenders offer it free as part of the mortgage package. Whether part of the mortgage package or not, many people take out this insurance through their lender, but this is not necessarily a good idea: your lender might charge more than you would pay arranging your own cover, and some policies do not let you transfer the cover if you switch to a new lender. Although it is common to take out cover at the time you start a mortgage, you can arrange it later.

If you pay off part of your mortgage early, don't forget to tell the insurer and get the premium for your payment protection insurance revised.

House insurance

Insurance companies pay commission to agencies which arrange the sale of their policies. Banks and building societies have found this to be a useful source of extra income, so you may well find that you are expected to take out house buildings and even house contents insurance through the society or bank as part of the mortgage package. But check both the cost and cover carefully: you may be able to get better value insurance elsewhere, especially if you qualify for discounts with some companies because of your job. In the past, it was common for lenders to insist that you took out their insurance as part of the particular mortgage deal, so you had little choice. But a change in the law outlawed this practice. Another ruse is where the bank or building society makes an administration charge if you choose to buy your house insurance elsewhere – you will have to weigh up the impact of the charge against the amount you stand to save by insuring elsewhere. Check whether the new insurer will pay the administration charge for you – at least one company does this.

Switching your mortgage

Having taken out a mortgage, you are not locked into that particular loan for the full mortgage term. Lenders compete fiercely for your custom and you may be able to reduce the cost of your mortgage by switching to a new lender. Against this you must set the costs of making the switch. These might include: valuation, legal and land registry fees; arrangement fee and mortgage indemnity insurance premium charged by the new lender; discharge fee, deeds fee and any early redemption charge levied by the old lender. The costs can easily come to £1,000 or more, but the savings can be substantial too. For example, each 1 per cent cut in the mortgage rate on a 25-year

£50,000 loan could save you around £360 in interest each year. Although this is not widely advertised, rather than losing you to another lender, your existing mortgage lender might be willing to give you a better deal: for example, by extending to you discounted rates normally available only to first-time buyers. It is certainly worth talking to your existing lender before going ahead with any switch, since it will cost you less to stay put.

If you are interested in switching mortgage, check what deals are currently on offer (see 'More information' on page 151). Get quotes for the loans you are interested in, including the associated charges. Check what fees your existing lender might charge and check out whether your existing lender might be prepared to offer you a better deal than your current loan in order to keep your custom.

Bear in mind that switching mortgage counts as taking out a new loan, so you could be entitled to less help from the state if you ran into problems keeping up the payments – see page 144.

Deciding how much to borrow

When you take out a mortgage, the amount you borrow is driven by three main factors:

- **the price of the home you want to buy** The amount you can borrow will generally restrict your choice of properties. But, often, if you need to live in a particular area – for work, say – there will also be a minimum amount you must borrow if you are to buy anything at all.
- **the value of the home you buy** The lender will have the property valued. Usually, they will not be prepared to lend you the full value of the property. Commonly, the maximum will be 90 per cent or 95 per cent of the property's value – called a 90 per cent or 95 per cent loan-to-value (LTV) proportion. Bear in mind the value of the property for this purpose may be less than the price you are required to pay for it.
- **what you can afford to pay** Lenders often work on the basis of crude income multiples. For example, you might be able to borrow three times your gross salary. If you are a couple, you might get, say, two-and-a-half times your joint salaries. But you should never take out the maximum loan offered unless you have worked out that this is an amount you can afford to pay.

What you can afford

Write down your monthly budget:

- Look at the money you have coming in each month – your pay after tax and other deductions, income from investments, any child benefit or other state benefits, maintenance payments from a former partner, and so on.
- Deduct your monthly expenses for, say, council tax, water, heating and lighting, food, travel to work, telephone, and so on. Apportion annual and quarterly bills as if they were spread out monthly. Do not include rent or current mortgage payments if these will be saved once you have bought your new home.
- In the first instance, deduct non-essential spending – for example on holidays, meals out, cinema trips and so on. But, if it looks unlikely that you can afford the size of mortgage you want, go back and consider what non-essential spending you could do without. Be realistic – you must not count on savings which in practice you will not really make.
- Deduct your total spending from your income to see how much you can afford to pay each month for a mortgage. If you plan to choose a variable-rate mortgage, bear in mind that your mortgage costs will increase if interest rates rise. Similarly, if you choose a discounted mortgage, make sure you have allowed for the increase in payments once the discount period has finished.

Once you know how much you can afford to pay each month, compare this with the cost of a mortgage to find out the maximum loan you can afford to borrow – see below.

How much your mortgage might cost

The table opposite shows how much you can expect to pay each month for each £1,000 of mortgage loan depending on the term of your mortgage and the interest rate. Find the interest rate you will pay in the left-hand column and your chosen mortgage term across the top, or go straight to the last column if you plan to have an interest-only mortgage. The corresponding figure in the table tells you broadly how much you will have to pay for each £1,000 of loan. Divide the amount you can afford to pay each month by this figure, to find out the maximum loan you can afford – see Example opposite.

Monthly mortgage payments for each £1,000 of mortgage loan*

Interest rate % pa	Repayment mortgage with term of:						Interest-only mortgage
	5	10	15	20	25	30	Any term
1%	£17.09	£8.76	£5.98	£4.60	£3.77	£3.22	£0.83
2%	£17.51	£9.19	£6.43	£5.06	£4.24	£3.69	£1.67
3%	£17.95	£9.65	£6.90	£5.54	£4.74	£4.21	£2.50
4%	£18.39	£10.11	£7.39	£6.05	£5.27	£4.77	£3.33
5%	£18.84	£10.59	£7.90	£6.59	£5.84	£5.36	£4.17
6%	£19.29	£11.08	£8.43	£7.16	£6.44	£5.99	£5.00
7%	£19.75	£11.59	£8.97	£7.74	£7.06	£6.65	£5.83
8%	£20.22	£12.11	£9.54	£8.35	£7.71	£7.33	£6.67
9%	£20.70	£12.64	£10.13	£8.99	£8.38	£8.04	£7.50
10%	£21.18	£13.18	£10.73	£9.64	£9.08	£8.77	£8.33
11%	£21.67	£13.74	£11.35	£10.31	£9.79	£9.52	£9.17
12%	£22.17	£14.31	£11.98	£11.00	£10.52	£10.28	£10.00

* Different lenders use different calculation methods, so figures may vary slightly from those shown here.

Different lenders use different methods to work out your payments, so the amount you pay might not be exactly the same as the amount from the table but it should be close.

In the table, payments for repayment mortgages assume that the interest you must pay is recalculated daily using the latest mortgage balance. Some lenders calculate the interest only monthly or even once a year. This means that there is a delay before loan repayments work through to reduce the interest charge. Overall, you will pay more for a mortgage if the interest is recalculated infrequently.

The column for interest-only mortgages shows just the interest you would pay for the mortgage. To this you must add whatever you would pay each month to any investment you will use to pay off the mortgage.

Example

Rachel and Ben are thinking about taking out a repayment mortgage. Ben earns £36,000 a year and Rachel, who has just had a baby, currently earns just £10,000 a year. They've been told by one lender that they can borrow up to three times Ben's salary plus Rachel's earnings – a total of $(3 \times £36,000) + £10,000 = £118,000$.

Rachel and Ben work out their monthly budget. They reckon they can afford to spend £400 a month on a mortgage. They are thinking about a 25-year-term repayment mortgage and expect to borrow at 5 per cent a year.

They find 5% in the left-hand column of the table and read across to the 25-year column. This tells them that they'll have to pay about £5.84 a month for each £1,000 they borrow. Dividing this into the £400 they can afford gives a figure of £400 ÷ £5.84 = 68.5. This suggests that the maximum loan they can afford is £68,500 – considerably less than the maximum they can get according to the lender's formula.

If Ben and Rachel borrowed £118,000 at an interest rate of 5 per cent a year for 25 years, it would cost them 118 × £5.84 = £689 a month. This is much more than the amount they feel they can afford.

As interest rates are low at the time Rachel and Ben are looking for their mortgage, they should also consider whether they would cope financially if there was an increase in the mortgage rate.

Mortgage problems

Payment difficulties

According to official figures, as a nation we owe over £850 billion in mortgages. For a minority of people this debt becomes a problem. Usually this happens because of some unforeseen crisis, such as redundancy or divorce. It can be very tempting to close your eyes to mounting bills and simply hope the problem will go away. But debt problems nearly always get worse the longer you leave them. It's essential that you take action as soon as you can.

Your mortgage is a priority debt, because failing to tackle the problem could mean losing your home. Contact your lender immediately and let them know that you are having problems. They are as anxious to find a solution as you, and in most cases will take drastic action only as the very last resort. Some building societies and banks run in-house debt counselling services or will refer you to the Consumer Credit Counselling Service★, an independent debt management service to which some lenders subscribe. These services will help you to prioritise your debts, advise on any state benefits for which you might qualify and will try to set a realistic target for clearing your mortgage arrears, taking into account your whole financial position. Most mortgage lenders stress that repossessing

> **Warning**
> If you run into difficulties in paying your mortgage, contact the lender immediately. Debt problems have a nasty habit of getting worse if you ignore them.

your home is the last thing they want to do. Extending the term of the loan and thus reducing the monthly payments is a possible solution. Where repossession is unavoidable, a few societies have successfully used mortgage-to-rent schemes to allow people to stay in their old home but as tenants of a housing association.

You can get independent help with your debt problems from your local Citizens' Advice Bureau★, National Debtline★, Consumer Credit Counselling Service★ and independent money advice centres★.

Negative equity – where the mortgage on your home is greater than the value of your home – can be a problem, because even if your home is repossessed, there may still be a big mortgage debt outstanding. Your lender may insist on your paying for a 'mortgage indemnity guarantee' when you first take out your mortgage. This is insurance to ensure that your lender can recover their money if you default on the mortgage, but it does not protect you. The insurance company which reimburses the lender can still chase you for the outstanding mortgage debt.

More information

You can get information about mortgages direct from lenders but that is a laborious way of shopping around. If you have access to the Internet, there are some useful mortgage websites★ (including Switch with *Which?*) that do the shopping around for you and have handy calculators to help you work out how much you can borrow and to filter the huge number of mortgages available (estimated to be about 4,000) down to a selection that is particularly suited to you. The Financial Services Authority (FSA)★ comparative tables cover both mortgages and mortgage endowment policies. These are available on the FSA website, and you can also order paper versions of the tables from its consumer helpline.

See also the regular surveys of mortgages in *Which?*★ and specialist personal finance magazines. *What mortgage*★ gives listings of mortgages on offer, as does *Moneyfacts*★ magazine. Moneyfacts also operates a website and a fax information service.

The FSA★ publishes a number of useful booklets and factsheets about mortgages, including information about what to do if you have an endowment mortgage and the policy looks unlikely to repay your full mortgage. These include *The FSA guide to repaying your mortgage*, and FSA factsheet *Your endowment mortgage – time to decide*.

For information about mortgage payment protection insurance, either ask your lender or, if you want to arrange your own cover, talk to an insurance broker. *Which?* magazine publishes occasional surveys of this type of insurance.

If you don't ask, you don't get

Mona saved £900 by making a single phone call to her mortgage lender. Three years earlier, she had taken out a 25-year mortgage with a fixed interest rate of 6.59 per cent for three years. In August, the lender wrote to Mona to tell her the fixed deal was coming to an end and her new rate would be its standard variable rate of 5.99 per cent. Mona used a couple of mortgage-search websites to see what else was available. She phoned her existing lender to see if it would match a better deal she had found. The lender agreed that instead of paying its standard variable rate, Mona could switch to one of its new fixed-rate deals. This gives her a rate of 4.95 per cent fixed for 12 months, saving her just over £900 over the year. It will cost her nothing to switch and she will be free to switch again without penalty at the end of the 12 months.

Which? November 2001

Tied insurance

One of the supermarket insurers offered to insure Judy's house for £200 – almost two-thirds less than the £582 her mortgage lender wanted to charge. But her lender said she could not cancel her existing policy as it was a condition of her mortgage that she keep it for five years. Judy knew she had been tied in but thought it was for just two years and not, as it turned out, five. 'It made me think about switching mortgages, so now I'm looking at where I can get a better deal,' Judy told *Which?*

Which? May 2004

Chapter 10

Helping your children

If you are planning to start a family or you already have children, this will have a big impact on your financial planning. The needs of children are generally fairly immediate, so helping your children is likely to be a high-priority goal and may result in your putting some other financial goals on the back burner for a while.

Bringing up children

According to a survey for Woolworth's, the typical cost of bringing up a child from birth through to university is £164,000. That's a big drain on any family's finances, though you normally get some help from the state and your employer might chip in too.

Main help from the state

Child benefit
The most universal state help is child benefit. This is available tax-free to every family, rich and poor alike, in respect of each child from birth up to reaching age 16, and aged 16 up to reaching age 19 if in full-time education. In 2005–6, you get £17 a week (£884 a year) in respect of your only or eldest child, and £11.40 a week (£593 a year) for each other child. For example, a family with three children would receive £2,070 a year.

Child tax credit
Child tax credit can be claimed by most families with children. It is a tax-free means-tested benefit – in other words, whether you get it and how much depends on how well off you are. But, unlike many

means-tested benefits, even fairly wealthy families can qualify for some child tax credit.

To work out how much you can claim, you start with the maximum available and reduce this according to how much income your household has over certain thresholds.

Child tax credit has two main elements, as shown in the table below. The majority of families qualify for the family element (usually £545 in 2005–6) but this is reduced by £1 for each £15 of household income over £50,000 a year. This means that a family ceases to qualify for any child tax credit in 2005–6 if its income is more than £58,175, or £66,350 in the year a new child is born.

Families can also claim the child element, usually £1,690 per child in 2005–6. This is reduced by 37p for every £1 by which household income exceeds a certain threshold. If the family qualifies for child tax credit but not any working tax credit (see opposite), the threshold is £13,910. If the family also qualifies for working tax credit, this credit is reduced by 37p for each £1 by which the household income exceeds £5,220 in 2005–6. Once all the working tax credit has been tapered away, any further income starts to reduce the child element(s) of child tax credit.

For example, a family with two children over the age of one would in 2005–6 initially qualify for the family element of £545 and 2 x £1,690 (child element) = £3,380. If the household income is £16,000 a year, this is too low to affect the family element, but £2,090 above the limit at which the child elements start to be lost (assuming the family does not qualify for working tax credit). This means the child elements are reduced by £2,090 x 37p/£1 = £773.30. Therefore the family receives £545 + (£3,380 – £773.30) = £3,151.70 in child tax credit.

Child tax credit in 2005–6

Family element

Family element (usual amount)	£545
Baby addition (extra in year child born)	£545

Child element

Child element (usual amount)	£1,690
Disabled child element (extra if child is disabled)	£2,285
Severely disabled child element (further addition if child is severely disabled)	£920

> **Tip**
>
> The household income on which your eligibility for child tax credit and working tax credit is based is broadly your income for tax purposes (see Chapter 4). Things which reduce your taxable income may also increase the amount you can claim in credits. For example, paying into a pension scheme, claiming business losses if you are self-employed, or switching from taxable to tax-free investments (such as individual savings accounts) can all increase your tax credits.

Working tax credit

This is also a tax-free means-tested benefit available to many people who are working whether or not they have children. In general, this benefit is aimed at people on a low income but even fairly well-off families may qualify if they have high childcare costs.

Working tax credit is made up of various elements – see table below. To work out how much you'll get, you first add up all the elements for which your household is eligible. Next you reduce the total by 37p for each £1 by which the household income exceeds a given threshold (£5,220 in 2005–6). Any childcare element is the last part to be reduced.

If a family qualified for the basic, couple or lone parent and 30 hour elements and the maximum childcare element for two or more children, the initial award of working tax credit would be £1,620 + £1,595 + £660 + (70% x £300 x 52) = £14,795. The full amount would be lost only if the household income exceeded £45,206.

Any child tax credit (see above) is paid on top of working tax credit. For example, take a family with two young children, with single parent or couple working at least 30 hours a week, paying at least £300 a week for childcare for the two children for 46 weeks a year. Initially, in 2005–6 the family would qualify for working tax credit of £1,620 (basic element) + £1,595 (couple or lone parent element) + £660 (30 hour element) and 70% x £300 x 46 (childcare element) = £13,535. The family would also qualify for child tax credit of 2 x £1,690 (child element) + £545 (family element). If the household income is £16,000 a year, this is £10,780 more than the threshold of £5,220, so working tax credit and the child element of tax credit are reduced by £10,780 x 37p/£1 = £3,988.60. This leaves most of the childcare element and all of the child tax credit intact. The family receives total tax credits of (£13,535 – £3,988.60) + £3,380 + £545 = £13,471.40.

Working tax credit in 2005–6

Basic element	£1,620
Couple or lone parent element	£1,595
30 hour element	£660
Disabled worker element	£2,165
Severe disability element	£920
Age 50+ return to work payment (working 16 – 29 hours a week)	£1,110
Age 50+ return to work payment (working 30+ hours a week)	£1,660
Childcare element	70% of eligible costs. Eligible costs are £175 a week (one child) or £300 a week two or more children) [1]

[1] In the 2004 Pre-Budget Report, the government proposed increasing the percentage of eligible costs which you can claim to 80 per cent from April 2006.

Tip

Tax credits are means-tested state benefits paid in addition to any child benefit. Unlike most other means-tested state benefits, even reasonably well-off families may qualify for significant payouts, especially if they have many children and/or high childcare costs. You must claim tax credits from the Inland Revenue* – they are not paid automatically.

Help from your employer

Paid maternity leave

An employer is required by law to give most pregnant women and new mothers at least some paid maternity leave if they request it. In 2005–6, you can take off at least six months paid leave (and a further six months unpaid leave). Statutory maternity pay is 90 per cent of your previous average pay for the first six weeks and then 20 weeks at a flat rate (£102.80 a week in 2004–5). The government has said that it intends to increase paid maternity leave from April 2007 to 39 weeks and eventually to a full year. It is also likely that part of a mother's paid maternity leave will eventually be transferable to the father.

Similar paid leave is available to a parent on newly adopting a child. Partners of people claiming statutory maternity pay or statutory adoption pay may be eligible for statutory paternity pay, but this is available only for a maximum of two weeks.

Employer-funded childcare

In general, you pay income tax on all types of pay and benefits from your work, but some fringe benefits are specifically tax-free. For several years, employers have been able to provide workplace nurseries for employees' children tax-free, but from April 2005 you can receive a wider range of help from your employer as a tax-free benefit. Broadly, the tax exemption covers the following types of arrangement:

- childcare arranged, financed and managed by your employer either directly or in partnership with others – this could be a nursery at work or at other premises
- up to £50 a week of other qualifying childcare contracted by your employer on your behalf; for example, with a registered child-minder, or at an independent nursery or out-of-school club, or
- up to £50 a week of childcare vouchers which you can exchange for the qualifying childcare.

There is no tax relief if you arrange and pay for the childcare yourself and your employer reimburses you. Qualifying childcare means care by a registered childminder or through other arrangements formally approved by the government. The rules specifically exclude childcare provided by your husband, wife or unmarried partner, or care provided in your own home by a relative.

You can only receive one lot of £50-a-week childcare tax-free regardless of how many children you have. But both parents can receive this benefit from their respective employers for the same child, so a family could receive up to £100 a week of tax-free childcare through work.

You can't claim the working tax credit childcare element in respect of childcare which is paid for by your employer.

Paying for education

Private schooling

The typical £164,000 cost of bringing up a child assumes a state education. You'll spend a lot more if you opt for private schooling.

The Independent Schools Council puts the average cost if your child boards at around £16,800 a year. Even the cheapest independent schools charge around £1,000 a term for day pupils. There are basically three ways in which you can cope with school fees: borrow, pay-as-you-go or plan ahead.

Borrow

If you need to pay school fees now, borrowing or a combination of borrowing and pay-as-you-go (see below) might be your only options.

For most parents, borrowing on this scale is likely to mean extending the mortgage. Take care choosing how much to borrow and the period over which you intend to repay the loan. If repayments continue too long, you could jeopardise other goals, such as an intention to retire at a particular age. Do bear in mind that a mortgage is a secured loan, so if you do not keep up the payments you could lose your home. See Chapter 9 for more about mortgages.

Sometimes grandparents are willing to help with the cost of school fees. If they can't do this out of income or savings, they might consider an equity release scheme (see Chapter 13), raising money either by borrowing against their home or selling part of it. This might form part of an inheritance planning strategy (see Chapter 15), but in general grandparents should be wary of helping in this way since it will reduce the scope for them to raise extra income or cash in future for their own needs.

Pay-as-you-go

This means paying the fees out of your current income and/or savings already built up – or perhaps out of an inheritance. You might need to cut back on other spending or look at ways to boost your income by, for example, taking on extra work or taking in lodgers.

The task might be a bit less daunting than it at first seems because, according to the Independent Schools Council, nearly a third of pupils receive some financial help from their school in the form of bursaries or scholarships. Check with the school to see what awards are available.

Sometimes local authorities or charities might help with the cost, but generally there must be some out-of-the-ordinary situation. For example, local authorities might help if your child has special educational needs. Charities might help if there are emotional or social problems or, in some cases, if your child is especially gifted in, say, music or sport. But in general these sources can't help if you simply have a bright child who would benefit from private education but you can't afford it.

Plan ahead

This entails starting to save before your child gets to the entry age for the level of schooling you are interested in. A survey by the Independent Schools Council found that less than a third of private school parents do this.

In most respects, saving ahead for school fees is little different from any other form of saving and investing for growth and the main options are discussed on page 162. But there is one method of saving which is specific to this area of planning: a school's own prepayment scheme. The range of options is summarised in the chart on page 160.

Provided you have already chosen a particular school, contact the bursar to find out whether the school does have a prepayment scheme (sometimes called a 'composition fee scheme'). This can be a very efficient way to save because your money goes into a charitable trust where it currently builds up largely tax-free until needed. (However, this might change in future. Proposed new legislation might prevent private schools having charitable status in future unless they can show they offer some public benefit.) The main drawback of these prepayment schemes is that they are school specific, so you need to check what would happen if later you wanted to change your choice of school or could not go ahead as planned for some other reason.

Going to university

The National Union of Students (NUS) estimates that, in 2002–3, it cost £8,400 a year to be a student in London and £7,317 a year outside London (living away from home). And these figures are set to rise when increased tuition fees come into effect from 2006. In total it's reckoned that the cost of three years at university could amount to some £39,000. Parents are not expected to pay all of this and don't have to pay any of it. However many parents would like to help their children through this stage so that they can start their working life without large student debts hanging over them.

Providing for your child's school education

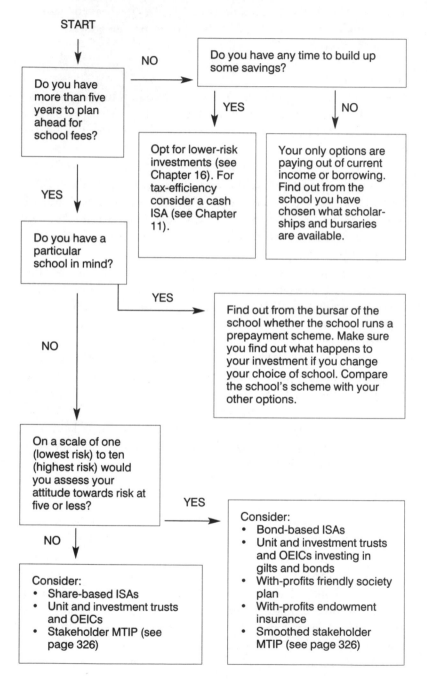

Your options are very much the same as those described above for financing your child's school education. Namely, you could borrow, pay-as-you-go out of your income, plan ahead by building up some savings, or use a combination of these options. If you decide to save, the types of investment that are suitable are discussed overleaf.

However, there is one other point worth bearing in mind. Although you may not want your child to run up large debts, student loans are in fact a very cheap way of borrowing. The amount that must be repaid increases in line with price inflation (running at around 2.5 to 3 per cent at the time of writing) but there is no other interest added. So it may be worth encouraging your child to take out the maximum available student loan. This allows you to keep some of your savings invested while your child is at university. Provided the savings grow faster than inflation (i.e. the effective cost of the student loans), this will be a better use of your finances. You can then use the sum built up to help your son or daughter after graduation. This could take the form of paying off their accumulated debts. But an even more efficient strategy might be to leave your graduate son or daughter to pay off the student loan over a longer period and instead use the savings you've built up to help him or her, say, buy a home (see page 170).

Saving for further education

Duncan and Sheena are both teachers in their mid-thirties. Since the birth of their daughter, Poppy, last year, Duncan has gone part-time but Sheena still works full-time. Poppy's arrival has changed their circumstances dramatically and they need to review their finances. One of their longer-term goals is to build up a fund for Poppy's further education.

They have enough savings to cover their short- and medium-term goals. In particular, their emergency funds (in mini cash ISAs) are pretty high. They should start a stocks-and-shares ISA via a unit trust, for example. This would allow them to invest tax-free, which is important as Sheena is nearly a higher-rate taxpayer. It would be a good way to save for Poppy's further education. As they have a fairly cautious attitude towards risk, Sheena and Duncan should choose a low-risk investment fund.

Which? August 2001

For more details about student loans, tuition fees and what parents may be required to contribute towards university costs, see *The Which? guide to financing your child's future* available from Which? Books★. For an outline of how the system may change from 2006, see the Department for Education and Skills (DFES)★ booklet *The future of higher education. What it means to students and parents*.

A savings strategy to pay for school or university

Assuming you have time to plan ahead, the aim is to save regularly to build up a fund which will cover at least part of the cost of either school fees (if you are looking at private education) or tuition fees and living costs when your son or daughter goes to university.

Investment tools for paying for education

This section suggests various savings and investments you might use. You will find explanations of these on the following pages:

- individual savings accounts, page 180
- child trust fund (for costs from age 18), page 164
- Stakeholder products, page 326
- bank, building society and National Savings & Investments (NS&I) savings accounts, Chapter 16
- endowment insurance, pages 314 (with-profits) and page 336 (unit-linked)
- friendly society plans, page 318
- unit trusts, pages 320 (bond-based) and page 341 (share-based)
- investment trusts, page 345.

Low-risk strategy

The type of savings you choose will depend primarily on how long you have until you start paying out and your attitude towards risk. If you have only a few years to go or you have longer but are very uncomfortable with risk, you have little choice but to build up what you can in bank, building society and National Savings & Investments (NS&I) accounts. These tend to grow only modestly, so you'll need either to save a lot or to accept that you're unlikely to accumulate enough to cover the full cost. See Chapter 16 for details of specific products.

Higher-risk strategy

If you have more than five years over which to build up your savings and you are comfortable taking some risk, consider putting at least part of your savings into investments where the return is linked either directly or indirectly to the stock market. Over the medium to long term, stock-market investments have tended to produce much higher returns than lower-risk investments. However, the value of stock-market investments can fall as well as rise. To avoid a fall in the value of your savings just at the time you need to start cashing them in, you should normally aim to shift into lower-risk investments, such as a building society account, during the last few years in the run up to starting to pay for school or university.

You do not have to put all your money into one basket. You can tailor the level of risk you take by mix-and-matching different investments – for example, some share-based and some linked to gilts and other bonds. For more about this, see Chapter 11.

Some insurance companies and friendly societies promote savings plans specifically as tools for saving for education. These are usually based on endowment insurance (see page 318) and three particular advantages are often cited:

- you pay in regular premiums. This may be a useful discipline if you find it hard to save
- built-in life cover ensures that your child's education plans need not be upset if you were to die
- medium-risk if you choose a with-profits plan (see page 314).

But endowment policies are inflexible and most have relatively high charges. And, apart from friendly society plans (see below), the tax treatment is a further disadvantage.

Other investments, in particular unit trusts and investment trusts are more flexible and cost-efficient. Admittedly, you do need more discipline to keep up a pattern of regular saving, but you could set up a standing order to automatically pay a set amount from your bank account each month. There is no built-in life cover with these investments, so you should take into account your commitment to paying for schooling or university when assessing your overall life insurance needs (see Chapter 6). Unit and investment trusts both give you a wide choice of funds (see page 337). If you want a medium-risk course, spread your savings with some invested in share-based trusts and some in bond-based trusts.

Making your strategy tax-efficient

A few of the savings products you can choose are tax-free – for example, some NS&I products (see Chapter 16). And many of the savings and investments discussed above can be put into 'tax-efficient wrappers', such as individual savings accounts (ISAs) or the new child trust fund (CTF). Saving tax either increases the fund you build up or reduces the amount you need to save.

If you are looking at the lower-risk investments (bank and building society accounts and NS&I products), consider using cash ISAs. The return is completely tax-free. For the higher-risk investments, consider a stocks-and-shares ISA. Income from shares and share-based investments within an ISA is taxed at 10 per cent but the rest of the return is tax-free. And the return from a bond-based stocks-and-shares ISA is completely tax-free. For more about ISAs, see Chapter 11.

If you have savings already built up in personal equity plans (the forerunners of ISAs), consider earmarking these to cover education goals if they are not already needed for another financial target.

A child born on or after 1 September 2002 is eligible for a CTF. These are described in detail on page 168. A CTF can be a useful way to save at least some of the money needed for university (though you can't force your child to use their CTF for this purpose). In addition to the government vouchers paid into the CTF, you and/or anyone else can add up to £1,200 a year in total to the CTF to build up a fund by age 18. Taxwise, CTFs are treated in the same way as ISAs – so income from shares and share-based investments is taxed at 10 per cent but other income and all growth are tax-free. You can choose to invest the CTF either in lower or higher-risk investments.

Friendly societies can offer tax-efficient plans. These are insurance policies but are treated in a special way for tax – the underlying investments in the plan are taxed in the same way as ISAs, so the return is largely tax free. However, the maximum you are allowed to invest in these plans is low (£25 a month or £270 a year) so they could form only part of your savings for education.

Savings and investments for children

There are two main reasons for considering children's savings and investments. The first is to help the child to understand how to value and use money; the second is to build up a nest egg for the child to use in later life. The chart on page 167 summarises the most useful options.

Learning about money

It's hard to beat a building society or bank account for teaching children to handle money sensibly. Essential features are an accessible branch, a low minimum balance, instant access and tolerant counter staff who don't mind counting a box full of change. Many banks and building societies have accounts especially aimed at children, often including free gifts, such as piggy-banks, magazines and birthday cards, but the interest offered is often pitifully low (though, if you are lucky, a small local society may offer better returns). Once your child reaches 11 or so, consider an account with a cash card (particularly useful as school-bound children may find it hard to visit a branch). From age 14 or so, a few accounts include a debit card which can be a good introduction to using plastic in shops or online. For the child's own larger sums, such as birthday money, consider too the NS&I investment account (see page 292).

Providing a nest egg

Tax complications

Parents giving, or building up, relatively large sums for their offspring (more than £2,000–£3,000, say) need to watch the tax rules. Even a child has a personal allowance to set against income tax – £4,895 in 2005–6. This means that most children are non-taxpayers (so make sure they receive income *gross*, that is, without tax deducted). A child can also make capital gains (over and above reliefs) of up to £8,200 in 2004–5 (2005–6 allowance not available at time of writing) tax-free. However, to prevent tax avoidance, if you give money or an asset to your own child, any income it produces during a tax year counts as *your* income, not the child's, and is taxed at your top rate. This rule is waived if the total before-tax income from all sources produced by all gifts from a parent comes to no more than £100 during the tax year.

Tip

You may need to give the Inland Revenue proof that a gift to your child was not from you, so ask grandparents, godparents etc. to send a letter with money or investments they give your child.

This means that a child could receive up to £200 without problem if both parents made gifts. If the income exceeds that limit, then all of it (not just the excess) is taxed as your own. To avoid falling foul of these rules, choose investments for your child which count as producing a tax-free return (including the new child trust fund) or capital gains rather than income. Income produced by gifts from people other than parents counts as the child's own.

Note that, even though the return from ISAs counts as tax-free, the gross income from a cash ISA taken out by someone under age 18 still counts as income of the parent if the ISA investment was the result of a gift from the parent and the £100 limit is breached.

A general strategy

To build up a nest egg to help a child in later years, longer-term investments offer the best prospect. As always, the particular choice of investment depends partly on the degree of risk you're willing to take. At the lowest end of the risk spectrum is the NS&I children's bonus bond (see page 299) or a child trust fund investing in deposits (see below). As this offers a tax-free return, it is suitable as a gift from a parent.

A medium- to higher-risk product aimed specifically at children is the the so-called 'baby bond' (see page 318). These are variants of the tax-efficient insurance policies offered by friendly societies. They are useful for parents investing for children because there's no tax on the eventual payout. But what makes them special is that, unlike other insurance policies, there's also little tax on the fund in which the premiums are invested. Premiums are invested on either a with-profits or a unit-linked basis. Unit-linking is more risky than with-profits because investment values may have taken a tumble at the time your child wants to cash in the bond. Over the long term, a unit-linked bond should tend to outperform a with-profits one.

Investing for children

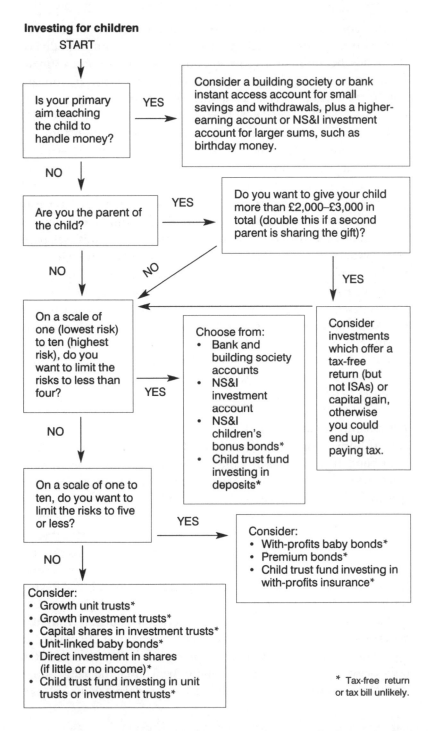

START

Is your primary aim teaching the child to handle money?

YES → Consider a building society or bank instant access account for small savings and withdrawals, plus a higher-earning account or NS&I investment account for larger sums, such as birthday money.

NO ↓

Are you the parent of the child?

YES → Do you want to give your child more than £2,000–£3,000 in total (double this if a second parent is sharing the gift)?

NO ↓   NO ↙   YES ↓

Consider investments which offer a tax-free return (but not ISAs) or capital gain, otherwise you could end up paying tax.

On a scale of one (lowest risk) to ten (highest risk), do you want to limit the risks to less than four?

YES → Choose from:
- Bank and building society accounts
- NS&I investment account
- NS&I children's bonus bonds*
- Child trust fund investing in deposits*

NO ↓

On a scale of one to ten, do you want to limit the risks to five or less?

YES → Consider:
- With-profits baby bonds*
- Premium bonds*
- Child trust fund investing in with-profits insurance*

NO ↓

Consider:
- Growth unit trusts*
- Growth investment trusts*
- Capital shares in investment trusts*
- Unit-linked baby bonds*
- Direct investment in shares (if little or no income)*
- Child trust fund investing in unit trusts or investment trusts*

* Tax-free return or tax bill unlikely.

167

In theory, the baby bonds' tax-free status should ensure very competitive returns, but charges have a big impact on the value of the bonds, because the government limits each person's investment in them to a very low maximum (£25 a month). If you are comfortable with the risk of a share-based investment for your child, you could do better by looking at unit trusts (see page 341) and investment trusts (see page 345). Ideal for children's investments are the savings schemes run by many unit and investment trust managers. Some accept investments as low as £20 a month on a regular basis, and *ad hoc* lump sums from £200.

Since April 2005, you can invest in insurance policies, units trusts and investment trusts through your child's trust fund (see below).

A popular gift for children are NS&I premium bonds (see page 300). Strictly speaking, these are not investments, although if the holding is big enough and the child has average luck, the 'return' can compare reasonably with middle-of-the-road bank and building society rates and, of course, there's always that outside chance of making a million. Children aged 16 or over can buy premium bonds themselves. Otherwise, only parents, grandparents, great grandparents and guardians can buy bonds for a child. Anyone else would need to give cash to, say, the parent who could then make the purchase in the name of the child.

The child trust fund (CTF)

A child born on or after 1 September 2002 is eligible to have a child trust fund (CTF). This is a new scheme from the government designed to 'strengthen the savings habit of future generations and spread the benefits of asset ownership to all'.

The scheme, which started on 6 April 2005, is a long-term savings scheme and aims to build up a pot of money available to your child when they reach age 18. At that time, your child can use the money in any way he or she chooses – for example, reinvesting it, funding university or vocational training, starting a business, for travelling or for spending in any other way.

The parent of an eligible child receives a voucher from the government for £250 and an extra £250 if your household income is less than a given amount (£13,910 in 2005–6). (If your child was born between 1 September 2002 and 6 April 2005, the value of the voucher is increased to compensate for the delay.) Vouchers are issued automatically once you are registered to receive child benefit for the child.

You use the voucher to open a CTF for your child. (If you haven't done so within a year, the government will step in and do this for you.) The government has proposed that it will add a further £250 (or £500 for low-income families) to the CTF on the child's seventh birthday.

In addition to the government money, you and/or anyone else can add up to £1,200 a year in total to your child's CTF. This means that by age 18, a total of over £22,000 could have been paid in. The table shows in today's money how much the fund might have grown to by age 18.

How a child trust fund might have grown by age 18

Amount you and/or friends or family invest each month [1]	No adjustment for inflation		Adjusted for inflation
	Total paid in	Possible value of fund by age 18 [2]	Value of the fund in today's money [3]
£0	£500	£840	£540
£10	£2,660	£3,840	£2,460
£20	£4,820	£6,830	£4,390
£30	£6,980	£9,830	£6,310
£40	£9,140	£12,820	£8,240
£50	£11,300	£15,820	£10,160
£75	£16,700	£23,310	£14,975
£100	£22,100	£30,800	£19,790

[1] In addition, assumes government pays in £250 at birth and £250 at age seven.
[2] Assumes growth of 5 per cent a year and charges of 1.5 per cent a year.
[3] Assumes inflation averages 2.5 per cent a year.

The guidance pack you receive with the government voucher lists the banks, unit trust companies, investment trusts, friendly societies, insurance companies and other organisations which offer CTF accounts and tells you how to invest.

There is a wide choice of CTFs. Some are invested in deposits which work like bank or building society savings accounts. Others are invested in a spread of shares and/or bonds. Although you might be attracted to the low risk of deposits, in general share-based investments are more suitable for long-term investing (see Chapter 11). All providers must either offer or give you access to a 'stakeholder CTF'. A stakeholder CTF is invested in a broad spread of different assets including shares until the last five years before your child reaches 18 by which time the investment must automatically shift towards deposits in order to lock in past gains – this is sometimes called 'lifestyling'. The maximum charges for a stakeholder CTF are 1.5 per cent a year of the value of the fund. If you want to add to the amount the government pays in, the provider may set a minimum investment but a stakeholder CTF must accept one-off payments as low as £10.

Whatever sort of CTF you choose, while the fund is invested, the savings and investments in the CTF are taxed in the same way as ISAs (see page 180). This means that income from shares and share-based investments is taxed at 10 per cent but other income and gains build up tax free. There is no tax to pay when the young person cashes in the CTF.

In some respects the tax benefits are less valuable than they seem at first sight. Most children do not use up their full income tax allowance (£4,895 in 2005–6) or capital gains tax allowance (£8,200 in 2004–5) and so are non-taxpayers anyway. But bear in mind that normally income from money you give to your child may be taxed as your income (see page 165). This does not apply to gifts you invest in your child's CTF, so adding extra over and above the government vouchers could be a tax-efficient way to help your child.

Buying a first home

Even graduates who can expect to earn £18,000 to £25,000 a year in their first job struggle to buy their first home. In late 2004, first-time buyers were paying on average £123,000. Typically, the maximum mortgage offer is three times salary, leaving most young people well short of the amount they need to get a foot on the housing ladder. Parents can help in a variety of ways.

Buy-to-let

If you are interested in owning residential property as an investment (see Chapter 18), you might consider buying in the place where your son or daughter is studying or working. They can live in the property either rent-free or paying you something and possibly let out surplus rooms.

Provide a deposit

You can reduce the amount your child needs to borrow for house purchase by helping them to find a large deposit. If you had planned to help your student son or daughter with university costs (see page 159), bear in mind that student loans are cheap compared with other loans, such as mortgages. Instead of paying off their student debts, it may be more useful if they keep the debts and instead you now provide a lump sum that they can put towards house purchase.

Helping with the deposit means you need to raise a lump sum. This might come out of money you already have saved. Alternatively, you might consider borrowing – for example, by taking out or extending a mortgage on your own home. Before doing this, make sure that you can afford the repayments. A mortgage is a secured loan, so if you don't keep up the monthly payments you could lose your home. See Chapter 9 for more information about mortgages.

Act as guarantor

Your son or daughter may be able to get a larger-than-normal mortgage relative to their salary if you agree to act as guarantor for all or part of the loan. This means if your child does not keep up the mortgage payments, the lender can turn to you to make the payments instead. This could be a big financial commitment, so don't agree to act as guarantor unless you are sure you would be able to make the payments if the worst happened. Being a guarantor could also affect your own ability to borrow in future since any lender may take into account the potential payments when deciding whether and how much to lend to you.

Take out a joint loan

At least one lender now offers a mortgage which can be based on the joint income of a young person and their parents. You are required to own the property jointly and legally you are both responsible for the monthly payments. In practice, many young people can manage to make the full repayments on their own, so you might not need to pay anything out of your own income. But bear in mind that, if your son or daughter couldn't keep up the payments or meet the full amount, you would be required to meet the shortfall.

Use an all-in-one mortgage

Some mortgages are bundled together with a current account and savings accounts. The positive balances in these accounts are deducted from the outstanding mortgage loan before the monthly interest is worked out and so reduce the monthly mortgage payments (see Chapter 9). With some of these mortgages, the savings of different family members can be included in the bundle. You as a parent could elect to have your savings set off against the outstanding mortgage of your son or daughter, so reducing their monthly payments. From your point of view, you will be forgoing the interest that your savings would normally earn. However, because your savings instead in effect earn at the mortgage rate and tax-free (see page 290), this is a very efficient way to help out.

Chapter 11

Saving or investing for growth

Many financial goals involve building up a sum of money – for example, for a deposit on a house, to pay for a once-in-a-lifetime holiday or to supplement your pension (see Chapter 12) when you retire. Or these goals might be met by investing a lump sum – perhaps an inheritance, winnings, redundancy pay or the payout from a savings plan. Sometimes the goals are less specific. The intention may simply be to build up or preserve a nest egg to provide security or opportunities later on, or to pass on to the next generation. What all these goals have in common is that you are saving or investing for growth.

There is a bewildering array of products that you might use. The charts on the next few pages summarise how you might narrow down your choice. A wide range of factors should be taken into account; these are discussed in the following pages. Details of the specific investments are given in Chapters 16 to 18.

The charts concentrate largely on risk, because this is the factor above all others which most often seems to cause problems. Numerous financial scandals have revolved around investors being seduced into products which promised exceptional returns at seemingly little or no risk. Sometimes governments might issue such investments, but in the commercial world risk and reward *always* go hand in hand. If you want the chance of high returns, you must be prepared to take on extra risk.

You should always treat a high-return, low-risk deal with suspicion. When interest rates are low and the stock market is in the doldrums, it can be especially tempting to believe the marketing hype for a deal offering above-average safe returns, but there is bound to be a catch. An example from recent times has been some types of split-capital investment trusts (see page 345). These could offer some very sensible, moderate-risk ways to save. But during the stock-market slump of 2000 to 2003, some variants were offering unusually high returns. Closer inspection revealed that, unlike their less risky counterparts, these trusts were often heavily reliant on borrowed funds and/or investment in other split-capital trusts. This made the trusts much more risky and vulnerable to a collapse in share prices. Unfortunately the scandal tarred all split capital trusts with the same brush even though some remained useful investment tools.

The charts that follow invite you to think of risk as a continuous scale from one to ten. If you place yourself at one, you are very averse to risk and should select savings and investments which carry the minimum of risk. Moving along the scale, you become more comfortable with risk and, at ten, you positively enjoy taking a gamble. How you assess your attitude towards risk was looked at in greater detail on page 64. As mentioned there, for a particular financial decision, your attitude towards risk may be influenced by the extent to which you are already on course to meet your most important financial targets. You should work through the charts for each financial target you have identified, bearing in mind the priority attached to each one. For example, if you are at the start of your financial plan, needing to build up an emergency fund and with little cash to spare, you should normally be very averse to risk. But as your main financial building-blocks fall into place, you may be comfortable taking greater risks with the lower-priority targets – see the diagram opposite.

How to choose savings and investments

You need to consider a combination of factors when thinking about whether one type of savings or investments or another will best meet your needs. Here, the main factors are looked at in turn.

How much can you save or invest and how regularly?

With most savings and investments, there is a minimum amount you can invest. Sometimes, where there is no minimum, charges still make it uneconomic to pay in small sums. Where a type of saving or investment enjoys favourable tax treatment, there is usually a maximum you can invest. This can apply to other products too.

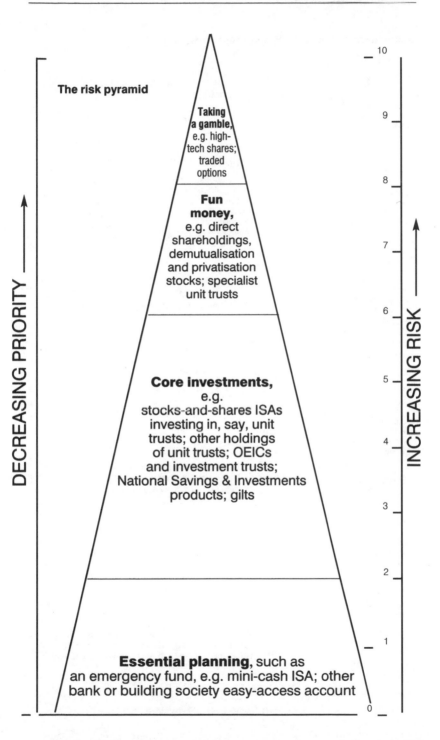

The risk pyramid

DECREASING PRIORITY ⟶

INCREASING RISK ⟶

10
9
8
7
6
5
4
3
2
1
0

Taking a gamble, e.g. high-tech shares; traded options

Fun money, e.g. direct shareholdings, demutualisation and privatisation stocks; specialist unit trusts

Core investments, e.g. stocks-and-shares ISAs investing in, say, unit trusts; other holdings of unit trusts; OEICs and investment trusts; National Savings & Investments products; gilts

Essential planning, such as an emergency fund, e.g. mini-cash ISA; other bank or building society easy-access account

Building up a lump sum through regular saving

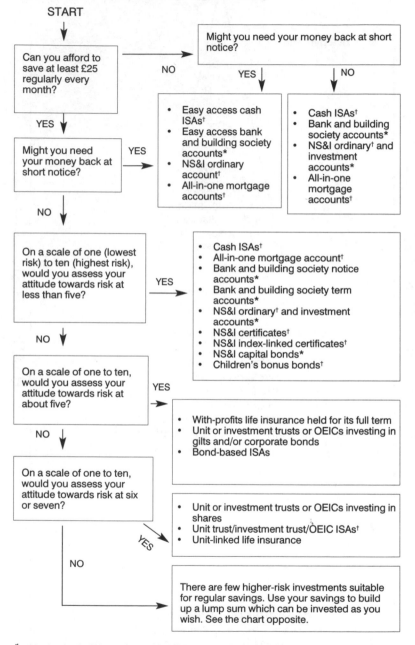

START

Can you afford to save at least £25 regularly every month? — NO → **Might you need your money back at short notice?**

- YES ↓ (from "Can you afford...")
- YES ↓ / NO ↓ (from "Might you need your money back at short notice?")

Might you need your money back at short notice? — YES →
- Easy access cash ISAs†
- Easy access bank and building society accounts*
- NS&I ordinary account†
- All-in-one mortgage accounts†

(NO branch from top-right question):
- Cash ISAs†
- Bank and building society accounts*
- NS&I ordinary† and investment accounts*
- All-in-one mortgage accounts†

NO ↓

On a scale of one (lowest risk) to ten (highest risk), would you assess your attitude towards risk at less than five? — YES →
- Cash ISAs†
- All-in-one mortgage account†
- Bank and building society notice accounts*
- Bank and building society term accounts*
- NS&I ordinary† and investment accounts*
- NS&I certificates†
- NS&I index-linked certificates†
- NS&I capital bonds*
- Children's bonus bonds†

NO ↓

On a scale of one to ten, would you assess your attitude towards risk at about five? — YES →
- With-profits life insurance held for its full term
- Unit or investment trusts or OEICs investing in gilts and/or corporate bonds
- Bond-based ISAs

NO ↓

On a scale of one to ten, would you assess your attitude towards risk at six or seven? — YES →
- Unit or investment trusts or OEICs investing in shares
- Unit trust/investment trust/OEIC ISAs†
- Unit-linked life insurance

NO →

There are few higher-risk investments suitable for regular savings. Use your savings to build up a lump sum which can be invested as you wish. See the chart opposite.

* May be particularly worth considering if you are a non-taxpayer.
† May be particularly worth considering if you pay tax at the higher rate.

Investing a lump sum to make it grow

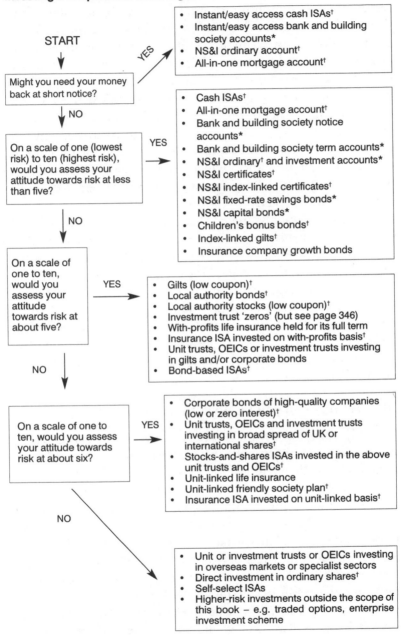

START

Might you need your money back at short notice?

YES →
- Instant/easy access cash ISAs†
- Instant/easy access bank and building society accounts*
- NS&I ordinary account†
- All-in-one mortgage account†

NO ↓

On a scale of one (lowest risk) to ten (highest risk), would you assess your attitude towards risk at less than five?

YES →
- Cash ISAs†
- All-in-one mortgage account†
- Bank and building society notice accounts*
- Bank and building society term accounts*
- NS&I ordinary† and investment accounts*
- NS&I certificates†
- NS&I index-linked certificates†
- NS&I fixed-rate savings bonds*
- NS&I capital bonds*
- Children's bonus bonds†
- Index-linked gilts†
- Insurance company growth bonds

NO ↓

On a scale of one to ten, would you assess your attitude towards risk at about five?

YES →
- Gilts (low coupon)†
- Local authority bonds†
- Local authority stocks (low coupon)†
- Investment trust 'zeros' (but see page 346)
- With-profits life insurance held for its full term
- Insurance ISA invested on with-profits basis†
- Unit trusts, OEICs or investment trusts investing in gilts and/or corporate bonds
- Bond-based ISAs†

NO ↓

On a scale of one to ten, would you assess your attitude towards risk at about six?

YES →
- Corporate bonds of high-quality companies (low or zero interest)†
- Unit trusts, OEICs and investment trusts investing in broad spread of UK or international shares†
- Stocks-and-shares ISAs invested in the above unit trusts and OEICs†
- Unit-linked life insurance
- Unit-linked friendly society plan†
- Insurance ISA invested on unit-linked basis†

NO ↓

- Unit or investment trusts or OEICs investing in overseas markets or specialist sectors
- Direct investment in ordinary shares†
- Self-select ISAs
- Higher-risk investments outside the scope of this book – e.g. traded options, enterprise investment scheme

*May be particularly worth considering if you are a non-taxpayer.
† May be particularly worth considering if you pay tax at the higher rate.

177

Some investment products are specifically designed to accept regular savings – monthly or annual sums, for instance – and there may be penalties if you fail to keep up the payments. There is quite a debate, especially in the insurance and pensions world, over whether regular saving is a 'good thing'. Regular saving has the advantage of creating a discipline which you might find helpful. It also takes away tricky decisions about when is the right time to buy investments, the price of which rises and falls. On the other hand, by committing yourself to regular saving, you lose flexibility over what, when and with whom you invest, because you are locked into the savings arrangement. This can be a problem if either your circumstances change or better products come on to the market.

It is also commonly argued that charges from regular-savings insurance and pensions products are higher than for equivalent single-premium products (where you pay in a single lump sum). On the face of it, this is true. However, you must consider how you would use single-premium products. If, for you, the alternative to taking out a regular-premium plan would be to take out a series of single-premium plans as and when you could afford to, you must compare charges for the *whole* series of lump-sum plans (and not just one of them) against the charges for the regular-savings plan.

For how long can you tie up your money?

Crucially important when choosing any investment is: can you get your money back, when, and are there penalties for doing so? Some products are designed to last for a specified period – for example, five or ten years. Obviously, you should not invest unless you can leave your money for the full period. Other investments do not have a specified term, but they may clearly be best suited to long-term investment, and may make an unwise choice if you know you want to save only for a year or two or might need funds in a hurry.

However sensibly you choose your investments at the outset, life can be unpredictable, so you should check what happens if you need your money back sooner: maybe you simply would not be able to have it back, perhaps you would lose interest, there might be surrender charges or, with an investment where the price rises and falls, you might run the risk of a loss.

What type of return do you need?

This chapter considers investing for growth. With some financial goals, you may need to invest for income – see Chapter 13. A further consideration is whether you want a fixed return or one which varies. Fixed returns, which go hand in hand with investing for a fixed period, are attractive if you expect returns on competing investments to fall. If, in fact, the competing returns rise over the period, you will lose out, so do not assume that choosing a fixed return is necessarily less risky than a return which can vary.

A fixed return loses value, in terms of what it can buy, if prices rise. A few products offering index-linked returns, which protect your investment against the impact of inflation, are available.

What return will you get?

Only a handful of investments offer a fixed or guaranteed return. Even then, you should check carefully so that you understand the nature of the guarantee – for example, will you get the promised return regardless or does the guarantee hold only as long as certain conditions are met?

With most savings and investments, you cannot know in advance what return you will get. As a rough guide, there is a trade-off between risk and return. For example, an investment that promises you will not lose any of your original capital is likely to offer a lower return than an investment where there is some capital risk – see page 184 for more about risk.

Salespeople and advisers often make much of past performance data. They point out that an investment fund has grown strongly in the past, implicitly suggesting that it will do just as well in future. Take all this with a pinch of salt. Academic studies suggest only a weak link, if any, between past and future investment performance. What link there is suggests that investment funds that have performed poorly in the past are more likely than average to perform poorly in future. So there is some basis for avoiding the worst performing investments. But sadly there is no magic rule to help you pick the future winners.

How is the return taxed?

Chapter 4 examines the tax system to help you identify your own tax position. Now, you need to marry your personal tax treatment to the tax treatment of the investments you choose. Some investments and savings have particular tax advantages for certain types of investor, and this is highlighted as appropriate throughout Chapters 16 to 18. Most taxpayers can benefit from special rules which in effect put a tax-efficient wrapper around your choice of investments. These wrappers are pension schemes (see Chapter 12), individual saving accounts (see below) and the child trust fund (see Chapter 10).

Some broad tax points to consider are as follows:

- Look at the after-tax (net) return you will get personally, given your income tax rate and capital gains tax position, not the before-tax (gross) return.
- Non-taxpayers gain nothing extra from tax-free investments.
- It is more convenient for non-taxpayers to receive returns from which no tax has been deducted than to have to claim back such tax.
- Tax-free returns are especially valuable to higher-rate taxpayers.
- Even if your income is taxed, you can often make capital gains without having to pay any tax on them because of the generous tax allowances.
- Income from most types of savings is taxed only at the savings rate. Basic-rate taxpayers have no further tax to pay. Higher-rate taxpayers have extra to pay. Non-taxpayers can, in most cases, reclaim any tax already deducted and starting-rate taxpayers can reclaim some of the tax. This treatment applies to interest from bank and building society accounts, income from annuities and interest from gilts and corporate bonds.
- Dividends from shares and distributions from most unit trusts and open-ended investment companies (OEICs) are taxed in a special way. Even non-taxpayers pay some tax (at 10 per cent) on this type of income.

Individual savings accounts

An individual savings account (ISA) is not itself an investment. Think of it as a wrapper into which you can put various different sorts of savings and investments. The return from the savings or investments inside the wrapper is either completely or largely tax-free.

You invest through a plan manager who operates the ISA for you. Plan managers are usually the same organisations that offer the products within the ISA wrapper, so in practice you simply take out an ISA in the same way that you would take out the underlying savings or investments.

There are two types of ISA (mini-ISA and maxi-ISA) and two 'components' corresponding to different types of saving or investments. The components are:

- **cash** This is a type of bank, building society or National Savings & Investments (NS&I) account. It works like an ordinary savings account: your money earns interest and you get back your capital in full. This makes cash ISAs a low-risk product. Different providers offer different cash ISAs; some offer instant access, others are notice accounts, most pay a variable rate of interest but some offer a fixed rate. See Chapter 16 for more about these types of investment

- **stocks and shares** This can contain any of a wide range of investments, most commonly one or more unit trusts, open-ended investment companies (OEICs) or investment trusts, your own selection of shares and bonds, or an insurance policy. (There used to be a separate 'insurance component' for ISAs but from 6 April 2005 this became part of the stocks-and-shares component.) These are all medium- to high-risk investments.

A mini-ISA invests in just one of the above components – it is either a cash mini-ISA or a stocks-and-shares mini-ISA. You can take out one of each type each tax year and each has its own plan manager. Alternatively, you can take out one maxi-ISA each year. A maxi-ISA must have the stocks-and-shares component and can also have a cash component (but doesn't have to). You have just one plan manager for the maxi-ISA regardless of the number of components. You cannot start both mini-ISAs and a maxi-ISA in the same tax year – you have to choose which you want.

Each tax year you have an ISA allowance, as shown in the table overleaf. If you do not use up your full ISA allowance for a year, the unused part is lost for good – you can't carry it forward. If you want to invest as much as you can in stock-market investments, you should opt for a maxi-ISA, putting little or nothing into a cash component.

The government has said that ISAs will continue to be available until 5 April 2009.

Each tax year you can use your ISA allowance to open different ISAs from those you took out in previous years. Alternatively, you can add more to an ISA you started in a previous year.

You can transfer your existing ISAs from one plan manager to another without affecting your ISA allowance, provided you instruct the managers of your old and new ISAs to organise the transfer. Do not yourself withdraw money from the old ISA to pay into a new one – if you do this, you'll be treated as having cashed in the old ISA and what you pay into the new one will use up part of your current year's ISA allowance.

How much you can invest in an ISA each tax year from 2005–6 to 2008–9 [1]

ISA component	You can invest this much in mini-ISAs	Or, you can invest this much in a maxi-ISA
Cash	up to £3,000	up to £3,000
Stocks and shares	up to £4,000	up to £7,000 less anything invested in the cash component

[1] Assuming government Pre-Budget proposals to maintain current ISA limits go ahead. Originally, the limits had been due to fall to £1,000 for a cash ISA or component and £5,000 overall from 6 April 2006.

> **Tip**
> If you want to use your ISA allowance to invest the maximum possible in share-based investments, such as unit and investment trusts, choose a maxi-ISA rather than separate mini-ISAs.

Whether or not you benefit from using ISAs depends on the type of ISA you choose, your tax position and whether the plan manager charges for the ISA wrapper:

- **cash ISAs** – the return is completely tax-free and normally there are no charges for the ISA, so all taxpayers can benefit from having cash ISAs. If you are a non-taxpayer, there is no tax advantage, but sometimes the interest offered by cash ISAs is better than the return on non-ISA savings accounts, so it's worth checking out the ISA deals

- **bond-based stocks and shares ISAs** – for example, a bond-based unit trust (see page 320) held through an ISA. Again the return is completely tax free, so all taxpayers get a tax advantage. Some plan managers charge for the ISA wrapper, others don't. Check this and make sure that any charges do not outweigh the tax saved
- **share-based stocks and shares ISAs** – for example a share-based unit trust (see page 341) held through an ISA. Income from the shares is taxed at 10 per cent but other types of income and capital gains are tax-free. This means that higher-rate taxpayers are likely to gain from using the ISA, but other taxpayers stand to save tax only if they make a large capital gain when they cash in the ISA – see the table below. Check whether there are any ISA charges and, if so, that they do not outweigh any tax savings.

How your return is taxed if you hold shares, share-based unit trusts or similar investments

	If you are this type of taxpayer:			
	Non-taxpayer	Starting-rate taxpayer	Basic-rate taxpayer	Higher-rate taxpayer
Through an ISA				
Income taxed at	10%	10%	10%	10%
Growth taxed at	0%	0%	0%	0%
Not through an ISA				
Income taxed at	10%	10%	10%	32.5%
First £8,200 [1] of growth taxed at	0%	0%	0%	0%
Further growth taxed at	0%	10%	20%	40%

[1] Capital gains tax allowance per person for 2004–5. This allowance is usually increased each year. If unused in one year, it cannot be carried forward to the next.

What are the costs?

Just as you need to know the after-tax return for you personally, so you need to know the after-all-charges return to build a clear idea of what you stand to gain through a particular savings or investment medium. Some products are very straightforward. For example, when you save with a building society, you are quoted a particular rate of interest. The rate has been pitched at a level which (taking other factors into account) is expected to cover the society's costs. What you are quoted is what you get net of charges. Well, almost – you do have to watch out for interest penalties if you cash in term or notice accounts.

Most packaged products (life insurance, unit trusts, pension schemes) are more complex, with a variety of different charges – management fees, upfront charges, surrender penalties, switching fees, and so on. Trying to understand the impact of all these charges can be a nightmare. But life insurance and pension providers have to provide illustrations of the possible return from their products, netting out the impact of their own charges on the return you get (see Chapter 3 for details).

A third group of investments are those which run up dealing or transaction costs when you buy and sell them. These include most shares, gilts and corporate bonds. When assessing the return you might get, you should deduct what you will pay in stockbroker's commission, stamp duty, and so on.

What are the risks?

When people talk about investment risk, they usually mean the possibility of losing some or all of their original stake. But this is only part of the picture. There are four main types of risk:

- **capital risk** If you put your money into deposit-based savings, such as building society accounts, you know that you will always get back at least the amount of your original capital – that is, there is no capital risk. With investments like shares and unit trusts, which are bought and sold in a marketplace, you cannot be sure of this, because their price may have fallen during the time you have owned them. Another less obvious threat to capital is where charges are deducted from that capital rather than from the return. You also need to consider the standing of the organisation with whom you are investing. If you lend money to the British government, it is very unlikely that the government will default and be unable to pay you back as promised. But if you buy the bonds or shares of a small company struggling to break into new markets, there is a distinct possibility of your losing all your investment if the company goes out of business.

- **inflation risk** The big problem with deposit-type investments is that, over the long term, their returns tend to be lower than those from investments such as shares, and can be so low that they do not even compensate you for the impact of rising prices. This means that, although you can be sure of getting back your original outlay, it may be worth a lot less in terms of what you can buy with it. A few investments are specifically designed to protect you against inflation, but are not always the most appropriate choice. In the main, if you are investing for the long term, you should consider investments either in shares or linked to shares (such as unit trusts) as a way of hedging against inflation.

- **shortfall risk** If you have a set target – for example, saving enough to provide a certain level of retirement income, building up a lump sum to pay off a mortgage at the end of its term, or saving in advance to fund your child through university – there is often a risk that you will fail to meet your target. A way to reduce this risk would be to invest for a guaranteed return, or to stick to safe investments like deposits, though the return on these is usually relatively low. This means you would have to save more to reach your target, which could make the goal too expensive to be achievable at all. For example, the table below shows that for each £10,000 you needed in ten years' time, you would need to save £76 a month if you could get an after-tax return of only 2 per cent (as might be the case with, say, a building society savings account), but only £61 a month if you could invest at 6 per cent a year. Perversely, a more affordable way to reduce shortfall risk is to invest at least some of your money in equity-based investments which, although exposing you to capital risk, also give you the chance of a higher return over the long term.

Amount you would need to save to build up a lump sum of £10,000 over ten years through regular saving

If the yearly rate of return was:	10%	8%	6%	4%	2%
You would need to save this much each month:	£50	£55	£61	£68	£76

- **the risk of being locked in (or out)** Accepting a fixed return over a set period or agreeing to a contract with onerous early-surrender penalties can prevent you from benefiting from improved returns elsewhere. Equally, though, keeping your options open can mean that you have to accept falling returns when others have protected their position by taking on fixed-rate deals.

You can see that there is no such thing as a completely 'safe' investment. Inevitably, you have to trade risk against return, and the different risks against each other.

In the charts on pages 176–7 and in Chapters 16–18 each type of investment is given a risk rating of one (lowest risk) to ten (highest risk). These ratings attempt to take into account all the various risks and give you a rule of thumb for comparing the riskiness of one type of investment with another. However, the ratings are not based on objective measures of probabilities and volatility, and the riskiness sometimes varies depending on how you plan to use a particular type of investment: for example, holding it until repayment rather than selling in a volatile market, or combining it with other types of investment with a different degree of riskiness. Use the risk ratings as a rough guide which you can match to your assessment of the degree of risk which you are willing to take.

Building a portfolio

In general, each investment target you have will require its own strategy for achieving it. But you are not simply limited to the particular risk and return offered by each product. By combining different investments, you can build a portfolio which has its own balance of risks and rewards. This gives you the scope to tailor your savings and investments closely to your own targets, circumstances and preferences.

You can see how this works by considering the example of shares. Buying shares in just one company would be a high-risk strategy; you would face three levels of risk:

- **market risk** The whole stock market could fall – because of economic recession, say.
- **industry or sector risk** The particular industry your company is part of could suffer some blow – a sudden increase in the price of raw materials, for example.

- **company risk** Your particular company could run into difficulties – for example, fierce competition from an aggressive new player – and could even go bankrupt, in which case you would most likely lose all your investment.

You can reduce your exposure to company risk by investing in the shares of a number of different companies. And you can reduce your exposure to sector risk by making sure those companies come from a spread of different industries. Market risk can be lessened by investing not just in the UK stock market but in, say, Europe, Japan and the United States, and by investing in a range of other investments, such as bonds and property, which respond in a different way to economic factors.

In the same way, you can combine different 'asset classes' to adjust the mix of risk and return. The four main asset classes are:

- **cash** – deposit-based investments like bank and building society accounts. This is the least risky asset class
- **bonds** – in effect loans to governments and companies, but these can be bought and sold on the stock market. This class is more risky than cash, but less risky than equities
- **property** – either direct investment in property (usually commercial buildings like office blocks and shopping centres) or investment in the shares of companies that own and manage such properties. Views are divided, but property is generally considered less risky than shares, though money in property may be tied up for a long time
- **equities** – shares in companies. This is the most risky of the four classes.

By mixing assets from each class, you build an investment portfolio with the combination of risk and expected returns that suits you. You can buy into 'ready-made' portfolios by investing in 'pooled investments', such as unit trusts, investment trusts and investment-type life insurance.

There are no hard and fast rules about how much of your money you should have in each asset class. One rule of thumb suggests that the amount invested in equities (shares) should be 100 per cent less your age in years – for example, if you are 40, invest $100 - 40 = 60$ per cent in shares, and if you are 70, invest $100 - 70 = 30$ per cent in shares.

But such guides are simplistic. Factors that will tend to influence your asset mix include:

- **your overall resources**. In general, the better off you are the more freedom you have to put more of your money in riskier assets
- **the financial goal you are targeting**. You can afford to put a higher proportion of your money in higher-risk assets if you are investing for fun than if you are saving or investing to pay for something specific, such as the cost of university education
- **timescale**. As you approach the time when you will need to start drawing on your savings or investments, you should consider shifting towards lower risk assets so that you lock in gains you have made in the past
- **temperament**. However sensible it might be in theory to put some of your long-term savings and investments into share-based assets, there may be little point if such a strategy would cause you unacceptable worry.

More information

Chapters 16-18 outline the main investment and saving tools. Many books are devoted to developing your understanding of investment strategy and portfolio building: browse around a good bookshop. Regular journals to consider include *Which?*★, *Money Management*★, *Investors Chronicle*★, *Moneywise*★ and *Money Observer*★.

When it comes to organising your investments, you might find it helpful to use a computer. A spreadsheet program, such as Microsoft Excel, is ideal if you are comfortable setting up your own system for logging your investments, calculating their values, working out any tax due, and so on. But you can also get tailor-made packages: for example, for managing a portfolio of stocks and shares, handling your tax, and so on. Many personal finance and stock-brokers' websites include portfolio managers. If you prefer to install your own software, have a browse around a computer warehouse or the advertisements in the various computer magazines stocked by most newsagents to see what is available.

Chapter 12

Building up retirement income

One of your highest financial priorities should be ensuring that you will have an adequate income in retirement. In many areas of personal finance, the aim is to protect yourself against the *possibility* that certain events will happen. But with pension planning you are dealing with the very near *certainty* that you will retire and you will need an income.

Virtually everyone will need a pension. A few people are rich enough not to worry too much about where their retirement income will come from, but even they should take advantage of the tax incentives available for pension planning. If you run your own business, you might think that you do not need to make special plans for retirement. After all, you'll sell the business and live off the proceeds, won't you? But this is a very risky strategy: your business might fail before you reach retirement, or you might be unable to sell it at the time you want to retire or for enough to provide a comfortable income.

Do not underestimate the financial resources you will need for retirement. This is a phase of your life which can span two or three decades or more: see the table overleaf. To build up the resources you need, you should start your retirement saving as soon as possible.

How much retirement income will you need?

Your income needs are likely to be substantially different from your current needs. For example, in retirement you might no longer be paying out on a mortgage, and you will not have work-related expenses (although you might need to replace, say, running costs of a car previously met by your employer, out of your own pocket); on the other hand, you might spend more on travelling and holidays (being able to go away at off-peak times could reduce the outlay). Health problems tend to be more prevalent the older you are, so you might spend more in that area too, and so on. You should also consider how you will meet capital outlays once you are retired – for example, the cost of replacing a company car, the washing machine or the fridge. You may need to set aside a little of your income each month to meet such capital needs. Try to envisage what your expenditure patterns might be in retirement and fill in the Calculator starting on page 194, estimating how much you might spend each month, assuming *today*'s prices, on each type of expenditure. Fill in the figures up to amount B on page 196, then follow the instructions below.

Average length of retirement

If you retire at this age:	On average, you can expect this many years of retirement:	
	women	men
50	32	28
55	27	24
60	23	19
65	19	16
70	15	12
75	12	9
80	9	7
85	6	5

Source: Government Actuary's Department

The impact of tax

Amount B in the Calculator gives the total of your expected yearly spending in retirement. However, this makes no allowance for income tax. Both state pensions and pensions you build up for yourself are taxable, though you may enjoy higher age-related allowances once you reach 65 (see page 63). It is fairly pointless going into detailed calculations at this stage to estimate how much extra income you might need to foot the tax bills. After all, the tax system could be wildly different by the time you retire. As a very rough rule of thumb, you might adjust the value at B in the Calculator by the amount suggested in the table below. Follow the instructions in the Calculator to find amount D (the before-tax income you'll need). If you are a couple, decide how the income at B is likely to be split between you and work out the tax on each share.

Rough guide to tax on your future retirement income

If the after-tax income you need (B in the Calculator) is about:	This is the factor you enter as amount C in the Calculator:
£5,000	1
£10,000	1.1
£15,000	1.1
£20,000	1.2
£25,000	1.2
£30,000	1.2
£35,000	1.3
£40,000	1.3
£50,000	1.4

Example

Holly and Dan use the Calculator to estimate that they will need a starting income of about £21,000 at today's prices to cover their retirement spending (figure B).

Although Holly has a well-paid job now, she took a career break when their children were younger, so the couple expect that they will rely on Dan's pension savings for about two-thirds of their retirement income (say, £14,000) and Holly's for the remaining third (say, £7,000).

To check up how much extra they will need to cover their tax bills, Dan looks in the table above for an income of around £14,000 The table tells him to multiply value B by 1.1 to cover tax. This comes to 1.1 × £14,000 = £15,400.

Holly goes through the same procedure. But with an after-tax income of only £7,000, she needs to multiply value B by 1 – in other words, no increase.

Holly and Dan work out the before-tax retirement income they will need (at today's prices): £15,400 + £7,000 = £22,400 (figure D in the Calculator).

The impact of inflation

When planning for retirement, it is essential that you do not overlook the effects of inflation. Even relatively low rates of inflation can eat heavily into the spending power of your income. For example, if prices were to rise by just 2.5 per cent a year over the next 20 years, a loaf of bread costing 60 pence would then cost 98p and you would need an income of nearly £16,400 to be able to buy the same things that you can today with just £10,000.

The effect of inflation is important in pension planning for two reasons:

- **making sure you save enough in the years before retirement** Suppose you need a retirement income of £20,000 in today's money starting in 30 years' time. Because of rising prices, when 30 years are up, the amount of money that will buy the same as £20,000 today will be a much larger sum – for example, £42,000 if inflation averages 2.5 per cent a year. To check whether your pension savings were on track, until recently you had to convert amounts in today's money into what you would need in future money. Thankfully, you no longer need to make these adjustments because statements for state, occupational and personal pensions now give an estimate of the pension you have built up so far in today's money – see page 227
- **maintaining your living standards throughout retirement** On the day you retire, you might have a perfectly adequate income. But, unless that income increases over the years, its buying power will almost certainly fall as time goes by. The fall could be substantial, making it impossible to maintain a comfortable lifestyle. See page 239 for more information.

Are you on track?

Gather together your pension forecasts and statements for your state pension (see page 231) occupational pension(s) and personal pension(s) (page 227). From each select the figure showing the amount of pension you might get at retirement in today's money. Insert these amounts at E1 to E5 in the calculator. Add them together and subtract the total F from D. The answer G is your 'pension gap'.

If G is zero or less, you are on track for your desired retirement income. You probably do not need to make any extra savings but bear in mind that G has been worked out based on various

How much extra you might need to save each month to provide each £100 a year of extra pension[1]

Years to go until you reach your intended retirement age	If you are a man intending to retire at:					If you are a woman intending to retire at:				
	55	60	65	70	75	55	60	65	70	75
5	£28.61	£24.15	£19.79	£15.70	£12.11	£31.20	£26.89	£22.65	£18.57	£14.87
10	£13.13	£11.08	£9.08	£7.20	£5.55	£14.31	£12.34	£10.39	£8.52	£6.83
15	£8.01	£6.76	£5.54	£4.40	£3.39	£8.75	£7.53	£6.34	£5.20	£4.17
20	£5.49	£4.63	£3.80	£3.01	£2.32	£5.98	£5.16	£4.34	£3.56	£2.85
25	£4.00	£3.38	£2.77	£2.19	£1.69	£4.36	£3.76	£3.17	£2.60	£2.08
30	£3.03	£2.56	£2.10	£1.66	£1.29	£3.31	£2.85	£2.40	£1.97	£1.58
35	£2.36	£1.99	£1.63	£1.29	£1.00	£2.57	£2.22	£1.86	£1.53	£1.22
40	£1.87	£1.58	£1.29	£1.02	£0.79	£2.04	£1.76	£1.48	£1.22	£0.97
45	£1.50	£1.26	£1.04	£0.83	£0.63	£1.64	£1.41	£1.19	£0.98	£0.78
50	£1.22	£1.03	£0.84	£0.67	£0.51	£1.33	£1.15	£0.97	£0.79	£0.63

[1] The figures are based on the following assumptions: tax relief at the basic rate is added to the amount shown; you increase the amount shown each year in line with earnings inflation; price inflation averages 2.5% a year; earnings inflation averages 4.5% a year; your investments grow by an average 7% a year; the investment firm charges an average 1% a year; and at retirement you use the fund to buy an annuity whose income changes each year in line with inflation (see Chapter 13).

assumptions – the future could turn out to be very different – so you might want to set aside extra anyway as a buffer. In any case, you should recheck the position each year.

If G is positive, you are currently saving too little to achieve your retirement goal. The table on page 193 gives a rough guide to the extra you might need to save each month to provide each extra £100 a year of pension. The figures are based on assumptions about investment returns and inflation. Assumptions are just sensible guesses and the future may turn out to be very different, so it is important that you check regularly to see if your extra savings are proving to be enough to plug your pension gap. You can also check out how much pension your savings could produce by using an online calculator devised by the Financial Services Authority (FSA)* and Association of British Insurers* at www.pensioncalculator.org.uk.

Example

Holly and Dan reckon they will need a retirement income of about £22,400. Using their state pension forecasts and benefit statements, they check the pensions they are on track for so far and fill in amounts E1 to E5. The total comes to £19,000 (amount F). This falls short of their target income by £22,400 – £19,000 = £3,400 (amount G). They decide Dan should increase the amount he saves. He is now aged 40 and is hoping to retire at age 65. The table on page 193 suggests that he needs to save an extra £2.77 a month for each £100 of the shortfall; in other words, an extra £3,400/£100 x £2.77 = £94 a month.

Retirement Income Calculator

Write down how much you might spend on:	£/month
Household expenses	
Food shopping and household basics	a
Buying and repairing household equipment	b
Newspapers/magazines/books	c
TV licence/videos/music	d
Dog/cat/other pets	e
Clothes/shoes/cosmetics/hairdressing	f

	£/month
Other home-related expenses	
Mortgage/rent	g
Repairs/service charge/decoration/furnishing	h
Building and contents insurance	i
Council tax/water charges	j
Gas/electricity/heating oil/solid fuel	k
Home help/window cleaner/other paid help	l
Gardening	m
Telephone	n
Leisure and treats	
Sports and hobbies: materials/lessons/other	o
Dining out/theatre/cinema/concerts/exhibitions	p
Holidays/holiday home/second home	q
Other (e.g. smoking, drinking)	r
Transport	
Owning a car: tax/insurance/servicing/repairs/breakdown insurance	s
Renting a car: rental charges/insurance	t
Running a car: petrol/oil/diesel	u
Train fares/bus fares/coach fares	v
Other	w
Health-related	
Dentist	x
Optician	y
Private medical insurance/hospital cash plan	z
Long-term care insurance	aa
Other health-related expenses	bb

	£/month
Caring for others	
Spending on children and grandchildren	cc
Financial help for elderly relatives	dd
Christmas/birthday/other presents	ee
Gifts to charity/church collections	ff
Protection-type life insurance	gg
Other	hh
Saving and borrowing	
Saving to replace car/major household equipment	ii
Saving to finance home improvements	jj
Saving to cover higher health spending later on	kk
Other regular saving	ll
Loan repayments (other than mortgage)	mm
Other spending	
Postage/stationery, etc.	nn
Other	oo
TOTAL (Add items a to oo)	A
Multiply A by 12 to give yearly amount. This is the yearly after-tax income you need to cover your retirement spending at today's prices	B
Find the factor that corresponds to B, in the table on page 191	C
Multiply B by C to find the before-tax (gross) income you need	D
Estimated income at retirement in today's prices from pensions you are already building up from:	
– state pension (see page 231)	E1
– current occupational pension (see page 226)	E2
– occupational pension(s) from previous employer (see page 226)	E3

	£/month
– personal pension(s) you are currently paying into (see page 226)	E4
– personal pension(s) you are no longer paying into (see page 226)	E5
Total estimated pension(s) you are on track to get. Add together all the amounts you have listed under E1 to E5	F
Subtract F from D. This is your 'pension gap'.	G
Divide G by £100 and multiply by the relevant figure from the table on page 193. This is the extra you might need to save to plug your pension gap	H

Minimum income for pensioners

A difficulty with planning a pension when retirement is many years ahead is deciding how much attention to pay to current laws and regulations that might well have changed by the time you retire. It seems reasonable to assume that the state basic pension (see page 199) in broadly its current form might continue because this has been a fairly stable feature of state support for many decades and attempts to change it are politically very sensitive. But other areas of governments' pension policies have been subject to frequent change and so you should perhaps be wary of assuming that they will still apply many years ahead.

The latest change to state pensions was the introduction of the pension credit from October 2003. The credit has two elements:

- a guarantee that everyone aged 60 or over will have at least a minimum amount of income to live on.
- a savings credit to 'reward' people over 65 on modest incomes who have made their own savings for retirement over and above their state basic pension.

A brief outline of the pension credit income guarantee is given below and, as you plan your pension savings, you might bear these arrangements in mind because, if you were to qualify for the credit, it could reduce the amount you need to save. However, it is impossible to predict whether such a guarantee will still be available when you retire and, even if it is, it will be relevant only if your target retirement pension is fairly low (around £5,700 a year if you are single or £8,700 a year if you are a couple at 2005–6 rates).

The long-term future of the savings credit part of pension credit is more uncertain. Especially if you are many years from retirement, it is probably better to ignore its existence when planning how much to save.

The pension credit income guarantee

In 2005–6, people aged 60 and over whose income is less than a certain amount (£109.45 a week for a single person and £167.05 for a couple) can receive a state top-up to bring their income to that level.

Income includes state pensions, other pensions, some state benefits, earnings from any work, and so on. It does not include actual income from savings (such as interest and dividends). Instead, you are deemed to receive a 'tariff income' of £1 a week from each £500 of savings you have over a capital threshold (£6,000 in 2005–6). If your savings are less than £6,000, they are ignored completely.

Example

In 2005–6, Kitty is 62 and has a state pension of £82.05 a week and savings of £8,200. For the purpose of pension credit, she is treated as receiving a tariff income of £5 a week from these savings (because £8,200 – £6,000 = £2,200 which can be divided into four lots of £500 and a part-lot of £200). This brings her income up to £87.05 a week which is less than the income guarantee of £109.45. Therefore she qualifies for pension credit of £109.45 – £87.05 = £22.40 a week to bring her income up to the minimum level (she will also qualify for some savings credit too).

A pension from the state

You would be very unwise to rely on the state pension alone for your retirement income. Even with the pension credit it is too low to support a comfortable standard of living. However, it does provide a useful core to your retirement planning, and it is worth making sure that you maintain your entitlement to it.

How much pension?

State retirement pensions become payable when you reach state pension age (see page 200), regardless of whether you have stopped work. You can, however, choose to delay the start of your pension, in which case the amount payable is increased.

State pensions have three components:

- **basic pension** This is payable to everyone who has paid enough National Insurance contributions throughout their working life – see overleaf. In 2005–6 the full basic pension for a single person is £82.05 a week (£4,267 a year). A couple who both qualify for their own basic pension could get double this. Alternatively, a wife over state pension age can have a basic pension of up to £49.15 a week (£2,556 a year) based on her husband's contribution record, provided he is receiving his state pension. If the wife is under pension age, the husband gets the extra sum, but only if his wife earns no more than a given limit (£56.20 a week in 2005–6).

- **additional pension** Until April 2002, this was limited to employees who earn above a lower earnings limit (£82 a week in 2005–6) and who are not 'contracted out' of this part of the state scheme – see page 202. But, from April 2002, it has been extended to people who are caring for young children, certain other carers and some people who are unable to work because of illness or disability. If you are unemployed for any other reason, if you are self-employed or your earnings are below the lower earnings limit, you cannot build up additional pension. Until April 2002, additional pension was built up through the State Earnings-Related Pension Scheme (SERPS); from April 2002 onwards, additional pension is built up through the State Second

---

Husbands and same-sex couples

From April 2010, a husband will be able to receive a state pension based on his wife's National Insurance record in the same way as a wife. From the same date, same-sex couples who have registered their relationship as a civil partnership will also be able to claim a state pension based on their partner's National Insurance record.

How much additional pension?

The State Earnings-Related Pension Scheme (SERPS) was designed to provide pensions linked to your earnings. So if you have a well-paid job you could expect a bigger pension than if you were in a low-paid job. In 2003–4, the maximum SERPS pension a high earner could get was £138 a week but the average paid was just £21.86 a week for men and just £9.62 a week for women.

The amounts actually paid out are low, partly because breaks from work – for example, to care for children – reduce the pension, and partly because the people who stay in SERPS tend to be in low-paid jobs. Higher-paid employees are often 'contracted out' – see page 202.

The State Second Pension (S2P), which replaced SERPS from April 2002, is designed to improve your additional pension if your income is low or if you have to take breaks from work because of certain caring duties or health problems.

The government had said that S2P might some time in the future change to a flat-rate pension for everyone under a certain age – probably then aged 45. People on moderate to high earnings would be encouraged to contract out – see page 202.

Pension (S2P). See the box above for guidance on the amount of additional pension you might get.

- **graduated pension** This is an older, simpler but much less generous earnings-related scheme for employees which ran from 1961 to 1975. If you belonged to the scheme, the National Insurance contributions you paid were related to your earnings. The contributions you paid are divided into 'units'. You now get so much pension for each unit (9.93 pence per unit in 2005–6). In 2003–4 the average graduated pension was £4.24 a week for men and 87 pence for women.

All the state pensions are increased each year in line with inflation, and are taxable.

Working life and state pension age

In general, your entitlement to state pensions depends on the National Insurance contributions paid during your working life.

'Working life' is an official definition which, for most people, means the tax years from the start of the one in which you reach age 16 to the last complete tax year before you reach state pension age.

At present, state pension age is 65 for men and 60 for women. But for women born after 5 March 1955, their pension age is 65. There is a transitional period during which women's pension age gradually rises from the old level of 60 to the new level of 65. Women who were born between 6 April 1950 and 5 March 1955 are affected by the transitional rules. If they apply to you, your state pension age is calculated according to the following rule: pension age is 60 plus one month for each month (or part-month) that your birth date falls after 5 April 1950. For this purpose, a month runs from the sixth day of one month to the fifth day of the next. If you have access to the Internet, you'll find a calculator to work out your state pension date and age on The Pension Service* website.

If your state pension age is 65, you normally have a working life of 49 years. If your state pension age is 60, your working life is normally 44 years.

National Insurance contributions

Not all National Insurance contributions count for the purpose of building up state pensions. Broadly, you are building up basic pension if you pay Class 1 (employees) or Class 2 (self-employed) contributions or you are being credited with contributions while not working and claiming certain state benefits. You also qualify during periods when you choose to pay voluntary Class 3 contributions.

To build up state additional pension, you must normally be paying Class 1 contributions but employees earning too little to pay contributions but earning at least the lower earnings limit (£82 a week in 2005–6) do build up additional pension. And, if you are contracted out (see page 202), you are not building up any additional pension.

To qualify for the full basic state pension, you must have paid the right type of National Insurance contributions for at least nine-tenths of your working life. If you have paid these contributions for less than a quarter of your working life, you will get no basic pension at all. Contributions paid between a ~~~ tenths of working life qualify you for a re~~

If you do not pay contributio~ home caring for children o~

Home Responsibilities Protection (HRP). This, in effect, reduces the length of your working life, so that you need fewer years in order to qualify for a given rate of basic pension.

Tip

If you have gaps in your National Insurance record for any year the Inland Revenue should alert you. You normally have six years within which to make good the gap if you want to by paying voluntary Class 3 contributions. Exceptionally you have until 5 April 2008 to make good gaps between 6 April 1996 and 5 April 2002. Check whether filling the gaps would increase your entitlement to the state basic pension. If it would, consider paying voluntary contributions. Contact your local Inland Revenue* office for details.

Contracting out

'Contracting out' means opting out of the additional state pension (now S2P) and instead building up a private pension either through a pension scheme run by an employer or through a scheme you arrange for yourself.

If you contract out of a state scheme, the state will eventually save money because it will have to pay you less pension. In return, you get a rebate of the National Insurance contributions you are paying now. The rebate is given in different ways depending on how you contract out:

- if you are contracted out through an occupational pension scheme run by your employer, you (and your employer) get the rebate as a cut in the rate of National Insurance you pay
- if you contract out through a personal arrangement – a personal pension or a personal stakeholder pension scheme (see page 215) – you pay the standard National Insurance rate and the rebate is paid direct to your pension scheme.

ntracted out, you are building up either less or no Instead you build up a pension through the re is no guarantee that the pension will be as much as the state pension you give up. This will depend on various factors such as the amount of the rebate and the rate at which you expect investments to grow. At the time of writing, most advisers thought the decision was at best finely balanced and, for many people, tilted towards the state scheme. So, general advice was that, on the whole, it would be better to stay in, or contract back into, the state scheme. Bear in mind that if your employer runs an occupational pension scheme, it is usually a good idea to join whether or not it is contracted out and whether or not contracting out would be best for you personally. This is because occupational schemes have advantages (see page 210) which outweigh any gains or losses from contracting out.

If you can join an occupational pension scheme through work, ask your pension scheme administrator about the contracting out position. If you are saving through a personal pension or a personal stakeholder scheme, get advice from the salesperson providing the scheme or an independent financial adviser (IFA)★.

What state pension(s) will you get?

The state pension system is complicated and thankfully you do not need to work out for yourself what your state pension entitlement will be; instead, you can ask The Pension Service★ to provide you with a retirement forecast. This states what rights to pension you have built up so far and projects what your state pensions might be by state pension age if your circumstances continue unchanged. Note that the projection is in terms of today's money. The forecast also gives guidance on steps you might take to boost your entitlement: for example, by paying voluntary National Insurance contributions to fill any gaps in your record.

To obtain a retirement forecast, get form BR19 from The Pension Service★. You should receive your forecast within a few weeks of sending in the form. The Pension Service has started to send out forecasts automatically to people of working age, starting with the self-employed.

Increasingly, the annual statements you receive from any occupational pension scheme you belong to or personal pension you have will be in the form of 'combined benefit stateme: forecast of your state pension based on record. (Do not confuse this wit indicate the state pension t specific details.) If you receive a combined benefit statement, you will not need to obtain a separate forecast from The Pension Service.

At retirement

State pensions become payable from state pension age but you can earn extra (either as income or a lump sum) by putting off the start of your pension. This will be viable only if you have other resources, for example, because you carry on doing some work. From 6 April 2005 onwards, your state pension is increased by 1 per cent for each five-week period you put off claiming it (equivalent to 10.4 per cent a year). Provided you defer the pension for at least a year, you can take the extra as a lump sum rather than an increase in your weekly pension. A spouse claiming a pension on your contribution record also has their pension deferred and must agree to the deferral.

Whether or not deferring is worthwhile depends on how long you live or, if you take the lump sum, the rate of return you could get by investing your pension elsewhere. For example, at 2005–6 pension rates, if you are single and deferred your pension for a year you would forego 52 x £82.05 = £4,290. In return, your pension when it started would be increased to 110.4% x £82.05 = £90.57. You would need to survive for 9 years and 8 months to break even. Alternatively, you could opt for a lump sum. This is treated as if you have invested the deferred pension with the government which pays you interest at 2 per cent above the Bank of England base rate. At end-2004, you would have received 6.75 per cent (equivalent to 5.3 per cent after tax for a basic-rate taxpayer) which was higher than the return then available on lower-risk investments.

Private pensions

If you have filled in the Retirement Income Calculator on page 194 probably any state pension you expect falls far short of the income you would ideally like to enjoy in retirement. A key part of financial planning is ensuring that the shortfall is made good.

Any long-term saving could help you do this. But, in practice, ___ while tax advantages to using a dedicated pension

___u get tax relief at your highest ___ scheme

- **tax-free fringe benefit** If your employer pays into the scheme on your behalf, this normally counts as a tax-free fringe benefit
- **tax-free gains** Any capital gain on the money invested in your pension fund is tax-free
- **some tax-free income** Income earned by the investments in your pension fund is tax-free unless it is dividends on shares (and similar income, such as distributions from unit trusts) in which case it is taxed at 10 per cent
- **tax-free lump sum** At retirement, you can usually take a quarter of the savings you have built up as a tax-free lump sum. The rest of your pension fund(s) must be used to provide an income (your pension) which is taxable.

There are broadly two types of private pension scheme and plan: schemes run by an employer and plans you arrange for yourself. These are looked at in the sections below.

Changes on the way

At the time of writing, depending on the type of pension scheme or plan you use, different rules set out how much you can pay in and, particularly in the case of most occupational schemes, the amount of pension and other benefits you can have. From 6 April 2006, this complicated array of rules is being swept away and replaced by a single, simpler system. Under the new system, the following rules will apply collectively to all your savings through tax-favoured pension schemes and plans:

- the tax reliefs (see above) are unchanged
- by retirement, you are allowed to accumulate total pension funds up to a lifetime allowance. Initially the standard lifetime allowance has been set at £1.5 million and this will be increased each year broadly in line with price inflation. A tax charge will be levied on any pension fund or benefits in excess of the lifetime allowance (in order to claw back the tax reliefs given on the excess savings). If you are in a scheme which promises an amount of pension, you convert this into an equivalent lump sum (usually by multiplying the pension by 20) in order to compare it against the lifetime allowance
- you can take a quarter of your pension funds and benefits (up to the lifetime allowance) as a tax-free lump sum. The rest must be

taken as pension. (See Chapter 13 for information about the methods you can use to provide the pension)

- each year, your pension funds and benefits may increase up to an annual allowance. Initially this allowance is set at £215,000 and will increase each year broadly in line with inflation. A tax charge is levied on any increase in excess of the annual allowance. To compare additions to a promised pension against the lifetime allowance, you convert it into an equivalent lump sum (by multiplying the pension by 10)
- the most you can pay into your pension schemes and plans in a year is either £3,600 or the amount of your taxable income, whichever is higher.

There are other rules allowing people who have already built up substantial pension savings or tax-free lump sums by April 2006 which are over the permitted limits to protect these from extra tax charges. If this might affect you, there are steps you may need to take before the new rules come into effect, so you should urgently seek advice from an independent financial adviser (IFA)* specialising in pension planning. But for the vast majority of people the new limits exceed the amount of pension or other benefits you are likely to build up by retirement and offer you the freedom to save what you can afford when you can without hindrance.

Pension schemes run by your employer

Many employers, especially larger ones, have set up their own 'occupational pension schemes' (also called 'superannuation schemes' in the public sector). If you are eligible to join one, this is usually the best way to save for retirement because an occupational scheme has the following additional advantages:

- **employer contributions** In most cases, your employer must pay into the scheme on your behalf. Some schemes are even 'non-contributory' which means that the employer meets the full cost of the scheme and you don't have to pay anything at all.
- **package of benefits** Usually, the scheme provides more than just a pension at retirement. Common extra benefits are an early pension if you have to stop work because of illness, lump-sum life insurance, pensions for your spouse and sometimes other dependants if you die before or after retirement. Inland Revenue

rules limit the maximum pension and benefits you can have, but these limits are high and most people's pensions fall far short of the maximum allowed.

- **charges** The costs of the scheme may be lower than for pension schemes you arrange yourself and your employer might pay the charges direct instead of the costs being deducted from the pension fund.

There are two main types of occupational pension scheme: salary-related schemes and money purchase schemes – see below and page 211.

Tip

An occupational pension scheme is usually hard to beat as a way of saving for retirement. Not only does it benefit from favourable tax treatment, but your employer puts in money on your behalf and will often pay separately the major costs of administering the scheme instead of the costs being charged to the pension fund.

Salary-related occupational pension schemes

How much pension?

Salary-related schemes promise to pay you a pension worked out according to a formula. Typically you get a fraction (say, one-sixtieth or one-eightieth) of your pay for each year you have been in the scheme. In a final salary scheme, the pay used in the formula is your salary at or shortly before retirement (or the date you leave the scheme if that is earlier). In a career average scheme, the pay used is the average of your earnings over the whole period you have been in the scheme. Earnings from earlier years are normally increased in line with earnings or price inflation before being plugged into the formula.

A final salary scheme is best if your earnings (after taking out the effects of inflation) are likely to increase throughout your working life through promotions and career progression. A career average scheme tends to give a better deal if your earnings (net of the effects of inflation) flatten out mid-career.

Once your pension starts to be paid it must be increased each year. The rules are complicated, but the increase must generally be at least 2.5 per cent a year or in line with price inflation if this is less. Some schemes – particularly in the public sector – fully index pensions so that their buying power is maintained throughout retirement.

In an occupational salary-related scheme, other benefits – such as widow's pension and the tax-free lump sum at retirement – are worked out in a similar way, according to a formula.

Your employer must ensure that enough is paid into the pension scheme to provide the promised benefits. If the scheme is contributory, you have to pay part of the cost.

Example

Harry's employer runs an occupational final salary pension scheme. The scheme offers one-sixtieth of pre-retirement salary for each year of membership. By retirement, Harry expects to have clocked up 15 years in the scheme. If his earnings just before retirement are £30,000, he can expect a pension of:

$1/60 \times £30,000 \times 15 = £7,500$ a year.

On past experience the scheme usually increases pensions each year in line with inflation once they start to be paid. If that policy continues, the buying power of Harry's pension should be protected.

Contracted-out salary-related schemes

For periods when you belong to a contracted-out occupational scheme, you build up pension through the scheme in place of part or all of the pension you would have had through the state additional pension scheme (see page 199).

It is up to your employer to ensure that enough is paid into the pension scheme to provide the contracted-out benefits. In a contributory scheme, you are required to pay part of the cost.

You build up different benefits depending on the period for which you were contracted out. For periods from April 1997 onwards, to qualify as contracted-out, the scheme must provide most employees with benefits which are at least as good as those specified for a benchmark 'reference scheme'. In the reference scheme, pension equals one-eightieth of 90 per cent of earnings between a lower and upper earnings limit (£82 and £630 a week in 2005–6) for each year of membership plus a widow's or widower's pension of half that amount.

How much do you pay?

The government is proposing to radically alter the rules concerning the limits on contributions to pension schemes. The proposals which are due to come into effect from 6 April 2006, are outlined on page 205. Until then, the rules described below apply in the case of occupational schemes.

The Inland Revenue limits the amount you can pay into an occupational pension scheme, but there is no limit on the amount your employer can pay in on your behalf.

The maximum you can pay is generally 15 per cent of your earnings – see Example below. If you joined your scheme on or after 1 June 1989, or if you joined earlier but the scheme was set up on or after 14 March 1989 (or you opt to be treated under these rules), there is also a cap on the earnings which can count towards this limit. The cap usually increases each year – in 2005–6 it is £105,600.

In practice, your regular contributions to the scheme will generally be much lower than the maximum. Typically, you might pay, say, 5 or 6 per cent of your earnings. This will automatically be deducted from your pay before income tax is worked out, thereby giving you tax relief at your top rate.

Example

Harry currently earns £20,000 a year before tax. He pays 6 per cent of this into the occupational pension scheme:

6% × £20,000 = £1,200 a year.

In 2004–5, income tax on earnings of £20,000 would normally come to £3,114. When Harry's pension contributions are deducted, tax on the remaining income is £2,850. So paying £1,200 into the pension scheme saves Harry £264 in tax (in other words, 22 per cent of £1,200).

Pros and cons of salary-related schemes

A major advantage of salary-related pension schemes is that your employer, rather than you, takes on most of the risk of providing your pension. With most other types of pension scheme, the amount of pension you get depends heavily on the returns you can get from investments, particularly the stock market. With a salary-related scheme, you are promised a set amount of pension, expressed as a percentage of your pay. Whatever the stock market does, you are – in theory – promised the same amount of pension. If the stock market slumps, it's up to your employer to find the extra needed to provide the expected pension. The worth of the pension promise depends on your employer's financial strength and willingness to do this. If you work in the public sector, your employer (ultimately central or local government) can fall back on tax revenues. But private-sector employers do not have this advantage.

As a result of the long fall in share prices between 2000 and 2003, employers have been called upon to pay very large extra sums into their final salary schemes to ensure that the promised benefits are being adequately funded. Many employers have decided they can no longer afford this open-ended commitment and have closed their schemes to new members, in some cases closed them also to further contributions from existing members and even, in the most drastic cases, wound up the final salary pension scheme. When a scheme is wound up, the members are entitled to much lower benefits than they would have received at retirement. Moreover, if the pension fund does not have enough money to fund all the benefits, the pensions and other benefits may be scaled down. The government is in the process of setting up a compensation scheme (see page 47) to help protect members' pension rights in these situations. Despite some risk of your employer abandoning the scheme when the going gets tough, the advantages of final salary schemes mean that in general if you can join one it is usually a good idea.

Because your pension is linked to your pay, the amount of pension you will get automatically increases as your earnings increase. This gives in-built protection against inflation during the period that your pension is building up.

Salary-related schemes make pension planning fairly easy, because you can frame both your target retirement income and your expected retirement income as proportions of your pre-retirement income.

These schemes are less useful if you change jobs often. Your pension is then linked to your pay before you left the scheme – which might be low compared with what you will be earning by retirement. However, this 'preserved pension' as it is called must be increased up to retirement in line with inflation up to 5 per cent a year. You can opt to transfer the value of your preserved pension to another pension arrangement – see page 223.

Money purchase occupational schemes

How much pension?

Occupational money purchase schemes are a type of 'defined contribution' (DC) scheme. All defined contribution schemes provide you with your own savings pot, and the pension you get depends on:

* the amount paid into the scheme
* how well the invested payments grow
* how much is deducted in charges
* the amount of pension you can buy with your fund when you reach retirement (see Chapter 13).

Typically, the contributions made by your employer and you are invested in the stock market. Over the long term, shares and share-based investments have tended to produce good levels of growth and more than is needed to compensate for inflation. However, share prices can fall as well as rise. If the stock market slumped in the months leading up to retirement, your pension pot might fall in value. To guard against this, it is common to switch to less volatile investments, such as gilts, other bonds and money market deposits, as retirement approaches.

Following new legislation effective from April 2005, it is generally up to you to choose whether or not your pension increases each year once it has started to be paid (see page 239).

Example

Gill currently earns £20,000 a year and belongs to an occupational pension scheme at work. Her employer pays into the scheme on her behalf an amount equal to 3 per cent of Gill's earnings, and Gill pays in the same again. In total 6% x £20,000 = £1,200 is paid in each year. By retirement, after 15 years in the scheme, Gill's salary has risen to nearly £30,000 in today's money and she has built up a pension fund of around £25,000 in today's money. In December 2004, this could have bought her, say, an index-linked pension of £1,350 a year or a level pension of £1,950 a year.

Contracted-out money purchase schemes

For periods when you belong to a contracted-out occupational scheme, you build up pension through the scheme in place of part or all of the pension you would have had through the state additional pension scheme (see page 199).

In the case of a money purchase scheme, your employer must pay into the scheme an amount equal to the National Insurance rebate you and your employer receive as a result of being contracted out (see page 202); in a contributory scheme, your employer will require you to hand over some or all of your share of the rebate. The rebate is invested and must be used to provide 'protected rights' which are:

- **a pension for you** Under current rules the whole fund must be used for pensions – none can be taken as a tax-free lump sum. However, this restriction will cease to apply from April 2006.
- **a widow's or widower's pension** This is whatever pension the fund will buy if death occurs before retirement, or half your pension in the case of death after retirement.

How much do you pay?

The government is proposing to radically alter the rules concerning the limits on contributions to pension schemes. The proposals, which are due to come into effect from 6 April 2006, are outlined on page 205. Until then, the rules described below apply in the case of occupational schemes.

The Inland Revenue puts limits on the amount you can pay into an occupational money purchase scheme. In most cases, these are the same as the limits already described for occupational salary-related schemes – see page 207.

Pros and cons of money purchase schemes

Occupational money purchase schemes are reasonably simple to understand. They work much like any other type of saving or investment – money is paid in, it is invested and whatever fund builds up is yours to use for your pension.

But these schemes are unpredictable. You don't know how well your investment will grow or how much pension you will be able to buy with the resulting fund when you retire (see Chapter 13). This makes it more difficult to plan ahead for retirement and you directly bear the risk of your pension turning out to be less than expected.

In general, money purchase occupational schemes are not such a good way to save for retirement as salary-related schemes because you, rather than your employer, bear the risk of poor investment returns affecting your savings. In addition, although in theory your employer could pay just as much into either type of scheme, in practice employers' contributions to money purchase schemes tend to be substantially lower than to salary-related schemes.

On the other hand, if you move frequently from one job to another, a money purchase scheme can work out better than a salary-related scheme.

Other occupational pension schemes

Some occupational schemes offer a halfway house between final-salary schemes and money purchase schemes, spreading the risks between you and your employer.

In a hybrid scheme, you are offered the greater of a pension worked out according to a salary-related formula and the money purchase pension that could be bought with the fund that has built up to your credit. Often, the salary-related pension will be the higher amount if you are in the scheme until retirement, whereas the money purchase element may become the greater amount if you leave the scheme early (see page 223).

In a cash balance scheme, instead of promising you a given amount of pension at retirement, your employer promises a given amount of pension fund at retirement. Typically, your promised fund is a set amount for each year you have been in the scheme. Your employer shoulders the investment risk up to the time you retire, so if investment returns are poor, your employer has to pay extra into the scheme to ensure the pension fund promise is met. You then take over the risks from retirement onwards. Although you have a set amount of pension fund, it's up to you to turn this into pension (see Chapter 13) and you cannot know in advance how much pension you will be able to buy.

Other pension schemes available through work

Not all pension schemes available through work are occupational schemes. Instead of running its own scheme, your employer might instead give you access at work to one or more pension schemes run by other organisations – often insurance companies, but also banks, unit trusts and so on.

Often these alternative schemes are group personal pension schemes (GPPS). These are simply personal pensions (see page 215) but they may have advantages over a personal pension you arrange for yourself, for example:

- **employer contributions** Your employer does not have to pay into a GPPS on your behalf, though some do
- **special features** Your employer may have negotiated special terms with the pension provider. For example, charges may be lower or contributions might be more flexible, allowing you to vary your payments or stop them altogether without penalty.

Normally, when you leave your employer, you lose the special advantages of the GPPS, though the personal pension itself continues if you are still eligible to have one (see page 215).

Since April 2001, if your employer does not offer you membership of an occupational scheme, and does not offer you a GPPS to which it makes a contribution of at least 3 per cent of your pay, then it must usually give you access through work to one or more 'stakeholder pension schemes' (see page 215). However, this does not apply if your employer has fewer than five employees.

To earn the title 'stakeholder' these schemes must be low-charging and flexible. But your employer does not have to pay into a stakeholder scheme on your behalf. This means that, in general, you will still be better off joining an occupational pension scheme if you can.

Stakeholder pensions and personal pensions

If you can't join an occupational pension scheme you will need to build up your retirement savings in some other way. This will apply to you if, for example, you are an employee whose employer does not offer an occupational scheme, you are self-employed, or you are not working.

Any long-term savings or investment schemes would be suitable. But, as described on page 204, there are tax advantages to using a dedicated pension scheme or plan. Your main options are a stakeholder pension scheme or personal pension.

Under current rules, if you belong to an occupational pension scheme, you cannot normally simultaneously pay into a stakeholder scheme or personal pension unless:

- your occupational scheme is contracted into the state additional pension scheme (see page 199) and you are using the stakeholder scheme or personal pension simply to contract out (see page 202), or
- you have earnings which are not covered by your occupational scheme – for example from a second job, or
- you earn no more than £30,000 a year and you are not the controlling director of a company (as you would be if, say, you were owner-manager of your own company). In this case you can pay up to £3,600 a year into stakeholder schemes and personal plans in addition to your occupational scheme membership.

However, these restrictions will cease to apply when the new simplified regime starts from 6 April 2006 onwards (see page 205).

Stakeholder pension schemes

Stakeholder pension schemes are low-charging, flexible pension schemes available since 6 April 2001. Although occupational money purchase schemes can be stakeholder schemes, in practice most stakeholder schemes are personal pensions. In order to be described as a 'stakeholder scheme', the pension plan must have the features set out below.

Stakeholder condition 1: low charges

Charges must total no more than a set percentage of the value of your pension fund. This must cover all the costs of running the scheme and managing your investments. For a scheme started before 6 April 2005, the maximum charge is 1 per cent a year. For schemes started on or after 6 April 2005, the maximum is 1.5 per cent a year for the first ten years and 1 per cent a year thereafter.

The cost must include information and basic advice. If there is a fee for more detailed advice, this must be set out in a separate contract and charged separately.

Stakeholder condition 2: low and flexible contributions

The minimum contribution must be no higher than £20, whether it is a one-off payment or a regular contribution.

You can't be required to make contributions at regular intervals. It is up to you when or how often you pay.

Stakeholder condition 3: portability

You must be able to transfer out of a stakeholder scheme into another stakeholder scheme or another pension arrangement without penalty.

Stakeholder schemes must accept transfers from other stakeholder schemes and other pension arrangements.

Stakeholder condition 4: simplicity

The scheme must include a default investment option which determines how your money is invested if you don't want to choose an investment fund for yourself. From 6 April 2005 onwards, the default must be a lifestyle fund (see page 223).

Stakeholder condition 5: keeping you informed

The scheme provider must give you an annual benefit statement at least once a year showing you in straightforward terms the value of your rights under the scheme.

If the scheme's charges alter, you must be informed within one month of the change.

How much pension?

Stakeholder schemes and personal pensions are all money purchase arrangements. This means – just like the occupational money purchase schemes described on page 211 – you build up your own pot of savings with which to buy a pension. The amount of pension you get depends on:

- the amount paid into the scheme or plan
- how well the invested payments grow
- how much is deducted in charges
- the amount of pension you can buy with your fund when you reach retirement (see Chapter 13).

See page 213 for the pros and cons of money purchase schemes. Bear in mind the following additional disadvantages when taking out your own stakeholder scheme or personal pension. Usually there are no contributions from an employer to boost your savings, so saving this way typically costs you more than saving through an occupational scheme. Charges for a scheme or plan you arrange yourself may be higher than the charges for a money purchase scheme arranged through work.

Contracted-out stakeholder schemes and personal pensions

For periods when you have a contracted-out stakeholder scheme or personal pension, you build up pension through the scheme in place of part or all of the pension you would have had through the state additional pension scheme (see page 199).

Part of the National Insurance contributions you and your employer have paid is rebated and paid direct to your pension scheme. The rebate is invested and must be used to provide 'protected rights' which are:

- **a pension for you** Under current rules the whole fund must be used for pensions – none can be taken as a tax-free lump sum. However, this restriction will cease to apply from April 2006 (see page 205).
- **a widow's or widower's pension** This is whatever pension the fund will buy if death is before retirement, and half your pension in the case of death after retirement.

Current limits on what you can pay

You can pay up to £3,600 a year (before taking into account any tax relief) in total into stakeholder schemes and personal pensions, regardless of your earnings. Even if you have no earnings at all, you can still pay in up to £3,600.

If you want to pay in more than £3,600 in a year, you can do this provided the contributions do not breach a limit based on your age and earnings – see opposite.

In fact, contributions do not have to be paid by you – they can be paid by you, your employer, a relative or anyone else. For example, if you are a woman off work caring for children, your husband or partner could pay into your pension scheme for you. A parent, say, can pay contributions for a child.

You can use up to 10 per cent of the amount you contribute to pay premiums for life cover.

Any National Insurance rebates paid in because you are contracted out of the state additional pension scheme do not count towards the limit.

Contributions are paid after deducting tax relief at the basic rate. The scheme provider then claims the relief back from the Inland Revenue and adds it to your scheme. You keep the relief you have deducted, even if your income is too low to pay that much tax. This means that, if you have no earnings or are on a low income, the government effectively adds a bonus to your pension savings – see Example below.

If you are a higher-rate taxpayer, you can claim extra tax relief, which you receive through either the self-assessment system or PAYE.

Example

Rebecca works part-time while her children are at school. She earns £5,000 a year on which she pays £25.50 tax in 2004–5.

Rebecca was left some money when her mother died and she is using this to pay the maximum allowed into a stakeholder pension scheme. The maximum is a before-tax amount of £3,600. After deducting tax relief at the basic rate (22 per cent in 2004–5), Rebecca hands over 78% × £3,600 = £2,808 to the pension provider.

The pension provider claims £792 from the Inland Revenue and adds it to Rebecca's scheme. This means that £2,808 + £792 = £3,600 goes into the plan at a cost to Rebecca of just £2,808.

Rebecca gets the full £792 of basic-rate tax relief even though she actually pays tax of only £25.50. The additional £766.50 is pure bonus.

Maximum contributions to stakeholder schemes and personal pensions

Your age at the start of the tax year	Contribution limit as a percentage of your earnings or profits[1]	Overall cash limit on contributions in 2005–6[2]
Up to 35	17.5%	£18,480
36–45	20%	£21,120
46–50	25%	£26,400
51–55	30%	£31,680
56–60	35%	£36,960
61-74	40%	£42,240
75 and over	You can no longer contribute	

[1] The earnings on which your percentage contribution is based are your earnings for a basis tax year. You choose the basis year and are then deemed to have earnings at that level for the next five years, regardless of any change in your actual earnings. If you want to change the basis year – for example, because your earnings have subsequently increased – you can. The basis-year system enables you to continue paying contributions in excess of the £3,600 limit for five years if your earnings stop. After five years, the maximum you could pay would drop back to £3,600 a year.
[2] An earnings cap restricts the maximum earnings you can take into account and so the overall amount you can contribute in any one year. The earnings cap is usually increased each year and in 2005–6 is £105,600.

If you have not used up your contribution limit for the previous tax year, you can pay a contribution and claim to have it treated as if it had been paid in the previous tax year. The contribution must be paid on or before 31 January following the end of the year to which you want to carry back the contribution. For example, a contribution paid on or before 31 January 2006 can be carried back to the 2004–5 tax year. You must elect to carry it back either before or when you make the payment. Tax relief is given at the rates for the year to which the contribution is carried back (not the year in which it is paid). The option to carry back contributions ceases once the new simplified regime is introduced from April 2006 (see page 205).

Tip
Using the carry-back rule is worthwhile if you paid tax at a higher rate last year than you do in the current year since you will get more tax relief on the contribution. Carrying back is also useful if you are self-employed and, because of the delay in making up your accounts, do not know your earnings for a tax year until after the end of the year.

How your money is invested

With all defined contribution schemes – including stakeholder schemes, personal pensions and occupational money purchase schemes – what you and anyone else pays into the scheme is invested. With most schemes, you invest in one or more funds run by professional fund managers.

How well the invested contributions grow is the single most important factor determining how much pension you will get. Unfortunately it is also the factor which you cannot predict. You might be tempted to put your money in funds that have done well in the past. But countless studies show that past performance is not a good guide. Especially when considering long-term investments such as pensions, there is no correlation between the star funds of the past and the funds which do well today. Similarly, there is no evidence that the funds which do well today will be the stars of the future. So what can guide your choice of how to invest your pension fund?

- **Risk** If asked: 'Are you happy taking risks with your money?' your answer would probably be: 'No'. But it is a fundamental law of investment that to get higher returns you must take on extra risk. So you must ask yourself: 'How much extra risk am I happy to take to get a better return?' Different funds expose you to different levels of risk.
- **Charges** Although, at the end of the day, investment performance will far outweigh the effect of charges, a fund with high charges will obviously have to perform better to beat a fund with low charges. If you choose a high-charging fund, satisfy yourself that the extra costs are justified.
- **Consistent performance** There is no good evidence that even the funds which perform consistently well now will do so in the future, but there does seem to be weak evidence that poor past performers are more likely to continue to perform badly so you might do well to avoid consistently bad performers.

The main types of investment fund you can choose from are outlined below. Not all schemes will offer all choices, so if you want a wide choice you will need to shop around.

Most pension schemes let you invest in more than one fund if you want to and let you switch your contributions and the fund you have built up so far from one fund to another. But watch out for minimum investment levels for some funds and for charges if you switch.

Actively managed funds

Fund managers select the shares and/or other investments which they expect to do well. As market conditions change, they sell and buy other investments. Usually, they are aiming to beat some benchmark stock market index, such as the FTSE All Share. There is no evidence that they are consistently able to do this.

All of the funds below, apart from tracker funds, are actively managed.

Tracker funds

These invest in a range of shares which are selected to mimic the performance of a particular stock market index, such as the FTSE-100 index. There is relatively little buying and selling of shares once the fund has been set up so costs are a lot lower than for an actively managed fund. For this reason, tracker funds are likely to be a popular default fund for stakeholder pension schemes.

Tracker funds are generally considered suitable for people who don't like to take too much risk. But you do need to look carefully at the index being tracked. Provided the index covers a broad spread of companies and sectors (for example, industries), risk should not be high. But if the index becomes dominated by a few large companies or one or two particular sectors, you could end up with too many eggs in one basket. In general, a tracker fund is slightly less risky than an actively managed fund invested in a similar range of shares. The manager chooses the timing of sales and purchases in the hope of increasing returns, but some of the time the manager will get the timing wrong. Tracker funds do not have this timing risk.

Deposit-based funds

These invest in money market accounts – which are rather like bank and building society accounts but paying higher interest rates. Your money is very safe in the sense that you can't lose any of your capital, but over the long term, the return on your money would tend to be low compared with funds investing in shares. Deposit-based funds are useful when you are approaching retirement. By switching from shares into deposits, you can lock in past stock-market gains and protect yourself from any falls in share prices in the run-up to retirement.

With-profits funds

Your return is linked mainly to the performance of a wide range of investments such as shares, gilts, bonds and property but also depends on other factors connected with the provider's business. The key difference from other types of funds is that your investment grows steadily as bonuses are added year-by-year and can't usually fall in value. This generally makes with-profits funds less risky than funds linked directly to shares or bonds.

However, you are only protected from stock-market falls as long as you keep your pension with the same provider. If you decide to transfer your fund before retirement to another provider, the amount you can transfer may be reduced by the amount of a 'market value reduction' (MVR). The purpose of the MVR is to ensure that you do not take away more of the with-profits fund than would be fair to all the other policyholders who are staying with the old provider. When the stock market is rising, the MVR will often be zero. But when the stock market is falling, a high MVR might be imposed. This could reduce the transfer value of your pension fund by, say, a tenth or a fifth. For more information about investing on a with-profits basis, see Chapter 17.

Bond-based funds

These invest in gilts, corporate bonds and so on. They tend to be lower-risk than shares but, over the long term, generally do not perform as well. If you are young and a long way from retirement, bonds might not be for you, but as you get nearer to retirement it generally makes sense to spread your risks by putting some of your fund into bonds, increasing the proportion as retirement approaches. For more about gilts and bonds, see Chapter 17.

Share-based funds

The fund invests mainly in a spread of shares but sometimes other investments too. The value of your investment rises and falls with the value of the underlying investments. Provided you choose a fund with a broad spread of shares – typically going by names such as 'UK managed', 'UK growth', 'International growth' and so on – this is a medium-risk way to invest that is suitable for many people.

Specialist funds

These invest in the shares and/or other investments of a particular country or particular sector. Examples include Japanese funds, smaller companies and recovery stocks. Specialist funds tend to be high-risk – sometimes they turn in spectacular growth but equally there have been spectacular nose-dives too. Generally, these are not the place for the core of your retirement savings, but could be useful if you can afford to invest extra.

Lifestyle fund

This is a fund where the investments and degree of risk alter automatically as you approach your chosen retirement date. While retirement is a long way off the fund is invested largely in shares in order to maximise the potential for long-term growth. When you get within ten to five years of retirement, the fund is progressively switched into bonds and deposit-based investments so that, should share prices tumble, you will no longer be at risk of losing the gains you have made on shares in the past. In this way, the capital risk of your investment is automatically reduced as you approach retirement.

Self-investment

Some providers offer pension schemes where you yourself select the individual shares and other investments which make up your pension fund. Charges for self-invested schemes are usually higher than for managed schemes, and to manage risk you will need a good spread of investments, so this is generally an option only if you have a reasonably large sum to invest (say, £100,000 or more). Needless to say, you must be confident about your ability to select investments which will perform well.

Leaving a pension scheme or plan before retirement

Under the current rules, if you leave an occupational pension scheme after being a member for less than two years, the scheme does not have to give you any pension rights. Instead, it can refund your contributions (but not any paid by your employer) less income

> **Tip**
>
> Very few people can expect a pension which is as good as the maximum allowed under Inland Revenue limits, so there is plenty of scope for making extra contributions as a tax-efficient way of boosting your retirement savings.

tax at a special 20 per cent rate. From 6 April 2006 the rules change so that if you leave within the two years (or any shorter period specified by your scheme) but you have been a member for at least three months, you must be offered a choice of your contributions back or a transfer value which can be switched to another pension arrangement such as a new employer's scheme or stakeholder pension scheme.

In a money purchase scheme, the transfer value is the value of the pension fund you have built up so far. In a final salary scheme, the transfer value is a lump sum which, based on various assumptions, would if invested be enough to provide the pension you are giving up. Either way, the transfer value will be more valuable than a contribution refund because it includes the benefit of contributions made by your employer.

If you leave a pension scheme after two years' membership but before you have reached retirement, you must by law be given rights to a pension. You have a variety of choices about what to do with these rights. No general rule states which choice is best. Each situation has to be looked at on its own merits. To make a rational choice, you will probably need the help of an expert to evaluate the relative benefits of each choice. If a large sum is involved, it would be worth seeking help from an actuary (see page 233). If the cost of consulting an actuary cannot be justified, you could get advice from a couple of independent financial advisers (IFAs)★ who specialise in pensions.

Although the decisions facing early leavers cannot be generalised, there are some points worth considering:

- If you belong to a public-sector scheme, there may be a 'transfer club' which lets you transfer your pension, without loss, to another scheme within the public sector.

- Many public-sector schemes offer exceptional benefits, even to early leavers. Be wary of transferring your pension rights to a private-sector scheme; it is very unlikely that the new scheme could match the benefits you would give up.
- It may make sense to transfer your pension rights from one private-sector scheme to another as you switch jobs. It can be easier to keep track of your pension entitlements if they are not spread too widely across many schemes. But you might lose out each time you transfer.
- Be wary of transferring pension rights from an employer's scheme to a personal pension other than a stakeholder scheme. The charges for personal pensions are often a lot higher than for an employer's scheme (where the employer, rather than the pension fund, might be meeting the costs separately).
- When considering the relative merits of a possible transfer, make sure you look at the whole package of benefits under each option.

A personal pension or stakeholder scheme is personal to you regardless of your work, so there is no need to stop paying into your current scheme or plan just because you switch job. However, if it is a scheme or plan taken out through your workplace (see page 214), your employer might have negotiated special terms that cease on changing jobs.

If you are moving to a new employer who offers an occupational scheme, usually the occupational scheme will be a better deal than your personal pension or stakeholder scheme so you might want to stop paying into your personal arrangement. Similarly, if your budget becomes tight (for example, because you have to stop work for a while), you might want to stop paying into your personal pension or stakeholder scheme. With a stakeholder scheme, there is no penalty for stopping or transferring a plan. But check the position for any non-stakeholder personal pension – charges may eat heavily into a paid-up plan. Unfortunately, a personal pension with high charges is likely also to penalise you if you want to transfer your accumulated fund to a new pension arrangement. Deciding whether to stay with the old plan or cut your losses and transfer can be tricky and you may want to get help from an independent financial adviser (IFA)★ who specialises in pensions.

Keeping track of your pension target

When your pension is paid

Inland Revenue rules currently allow you to start most pensions at any age between 50 and 75. However, the earliest age is being increased to 55 by 2010. It is up to individual schemes and plans to decide how to phase in this increase.

Presently, most schemes have a normal retirement date at which your pension usually starts. You can start your pension earlier but it will normally be reduced. If you start your pension later it may be increased. But these rules are also due to change. New laws from 2006 to outlaw age discrimination are likely to prevent employers from setting a compulsory retirement age, though the concept of a 'normal' age at which your full pension first becomes payable is likely to continue.

Flexible retirement is also being encouraged with the government changing the rules from 6 April 2006 so that you can start to draw your pension while continuing to work for the same employer – perhaps using this as an opportunity to ease back from full-time into part-time work.

Checking how much pension you'll get

Whatever type of pension scheme or plan you belong to, you should receive regular benefit statements. With salary-related schemes, these statements have long shown the amount of pension you can expect at retirement as a proportion of your present salary. This means that you have an idea of your expected pension expressed in today's money.

The position used not to be so clear cut with money purchase schemes because, in the past, statements for these typically did not take into account the effect that inflation might have on your pension between now and retirement. But benefit statements issued from April 2003 onwards must include a forecast of your possible pension shown in today's money – see the example opposite. The forecast in today's money is worked out using standard assumptions, including that inflation will average 2.5 per cent a year. Of course, reality may turn out to be very different from the assumptions but, even so, having a forecast in today's money makes it very much easier to judge whether or not your pension savings are on track for the retirement income you want.

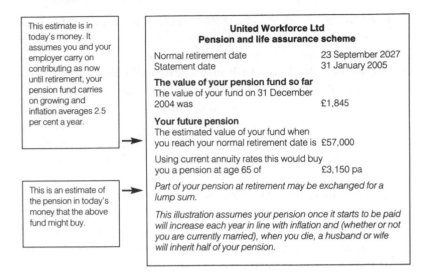

This estimate is in today's money. It assumes you and your employer carry on contributing as now until retirement, your pension fund carries on growing and inflation averages 2.5 per cent a year.

This is an estimate of the pension in today's money that the above fund might buy.

United Workforce Ltd
Pension and life assurance scheme

Normal retirement date   23 September 2027
Statement date   31 January 2005

The value of your pension fund so far
The value of your fund on 31 December
2004 was   £1,845

Your future pension
The estimated value of your fund when
you reach your normal retirement date is £57,000

Using current annuity rates this would buy
you a pension at age 65 of   £3,150 pa

Part of your pension at retirement may be exchanged for a lump sum.

This illustration assumes your pension once it starts to be paid will increase each year in line with inflation and (whether or not you are currently married), when you die, a husband or wife will inherit half of your pension.

If you have used the calculator on page 194 to work out how much retirement income you might need in today's money, you can subtract the amount shown on your benefit statement (or statements if you belong to more than one scheme) together with the forecast of any state pension (this may be shown on the benefit statement from your occupational scheme if it is a combined pension forecast – see page 192) to find out whether you are on track for the retirement income you want.

In all probability, you will belong to more than one pension scheme during your working years. You might transfer your pension rights from a former employer's scheme to another pension arrangement (see page 223). But if you leave pension rights in an old scheme, you can request a benefit statement to keep you up to date on the amount of pension you can expect at retirement.

Boosting your occupational pension

In simple terms, if your expected retirement income falls short of the desired amount, you need to save more. If you want to use pension schemes and plans – a good idea bearing in mind the tax advantages (see page 204) – the main options are:

- **occupational scheme in-house added-years scheme** You pay extra contributions and in return are credited with extra years in a salary-related scheme. The extra years feed through the formula to boost your pension and other benefits. Added-years schemes are generally available in public-sector occupational schemes

- **occupational scheme in-house additional voluntary contribution (AVC) scheme** You pay extra contributions into a money purchase arrangement organised by your employer. At retirement, the fund which has built up is used to buy extra pension and/or other benefits. Under current government rules, no part of the fund can usually be taken as tax-free lump sum but this restriction will cease to apply from 6 April 2006 (see page 205)
- **free-standing AVC (FSAVC) scheme** If you belong to an occupational scheme, you pay extra contributions to a money purchase arrangement you take out yourself. At retirement you use the fund which has built up to buy extra pension and/or other benefits. The scheme is personal to you and not tied to any particular occupational scheme. Under current government rules, no part of the fund can be taken as tax-free lump sum but this restriction will cease to apply from 6 April 2006 (see page 205)
- **stakeholder scheme** You start a stakeholder scheme or pay extra into an existing scheme. Some members of occupational schemes are not eligible under current rules
- **personal pension** You start a personal pension or pay extra into an existing plan. Some members of occupational schemes are not eligible under current rules.

Under current government rules, you might not be eligible for all the above options and a variety of rules limit the amount you can pay into each type of scheme. In particular, any added-years contributions, AVCs and free-standing AVCs plus your normal contributions to an occupational scheme must not exceed the 15 per cent limit on contributions described on page 209. Your total contributions to stakeholder schemes and personal pensions must be within the limits described on page 219. These restrictions will cease to apply from 6 April 2006, when the new simplified pension regime starts (see page 205).

The table on pages 230 to 231 compares the various options. The table also includes individual savings accounts (ISAs) as another tax-efficient option you might consider as a way to build up your retirement savings. For information about ISAs, see Chapter 11.

Early retirement comes at a cost

Barbara, 36, and Bruce, 41, are members of the local government pension scheme which is salary-related. They each pay the standard 6 per cent of their income in contributions to the scheme. To fulfil their wish to retire early, they both need to save more now. Under the local government scheme rules, to retire without losing pension benefits Bruce will have to work through to 56 and Barbara to 55. Their combined pension income at today's levels will then be just over £16,000 a year. They will also receive lump sums totalling £48,000 between them. If they invest these, they could receive a further £1,500 a year. But Barbara and Bruce will need just over £23,000 a year to maintain their current standard of living – a gap of around £6,000 a year. With inflation this rises to a shortfall of £10,000 a year by Barbara's retirement. To provide the additional income, they need to build up a fund of around £200,000 between them. To achieve this, they'll have to invest an extra £300 to £350 a month until they retire (and increase it by 3 per cent each year for inflation). This assumes their investment grows by at least 7 per cent a year; if growth is less, they'll have to invest more.

There are a number of ways in which they can build up this extra fund. The local government scheme allows employees to make AVCs which when invested boost the pension fund. The AVCs buy pension income but no tax-free lump sum. Another option is stakeholder pensions (for those earning no more than £30,000 a year) which allow a quarter of the built-up fund to be taken as tax-free cash. A further option is stocks-and-shares ISAs. The major advantage of these is that Bruce and Barbara would have complete control of their money and would not have to buy an annuity at retirement.

Whichever of these options they go for, Bruce and Barbara should also provide part of the extra income by buying 'added years' in their local government scheme. Under the rules, Barbara can buy one year and Bruce six. The cost of doing this between them would be £128 a month and would provide an extra £1,300 a year plus a lump sum of £3,900 at today's prices. This might seem expensive but it provides a guaranteed income not dependent on investment returns.

Which? December 2001

Comparison of ways to boost your pension

Feature	Type of scheme						
	In-house added years AVC scheme	In-house defined contribution AVC scheme	FSAVC scheme	Stakeholder pension scheme	Personal pension	Individual savings account (ISA)
Payments into the scheme						
Tax relief on amount you pay in	YES	YES	YES	YES	YES	NO
You keep the tax relief even if your income is too low to pay that much tax	NO	NO	YES	YES	YES	N/A
Your investment						
Wide choice of investments	N/A	Often NO	YES	Often NO	YES	YES
Gains on investments are tax-free	N/A	YES	YES	YES	YES	YES
Income from investments is tax-free	N/A	Partly NO	Partly NO	Partly NO	Partly NO	Partly NO
Charges						
Charges are low	N/A	Maybe	Often NO	YES	Often NO	Often NO

	In-house added years AVC scheme	In-house defined contribution AVC scheme	FSAVC scheme	Stakeholder pension scheme	Personal pension	Individual savings account (ISA)
You may face penalties if you switch to another scheme	NO	Often YES	Often YES	NO	Often YES	Often YES
Withdrawing your money						
You can make withdrawals at any time	NO	NO	NO	NO	NO	YES
Part of your money can be taken as a tax-free lump sum	YES	Usually NO [1]	NO [1]	YES	YES	YES
All your money can be taken as a tax-free lump sum	NO	NO	NO	NO	NO	YES
Most or all of your money must be taken as a regular income	YES	YES	YES	YES	YES	NO
On death						
Anything left to your survivors may be subject to inheritance tax	NO	NO	NO	NO	NO	YES

[1] From April 2006, government restrictions will cease to apply. However, whether or not you can then take part of the proceeds as a tax-free lump sum will depend on rules imposed by the scheme provider.

Example

By retirement, Harry (see Example on page 208) will have belonged to his pension scheme for 15 years, which would qualify him for a pension of £7,500 a year. By paying AVCs into an in-house added-years scheme, Harry 'buys' an extra three years' membership. This means he is credited with 18 years in the scheme, which increases his pension to:

$1/60 \times £30,000 \times 18 = £9,000$ a year.

In-house AVC scheme versus FSAVC scheme

Your in-house AVC scheme is often a better choice than an FSAVC scheme because:

- charges may be lower for the in-house scheme
- your employer might be prepared to match your AVCs and pay in extra contributions on your behalf.

Inland Revenue rules do not allow employers to contribute to FSAVC schemes, but FSAVC schemes may offer you a wider choice of investments and are not tied to a particular pension scheme.

More information

State pensions

Your main source of information about state pensions, both generally and your own entitlement, is The Pension Service* which is part of the government's Department for Work and Pensions (DWP)*.

For a forecast of your state pension, check whether any occupational, stakeholder or personal pension scheme you belong to issues combined benefit statements (see page 203). If not, contact The Pension Service* for a forecast.

The payment of National Insurance contributions (on which your state pension entitlement is based) is handled by the Inland Revenue*. Contact your local office if you have queries concerning your contributions or want to arrange to pay voluntary Class 3 contributions.

Occupational pensions

You should have been given a booklet giving a summary of the rules of your scheme and the benefits it provides. Benefit statements tell you about your own personal entitlement. Your main point of contact is your pensions administrator* usually located in the personnel or human resources department at work. Large public-sector schemes are often administered by a separate organisation – contact details should be given in the scheme booklet and any other literature.

If you interested in free-standing AVC schemes, check out surveys in specialist magazines such as *Money Management** and *Moneyfacts, Investments, Life & Pensions**. Then contact individual providers or get help from an IFA*.

Stakeholder schemes and personal pensions

There is a huge choice of personal pensions and a fair selection of stakeholder schemes. They offer different choices and have different charges, so it pays to shop around for the scheme or plan that best suits you. To help you do this, see the comparative tables published by the Financial Services Authority (FSA)* and regular surveys in specialist magazines such as *Money Management** and *Moneyfacts, Investments, Life & Pensions**.

If you are confident making your own shortlist, your next step can be to approach the providers or their agents direct for information about their specific schemes or plans. If you prefer more guidance, get help from an IFA*. Read Chapter 2 of this book and make sure any salesperson or adviser gives you an initial disclosure document (IDD) before you decide to do business. Check the IDD to make sure that the person can offer the type of advice and range of products that you want. Bear in mind that some providers do not offer advice at all – only information – if you are a direct customer.

The product provider, agent or adviser will give you a lot of information about the pension(s) he or she can offer. Head straight for the Key Facts document (see Chapter 3) which summarises the main features in a standard way that makes it easier to compare one pension with another.

Schemes with which you have lost touch

If you have lost contact with a previous employer or a stakeholder scheme or personal pension provider with whom you still have pension rights, contact the Pension Schemes Registry★ which operates a free tracing service.

Transferring a pension

If you are considering leaving an occupational scheme or switching from one stakeholder scheme or personal pension to another, consider getting advice from a pensions expert. This is especially important where you are thinking about switching from an occupational pension scheme to a personal arrangement. If you have built up substantial pension rights, it could be worth paying for an actuary to give you impartial advice. The Association of Consulting Actuaries★ can put you in touch with a member. The Society of Pension Consultants★ can refer you to members who are either actuaries or independent financial advisers with specialist pensions knowledge.

There are several other bodies who can also direct you to an independent financial adviser★. This will be a cheaper source of advice than using an actuary and so likely to be more suitable if your pension savings are modest. Any advice on transfers must be approved by someone in the firm who has a specialist pension qualification.

Pensions generally

For a more detailed guide to building up retirement savings, see *Planning your pension* from Which? Books★. To check how much extra pension you might get by saving more, see the website www.pensioncalculator.org.uk.

Free leaflets about pensions

Leaflet code	Name of leaflet	From
NP46	A guide to retirement pensions	The Pension Service*
PM1	A guide to your pension options	The Pension Service*
PM2	State pensions – your guide	The Pension Service*
PM3	Occupational pensions – your guide	The Pension Service*
PM4	Personal pensions – your guide	The Pension Service*
PM5	Pensions for the self-employed – your guide	The Pension Service*
PM6	Pensions for women – your guide	The Pension Service*
PM7	Contracted-out pensions – your guide	The Pension Service*
PM8	Stakeholder pensions – your guide	The Pension Service*
CA01	National Insurance for employees	Inland Revenue*
CWL2	National Insurance contributions for self-employed people. Class 2 and Class 4	Inland Revenue*
CA08	Voluntary National Insurance contributions	Inland Revenue*
	FSA guide to saving for retirement – starting to save	Financial Services Authority*
	FSA guide to saving for retirement – reviewing your plans	Financial Services Authority*
	Contracting out of the state second pension	Financial Services Authority*
	FSA guide to the risks of opting out of your employer's pension scheme	Financial Services Authority*
	FSA guide to the risks of occupational pension transfers	Financial Services Authority*
	FSA guide to topping up your occupational pension	Financial Services Authority*

Chapter 13

Providing income or extra capital

During your working life, you are likely to rely mainly on your job or business for the bulk of your income. When you stop working – typically at retirement, but also if you are ill or disabled for prolonged periods, or a woman divorcing late in life when prospects for a good job are slim – you have to look to other sources. This chapter considers:

- converting a pension fund into retirement income (see below)
- investing a lump sum (for example, from a pension scheme, a redundancy package, a divorce settlement or inheritance) to provide income (see page 251)
- if you are a homeowner, using an equity release scheme to raise extra income or capital (see page 256)
- the main state benefits you might be able to claim to boost your income (see page 258).

Converting a pension fund into pension

Chapter 12 looked at building up your retirement savings. At retirement, a salary-related pension scheme provides you with a specified amount of pension, but most other schemes and plans – for example, occupational money purchase schemes, additional voluntary contribution (AVC) schemes, stakeholder schemes and personal pensions – work on the money purchase principle. This means you build up a pension fund which you use at retirement to buy a pension. Usually you do this by buying an annuity (see opposite). The alternative is income drawdown (see page 249).

What is an annuity?

An annuity is an investment where you exchange a lump sum for an income. Once bought, you can't change your mind or cash in your investment to get your lump sum back.

Normally the annuity you buy with a pension fund (often called a 'compulsory purchase annuity') provides an income for the rest of your life. Non-pension annuities (also called 'purchased life annuities') may be for life or a set period.

The main difference between pension annuities and non-pension annuities is the way they are taxed: the whole income from a pension annuity is taxable whereas only part of the income from a non-pension annuity is taxable. See Chapter 17 for more about non-pension annuities.

Tax-free cash from your pension scheme or plan [C-HEAD]

In many cases, at retirement you can take part (typically, a quarter) of the pension fund you have built up as a tax-free lump sum. Even if your top priority is income, it is usually worth taking the maximum tax-free lump sum available because the rest of your pension fund must be drawn as a pension which is taxable. If you wish, you can invest the tax-free lump sum to provide an income. There are various ways you can do this (see page 251) and some offer a return which is completely or partly tax-free.

In the sections which follow, it is assumed that you have taken the maximum tax-free lump sum and are considering the choices for converting your remaining pension fund into pension.

Annuity choices

At retirement, most pension schemes and plans give you what is called an 'open-market option'. This means you do not have to buy your annuity from the provider with whom you have built up your pension fund. Instead you can shop around for the providers offering the best rate. Under FSA rules, the provider should draw your attention to the open-market option. Annuities are sold by insurance companies.

Usually, it will be worth exercising your open-market option. The difference between the best and worst providers can be hundreds of pounds of yearly pension – see Example below. If you are in poor health or a smoker, some companies are particularly worth looking at because they offer preferential rates (since you are not expected to live as long as someone in good health or a non-smoker).

You should be wary of exercising your open-market option if the company with which you have built up your fund offers a guaranteed annuity rate which is higher than the rates generally available now, or would levy a hefty penalty charge if you switched. If you have built up your pension fund on a with-profits basis, there should not normally be any market value reduction (MVR) when you use the fund to buy an annuity even if you use your open-market option to switch to another company.

You may be tempted just to choose the maximum possible pension from day one. But you should consider other factors. You need to look at how well your pension will continue to support you as retirement progresses and how to protect anyone who depends on you financially. Different types of annuity offer different features which can help you to meet these needs.

Example

Doug, 65, has been paying free-standing additional voluntary contributions (FSAVCs) into a scheme with XYZ insurance company and has built up a fund of £33,000. XYZ offers him an annuity of £632 a year for every £10,000 of fund. This would give him a pension of:

£632 / £10,000 × £33,000 = £2,086 a year.

But, if Doug shops around, he could get an annuity of £707 a year for every £10,000 of fund from ABC Insurers. This would give him a pension of:

£707 / £10,000 × £33,000 = £2,333 a year.

By shopping around, Doug has increased his yearly pension by £247 a year for the rest of his life.

Level annuities

This is the most basic type of annuity. It provides a level income which does not change from one year to the next. It pays you this income for the whole of your life and stops when you die.

A major problem with a level annuity is that there is no protection against inflation. If prices rise, your pension buys less and less as time goes on – see Example below. This might not be a drawback if the bulk of your retirement income is from another source – an occupational scheme, say – which does have built-in increases to counter the effects of inflation. But, if a level annuity is to be your main source of retirement income, you should be prepared to save some of your income now to use later on in retirement.

Example

Doug (see Example opposite) opts for the annuity from ABC Insurers and retires at age 65 on a pension of £2,333 a year. However, this is a level pension, so its buying power will fall if prices rise. How much the buying power falls depends on inflation.

For example, if prices rise by 2.5 per cent a year on average, by age 75, Doug's £2,333 will buy only the same as £1,823 today and Doug will have to go without a few luxuries.

If price increases averaged 5 per cent a year, the £2,333 would buy only the same as £1,432 today. That is a substantial cut in Doug's buying power and he will have to go without quite a few things he would have hoped to enjoy in retirement.

Increasing annuities

You can protect yourself either partially or fully from inflation by choosing an increasing annuity. There are three main options:

- **escalating annuity** Your income increases by a fixed percentage each year. For example, you might choose increases of 5 per cent a year. This protects you from rising prices, provided inflation does not rise above 5 per cent a year. If inflation is greater, the buying power of your pension still falls but not by as much as it would do without the increases. If inflation is consistently lower than 5 per cent, the buying power of your pension will gradually rise over the years.

- **RPI-linked annuity** Your income changes each year to keep pace with inflation as measured by the Retail Prices Index (RPI – the main measure of inflation used by the government). This means that your pension maintains exactly the same buying power throughout retirement. At the time of writing, inflation is running at less than 5 per cent a year and is expected to remain fairly low in the longer term. Therefore, the starting pension you can get from an RPI-linked annuity is currently higher than from an annuity escalating at 5 per cent a year.
- **limited price indexation (LPI) annuity** Your income changes each year to keep pace with inflation but only up to a set maximum of, say, 2.5 or 5 per cent a year. If inflation is less than the maximum, your pension also increases by less, but by just enough to fully compensate for inflation. If inflation is more than the maximum, your pension increases only by the maximum amount, providing only partial protection against inflation. Under government rules, the pension fund from some types of scheme had in the past to be used to buy this type of annuity, but from 6 April 2005 onwards the rules have been relaxed. It is now left up to you to decide whether or not to buy any built-in protection against inflation.

The big drawback with all increasing annuities is that your income at the start of retirement is a lot lower than the amount you would have had from a level annuity. In the past, unless inflation was running at very high levels, it would have taken many years before an escalating or RPI-linked annuity reached the amount of the equivalent level annuity. However, in recent years, the reduction in starting income has become much smaller. As the table in the Example opposite shows, within the space of ten years, a 5-per-cent escalating annuity would be giving you a better income than a level annuity. And, at all but the lowest levels of inflation, an RPI-linked annuity would be giving the highest income within ten years. Moreover, an RPI-linked annuity offers full protection against inflation, however rapidly prices rise. Although, at the time of writing, inflation was running at 2.5 to 3 per cent a year, back in the 1970s it reached 27 per cent a year. Even if it seems unlikely that such high rates of inflation will return, the impact that would have on a level annuity is so devastating that you might feel taking out the insurance of an RPI-linked annuity would be worthwhile.

On the other hand, even when the escalating annuity or RPI-linked annuity has caught up with the level annuity, it will be several more years before you will have received the same amount of income in total. If you are well disciplined, you might be better off choosing the level annuity but setting aside some of the income in the early years to help you cope with rising prices later on.

Example

Doug has a pension fund of £33,000. Instead of buying a level annuity, Doug could use his £33,000 fund to buy an increasing annuity. The table below shows how much his pension would be worth after 10, 20 and 30 years, depending on the type of annuity he chooses and the average level of inflation during his retirement.

Average yearly inflation	Years since start of retirement	Type of annuity					
		Level		Escalating at 5% a year		RPI-linked	
		Income you would get	Which would buy same as this much today	Income you would get	Which would buy same as this much today	Income you would get	Which would buy same as this much today
Starting income	0	£2,333	£2,333	£1,376	£1,376	£1,703	£1,703
2.50%	10	£2,333	£1,823	£2,241	£1,751	£2,180	£1,703
	20	£2,333	£1,424	£5,947	£3,629	£2,791	£1,703
	30	£2,333	£1,112	£25,703	£12,254	£3,572	£1,703
5%	10	£2,333	£1,432	£2,241	£1,376	£2,774	£1,703
	20	£2,333	£879	£5,947	£2,241	£4,519	£1,703
	30	£2,333	£540	£25,703	£5,947	£7,360	£1,703
10%	10	£2,333	£899	£2,241	£864	£4,417	£1,703
	20	£2,333	£347	£5,947	£884	£11,457	£1,703
	30	£2,333	£134	£25,703	£1,473	£29,716	£1,703

Investment-linked annuities

Investment-linked annuities give you the chance of a higher income than you can get from level or increasing annuities. But they are more risky because:

- increases in income are not usually guaranteed
- the size of the increases is unpredictable
- with many investment-linked annuities, your income can fall as well as rise.

There are two types of investment-linked annuity – 'with-profits' and 'unit-linked'. They are described below.

With-profits annuities

There may be two parts to your income:

- **guaranteed minimum income** This is the minimum pension you will get. Usually it is pretty low, but whatever happens you will never get less than this. Not all with-profits annuities provide a guaranteed minimum.
- **bonuses** These are used as the basis for increasing (or reducing) your income year by year.

Each year, the annuity provider announces its with-profits bonus rate. It depends on a variety of factors, but the most important is stock-market performance. However, the bonus is not simply added to your annuity. The system is a little more complex.

When you first buy the annuity, typically you must choose an 'assumed bonus rate' (ABR). You choose it from a range set by the insurance company, running from 0 per cent up to, say, 5 per cent. Once chosen, your ABR stays the same for the whole life of the annuity.

The ABR determines the amount of income you get at the start of the annuity and the likelihood of increases as your retirement progresses:

- **high ABR** If you choose a high ABR, your starting income is high. When the annual bonus rate is announced, if it exactly equals the ABR, your income stays broadly the same. (In practice, it might fall slightly due to the impact of charges.) If the bonus rate is higher than your ABR, your income increases. But, if the announced bonus rate is lower than your ABR, your income falls – see Example opposite.

- **low ABR** If you choose a low ABR, your starting income is low. But there is an increased chance that the announced bonus rate each year will be higher than your ABR, so it is likely that your income will increase each year. Only if the announced bonus rate is lower than your ABR will your income fall.
- **0 per cent ABR** If you choose the lowest possible ABR – in other words, 0 per cent – your starting income will be very low, usually just the guaranteed minimum amount. But, provided the company announces any bonus at all, your income increases. If, exceptionally, there is no bonus at all, your income stays the same – it can never fall.

Choosing a low or zero ABR can be useful if you want to retire gradually – see 'Gradual retirement' on page 248.

Because there is usually a risk of your income falling as well as rising, with-profits annuities are generally suitable only if you have a fairly large pension fund to invest – say, £100,000 or more – or you are using the with-profits annuity to provide only part of your retirement income.

Example

Malcolm, 60, is about to retire and has a pension fund of £150,000. If he used it to buy a level annuity, he could get an income of about £9,200 a year. But he decides to buy a with-profits annuity. His starting income depends on the assumed bonus rate (ABR) he chooses:

- **0 per cent ABR** This is the lowest ABR he can choose. His income would be only £5,200 a year, but is virtually certain to increase each year.
- **5 per cent ABR** This is the highest ABR the insurer is offering. The starting income would be much higher at £8,900 a year. But the income will increase only in years when the announced bonus rate is more than 5%. Every time the insurer announces a bonus of less than 5% Malcolm's income will fall.
- **ABR more than 0 per cent but less than 5 per cent** This will give Malcolm an income somewhere between £5,200 and £8,900 a year.

Malcolm chooses the maximum ABR of 5 per cent. The table overleaf shows how his income might vary over the first few years of his retirement.

Year of retirement	ABR (fixed for retirement)	Announced bonus rate	How income changes	Income for the year
Start of retirement	5%	n/a	n/a	£8,900
Year 1	5%	7%	× (1+7%)/(1+5%)	£9,070
Year 2	5%	6%	× (1+6%)/(1+5%)	£9,156
Year 3	5%	4%	× (1+4%)/(1+5%)	£9,069
Year 4	5%	5%	× (1+5%)/(1+5%)	£9,069
Year 5	5%	3%	× (1+3%)/(1+5%)	£8,896
Year 6	5%	6%	× (1+6%)/(1+5%)	£8,981

Unit-linked annuities

Unit-linked annuities work in a similar way to with-profits annuities, but they are more risky. This is because the amount of income you get is linked directly to the performance of a fund of underlying investments. Unlike the with-profits annuity, the worst investment performance is not limited to 0 per cent (no growth at all) – it can be less, because the underlying investments could actually fall in value. This means there is no guarantee that you will get at least a certain amount of income.

You should not consider a unit-linked annuity unless you can cope with the extra risk. In general, you will need a substantial pension fund to invest or other sources of retirement income to fall back on.

As with other types of unit-linked investments, you can choose which type of fund you will link your annuity to. For medium risk, you should normally choose a broadly based fund or a tracker fund. More specialist funds expose you to higher risks. See Chapter 18 for a summary of the unit-linked funds available. The more risky the fund you choose, the more your income will tend to swing up and down.

Limited-period annuities

Over the last 15 years, annuity rates have consistently fallen to around half the level they were at the start of the 1990s. This has been due to a combination of factors, including changing investment conditions, falling inflation and increasing longevity. Correctly or not, many people feel that annuity rates now represent poor value for money and resent being locked into a set level of income for the rest of their life when they buy an annuity at the start of retirement. To address this, the government is changing the rules to allow you to use part of your pension fund to buy a limited-period annuity.

A limited-period annuity provides an income for a maximum of five years and must end before you reach age 75. When the limited-period annuity ends, you can either use another slice of your pension fund to buy a further limited-period annuity or use the remaining fund to buy a lifetime annuity or for income drawdown (see page 249).

The advantage of a limited-period annuity is that you are not locked in for life. When the limited period ends, investment conditions might have improved and you get another chance to shop around for a better deal. The drawbacks are that investment conditions may have worsened and, in any case, you are exposed to 'mortality drag' – see the Box below for a brief explanation of this.

Mortality drag

Any arrangement – such as investment-linked annuities, phased retirement, limited-period annuities or income drawdown – which involves putting off the date at which you use your pension fund to buy a conventional annuity exposes you to 'mortality drag'.

Mortality drag refers to an additional return you need from your invested pension fund when you delay buying an annuity.

Annuities are a sort of reverse insurance, where you are insuring against living too long. If you had to provide your pension on your own, you would have to invest your pension fund and either just live on the income it produced (a cautious and costly approach) or gradually run down the capital as well (cheaper but more risky). If you knew how long you would live, you could time it exactly so that your capital ran out on the day you died. In practice, you don't know when you will die. If you lived longer than expected, your capital would run out and you would have nothing left to live on.

An insurance company can provide pensions by running down capital provided it does so for a large pool of people. It works on the basis of the average life expectancy of the people in the pool. Although some people live longer than average, their pension does not need to run out, because other people die sooner than average. The unused part of the pension fund of the people who die early produces a 'mortality gain' which is used to subsidise the pensions of the people who live longer than average.

The amount of cross-subsidy dwindles the later you leave buying an annuity. This is because an annuity rate is based only on the life expectancy of people who have reached a particular age. For example, if you buy an annuity at age 65, the rate is based on the life expectancy of people who are now aged 65. It does not take into account anyone who died before that age, so you do not get any cross subsidy from anyone who died before then. The later you leave buying an annuity, the smaller the pool of people on whom the annuity rate is based and the smaller the cross-subsidy. In the extreme, if you could leave buying an annuity to, say, age 105, you might be the only person in the pool and there could then be no cross-subsidy at all.

Therefore annuities become poorer value the later you buy them. If you are to be no worse off than you would have been buying an annuity straight away, your invested pension fund needs to grow by an extra amount equal to the decline in the value of the cross-subsidy. The amount of extra growth you need increases the older you are when you decide to defer annuity purchase and the older you are when you finally do buy an annuity. The Institute of Actuaries has estimated the extra return you need is generally in the region of 1 to 3 per cent a year provided you buy an annuity by age 75.

Annuities if someone depends on you

All types of annuity can be arranged on a 'single-life' or 'joint-life last-survivor' basis. A single-life annuity pays out just for the duration of your own lifetime. A joint-life last-survivor annuity pays out as long as both or one of two people are alive. On the first death, some annuities carry on paying the same amount to the survivor. With others, the amount is reduced – for example, by a third or by half.

The person you have the annuity with does not have to be someone who is financially dependent on you. But certainly if anyone is dependent on you – for example, your wife, husband or other partner – you should normally choose a joint-life last-survivor annuity – see Example opposite.

With contracted-out pension schemes, you have no choice – you must buy an annuity which provides a pension for a widow or widower equal to half your pension.

Example

Philip is 65 and his wife Doris is 60. Philip retires with a pension fund of £50,000. If he used this to buy a single-life level annuity, he could get a pension of £707 for each £10,000 of pension fund. This would give him:

£707 / £10,000 × £50,000 = £3,535 a year.

Doris and Philip would cope provided Philip was alive. But, if Philip dies before Doris, the £3,535 a year would stop and Doris would be left with nothing but her state pension to live on.

Therefore, Philip opts for a joint-life last-survivor level annuity reducing by one-third on the first death. This provides a pension while Philip is alive of £608 a year for each £10,000 of fund – in other words:

£608 / £10,000 × £50,000 = £3,040 a year.

If Philip dies, the pension is reduced by one-third to £2,027 a year and this reduced amount is paid to Doris for the rest of her life.

Guarantee period and capital protection

If you died soon after taking out an annuity, it would not have paid out for long, so would not seem a very good deal. You can insure against this possibility by choosing an annuity with a guarantee period. All the annuities described above can be set up with this option.

Typically, the guarantee ensures that the income is paid for at least five (or sometimes ten) years, even if you die within the guarantee period.

If you do die during the guarantee period, the remaining income generally continues to be paid out as a regular income. In some circumstances, the income may be rolled up and paid as a lump sum to your estate.

From 6 April 2006, another similar option will become available: a capital protection annuity. This is an annuity where, if you die before age 75, the balance of what you paid for the annuity less the sum of the pension payments already paid out can be paid to your heirs as a lump sum. This ensures that the annuity pays out in total as much as it cost, but the price of this protection will be a lower starting income.

Do not look on a guarantee period or capital protection as a way of providing for survivors who were financially dependent on you:

* you might survive the guarantee or capital protection period but still die before your dependant, in which case he or she will get nothing
* even if you die during the guarantee or capital protection period, unless your survivor dies soon after you, there will come the day when his or her income abruptly stops.

Gradual retirement

Occupational schemes

Your pension usually starts on a single date. However, from 30 June 1999 onwards, you can take the proceeds of money purchase AVC and FSAVC schemes at any time, regardless of whether you have started taking a pension from your occupational scheme and regardless of whether you have stopped work. Therefore you could use the AVCs or FSAVCs to provide a small pension to supplement your earnings while you reduce the hours you work.

Before 6 April 2006 you are not allowed to start drawing your occupational pension while continuing to work for the employer providing the pension – first you had to stop work. This is a strange rule because you can draw the pension while taking up work with a different employer and/or draw a pension from previous employers' schemes. Thankfully this restriction is to be removed from 6 April 2006, opening the way for you gradually to cut back the hours you work while starting to draw part or all of your pension in order to maintain your overall income at a reasonable level, provided your scheme's rules allow it.

Stakeholder schemes and personal pensions

You do not have to convert all the pension you have built up under a stakeholder scheme or personal pension into one annuity taken out on a single date. Instead, you can take out lots of different annuities on as many different dates as you choose.

In the past, this was done by dividing your pension scheme into a cluster of segments. Each segment was technically a separate pension scheme, so could be used to buy an annuity quite independently of the other segments. If your own scheme was not set up on a segmented basis, you could transfer to another which was – but there would normally be charges for making the transfer.

Since April 2001, even where a scheme is not segmented, it can have multiple pension dates, so you can buy several annuities each at a different time.

Other ways to phase a gradual retirement include:

- having several pension schemes with different providers and taking an annuity from each at different times
- opting for a with-profits annuity with a low or zero ABR (see page 242); the pension will be low at the outset but virtually guaranteed to increase as the years go by
- income drawdown (see below).

Income drawdown

Income drawdown is an alternative to buying an annuity. Instead you draw a pension direct from your pension fund while leaving the rest of the fund invested. Government rules currently allow income drawdown up to age 75 from personal pensions, stakeholder schemes and money purchase occupational schemes, but whether or not a particular scheme or plan offers this option depends on the rules of that arrangement. Under current rules, when you reach age 75, you must use the remaining fund to buy an annuity. From 6 April 2006 onwards, the rules are changing and it will be possible to continue with a restricted form of income drawdown after age 75.

Government rules limit the amount of income you can take from the pension fund. Currently the maximum is broadly the same as a level annuity for a single person (see page 239). You must take at least a minimum income which is set at 35 per cent of the maximum.

The insurance company you invest with must review your arrangement every three years. The minimum and maximum income limits will then be revised in line with changes in annuity rates and your increasing age. This means your pension may be reduced if you have been drawing the maximum or increased if you have been drawing the minimum. You must be able to cope with these changes in income.

There are two main advantages of pension fund withdrawal. First, you are not forced to commit yourself to an income based solely on the annuity rates available at the point of retirement. This gives you scope to avoid buying an annuity when rates are low. However, if annuity rates generally continue to fall as your retirement progresses, you could eventually be worse off. Second, with pension fund withdrawal until you reach age 75 your heirs can inherit whatever remains of your pension fund (after deduction of tax at 35 per cent in 2004–5). With an annuity, any of your pension fund not used up paying your annuity is usually kept by the annuity company. (However, see page 247 for ways in which your heirs could inherit a limited amount even if you bought an annuity.)

The main drawback of income drawdown is that you are exposed to mortality drag (see the box on page 245). This means that, to make pension fund withdrawal worthwhile, you will normally have to leave the bulk of your pension fund invested in shares and similar investments. This is more risky than buying an annuity, because your invested fund could fall in value or not grow fast enough to give you a better pension than an annuity would have done.

Because of the increased risks and the ongoing charges involved in leaving your pension fund invested, pension fund withdrawal is usually an option only if you have a substantial pension fund – say, £100,000 or more – or you are using pension fund withdrawal to provide only part of your retirement income. It is a complicated decision and you would be wise to get advice from an independent financial adviser (IFA)★ before going down this route.

More information

You can find out about your occupational pension scheme options from your scheme booklet and your occupational pension scheme administrator. The scheme should be in touch with you a few months before retirement to check what you would like to do and how you want your pension to be paid.

Find out about your choices under other schemes from the scheme literature and the pension provider. Again, they should be in touch in the months before retirement.

If you have lost contact with any pension schemes you have belonged to or had in the past, you may be able to trace them through the Pension Schemes Registry★.

To shop around for the best annuity, check out annuity rates. These are published in a variety of places, including personal finance sections of newspapers, specialist magazines such as *Money Management*★ and *Pensions Management*★. If you have access to a fax machine, try the fax services★ from *Moneyfacts*. The Financial Services Authority (FSA)★ publishes comparative tables for annuities.

If you want advice about choosing annuities, some IFAs★ specialise in this area and will select the best annuity for your circumstances, usually for a flat fee. The websites of these IFAs generally have useful background information as well as indications of the annuity rates currently available.

Investing a lump sum to provide income

This is the holy grail of many pensioners and a prime target in other situations where income from work has stopped or is low and a lump sum is available. It is also the target which seems most consistently to trigger cases of fraud and abuse among financial organisations. There is one basic lesson which you should never ignore: you cannot have an exceptionally high income without some risk to your capital. If you are offered a deal which promises high income from safe investments, be on your guard, take nothing at face value, ask questions, check documents and, ten to one, you'll find the deal is flawed. Don't touch it with a barge-pole, and report the providers to the main financial regulator, the FSA★, or to the police if you suspect a fraud.

The factors to take into account when investing for income are largely the same as those already discussed in Chapter 11 when you are investing for growth – see page 174. In particular, your choice will be informed by:

- **how much you can save or invest** In general, to provide a reasonable level of extra income, you need to have a fairly large amount to invest. You are likely to want to spread this across a range of different investments – some may specify a minimum investment, others may offer a higher return on larger balances
- **for how long you can tie up your money** If you will need an income over a prolonged period, you will be looking to invest for the long term and can happily consider investments that require investment for a fixed or minimum term. If you need income for a reasonably short period – for example, while you study or take a

career break to travel – stick to more flexible, short-term investments such as bank or building society deposits

- **the type of return you need** You are investing for income. However, this does not mean ignoring growth-oriented investments. You may need to invest partly for growth (see Chapter 11) in order to protect the value of your savings and income from inflation (see below). You can also provide yourself with an 'income' by regularly cashing in investments that produce growth (which might make sense for tax reasons – see below), though this is more cumbersome than choosing investments which automatically provide income

- **what return you will get** If this will be a major or only source of income, you might want to consider investments which offer a fixed return, so that your income does not fall every time interest rates go down. To maintain the income's value against inflation, you might consider indexed investments, such as National Savings & Investments index-linked savings certificates or index-linked gilts

- **how the return is taxed** Some savings and investments pay a tax-free income, which is especially valuable if you are a higher-rate taxpayer. Many investments can be put into an individual savings account (ISAs) – see box opposite – so that the growth and part of the income they produce is tax-free. If you are a taxpayer but have unused capital gains tax allowance (see page 63), it will be tax-efficient to create an 'income' by regularly cashing in your capital gains. Non-taxpayers can register to receive tax-free income from some investments (bank and building society accounts and annuities) that are normally paid with tax deducted. Be careful with insurance-based products, such as with-profits bonds, where there may be no tax for you to pay but the insurance company has already paid tax that you can't reclaim at a higher rate than you probably would have; in general these investments are tax-efficient only for higher-rate taxpayers

- **the costs** The higher the charges for a product, the harder your remaining capital has to work to maintain its value and provide your income

- **the risks** (See page 184 for a description of the main types of risk.) Make sure you are very clear about the risks inherent in any investment you choose. In particular, products which offer a higher-than-normal income usually involve some capital risk – for example, you might get your capital back in full only if the stock market has not fallen by more than a given amount. Check the terms and conditions carefully for hidden risks. Don't assume risks will never materialise; instead consider carefully how you would be affected if they did materialise, whether in that light you are comfortable taking the risk and how you can ensure that if it was realised the outcome would not be disastrous for you. Understandably many pensioners and others reliant on their savings for income are very cautious about capital risk, especially since it may be impossible to replace money that is lost. However, if you stick exclusively to deposit-type investments, the value of your savings and the income from them can be badly eroded by inflation – see table below. If you are investing for the long term, you need to strike a balance between income, security and capital growth. No one single investment will meet all these aims. Instead you should normally consider a portfolio of investments which will sustain the buying power of your income over a long period (see the case study below).

How inflation[1] can eat into the value of deposit-based savings[2]

	If you reinvest the interest		If you draw the interest as income			
Number of years your money is invested	Amount in your account	Buying power of money in your account	Amount in your account	Buying power of money in your account	Your yearly income	Buying power of your income
5	£1,276	£1,128	£1,000	£884	£40	£35
10	£1,629	£1,272	£1,000	£781	£40	£31
15	£2,079	£1,435	£1,000	£690	£40	£28
20	£2,653	£1,619	£1,000	£610	£40	£24
25	£3,386	£1,827	£1,000	£539	£40	£22

[1]The amount of money today that would buy the same, assuming that prices are rising by 2.5% a year.
[2]Assumes your money earns interest of 4% a year after tax at the savings rate has already been deducted (5% gross).

The investments in your portfolio, and their mixture, is a matter of personal choice, but will probably include some from each of the lower-risk, medium-risk and higher-risk investments described on page 187 and detailed in Chapters 16 to 18. So, for example, you might have a third of your money invested in monthly income building society accounts, cash ISAs and NS&I pensioners' bonds; a third in gilts, bond-based ISAs and insurance company guaranteed growth bonds; and a third in a range of unit trusts and share-based ISAs. The balance of the portfolio should shift as investment conditions alter: for example, with less in unit trusts if the stock market seems likely to fall, more in deposits if interest rates are high. If inflation is a particular concern, index-linked NS&I certificates and index-linked gilts would play a part in the portfolio too.

Investing for income

Eileen, 48, earns around £350 a month, has no dependants and owns her home outright. Her only other asset is £120,000 from a divorce settlement, currently invested in a building society account. The combined income from her earnings and savings comes to about £674 a month putting her just in the basic-rate tax bracket. Eileen needs all her income and wants to invest her capital to continue providing income, but also with sufficient growth to keep pace with inflation. She feels comfortable taking moderate risks with her money but, because her resources are limited, a cautious approach is suitable. At the time of investing (late 2002), investment conditions were exceptionally difficult. Interest rates were very low, gilts offered low returns to new investors and residential property prices had soared but looked to be near their peak. Commercial property prices were also starting to look high. Share prices were still volatile, but perhaps offered better value for longer-term investors than other assets, provided they could put up with some risk.

Financial plan: Eileen should continue to keep a sizeable chunk of her money (25 per cent) in deposit-based investments. She should use a spread of bonds (29 per cent of her money), property (8 per cent) and equities (38 per cent) to generate a bit more income (around £150 a month extra in late 2002) and give her a reasonable chance of enough capital growth to keep pace with inflation. Although some of the individual investments involve capital risk, it is important to look at all the investments as a whole. Collectively, they give a low to medium level of risk compatible with cautious investment.

Which? February 2003

Using a lump sum to provide an income immediately

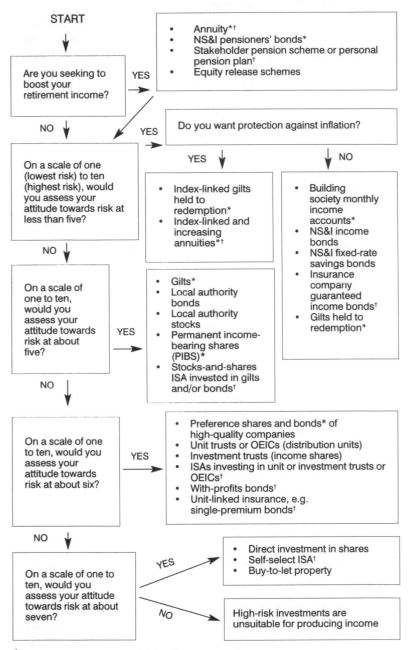

START

Are you seeking to boost your retirement income?

YES →
- Annuity*†
- NS&I pensioners' bonds*
- Stakeholder pension scheme or personal pension plan†
- Equity release schemes

NO ↓

YES → Do you want protection against inflation?

On a scale of one (lowest risk) to ten (highest risk), would you assess your attitude towards risk at less than five?

YES ↓
- Index-linked gilts held to redemption*
- Index-linked and increasing annuities*†

NO ↓
- Building society monthly income accounts*
- NS&I income bonds
- NS&I fixed-rate savings bonds
- Insurance company guaranteed income bonds†
- Gilts held to redemption*

NO ↓

On a scale of one to ten, would you assess your attitude towards risk at about five?

YES →
- Gilts*
- Local authority bonds
- Local authority stocks
- Permanent income-bearing shares (PIBS)*
- Stocks-and-shares ISA invested in gilts and/or bonds†

NO ↓

On a scale of one to ten, would you assess your attitude towards risk at about six?

YES →
- Preference shares and bonds* of high-quality companies
- Unit trusts or OEICs (distribution units)
- Investment trusts (income shares)
- ISAs investing in unit or investment trusts or OEICs†
- With-profits bonds†
- Unit-linked insurance, e.g. single-premium bonds†

NO ↓

On a scale of one to ten, would you assess your attitude towards risk at about seven?

YES →
- Direct investment in shares
- Self-select ISA†
- Buy-to-let property

NO →
High-risk investments are unsuitable for producing income

* May be particularly worth considering if you are a non-taxpayer.
† May be particularly worth considering if you pay tax at the higher rate.

Using ISAs to invest for income

ISAs are described in detail in Chapter 11. They are not just for growth investments, but can also be used for savings and investments that produce income. In that case, you should particularly bear in mind that:

- the income from share-based investments within an ISA is not tax-free. It is effectively paid with tax at 10 per cent already deducted – the same rate that most taxpayers would pay holding shares, unit trusts and so on without the ISA wrapper. Only higher-rate taxpayers gain a tax advantage when using share-based ISAs for income
- the income from cash ISAs and stocks-and-shares ISAs that are invested in bonds and gilts is tax-free, so these types of ISA could be useful if you are a taxpayer wanting to invest for tax-free income.

More information

The chart on page 255 summarises the main investments that you might consider if you are investing a lump sum to provide an income. You will find descriptions of the investments in Chapters 16 to 18, where the entry for each investment includes sources for more information.

For general discussion about overall strategies for investing for income, see specialist magazines such as *Money management** and *Money Observer** and occasional articles in *Which?** and the personal finance pages of newspapers.

Equity release schemes

How can you increase your income if you do not have a lump sum to spare? Many elderly people are 'cash poor, asset rich', having capital tied up, particularly in the home in which they live. Equity release schemes (also known as home income plans, or HIPs) let you release some of that capital. You can either take the proceeds as a lump sum or convert it into income. There are two basic types of scheme:

- **mortgage-based plans** (sometimes called 'lifetime mortgages') You take out an interest-only mortgage on your home (generally on up to 75 per cent of its value). If you are seeking an income, you usually use the proceeds to buy an annuity (see page 308)

> **Tip**
> If you are interested in taking out an equity release scheme, consider providers who are members of Safe Home Income Plans (SHIP)*. Always take advice from your own solicitor before taking out the plan.

which pays you a set income after the mortgage interest payments have been automatically deducted. The loan is eventually repaid out of your estate after your death (or the death of both you and your husband, wife or partner), or out of the proceeds of selling the home if you move before then. Essential features making these plans safe are that the mortgage rate is fixed, the interest is paid as you go along (and not added to the outstanding loan), and the income is set and payable for life (so you're not relying on stock-market performance)

* **reversion schemes** Instead of taking out a mortgage, you actually sell part or all of your home to the scheme provider, but have the guaranteed right to carry on living in it. To provide income, you use the proceeds to buy an annuity (see page 308) or to invest in other income-producing investments. The scheme offers some variations: the income you get could be fixed or, in the case of at least one provider, part or all of the income can depend on changes in property prices.

There are a number of variations on the theme, some of which gave equity release schemes a bad name in the late 1980s. The very worst combined two high-risk products: the mortgage allowed you to defer some or all of the interest, with the interest being added to the outstanding loan; and the investment gave you an income which depended on the performance of the stock market. When property prices collapsed and the stock market dipped, many planholders were left with unmanageable debts and the fear of their home being repossessed.

But there have always been perfectly sensible and sound versions of equity release schemes. In 1990 a group of companies formed Safe Home Income Plans (SHIP)*, an organisation to promote the safer versions of equity release schemes.

Warning

Beware of taking out an equity release scheme if you're getting pension credit, housing benefit or council tax benefit, as they are likely to be reduced. Bear in mind too that extra income may increase your tax bill, especially if your income is in the region where you are losing age allowance – see Chapter 4.

You usually need to be aged at least 65 or 70 to be eligible for a scheme; at younger ages, the annuity rates would simply be too low to make the scheme worthwhile. You'll need to own your own home outright – usually a freehold house or a long leasehold house or flat (though freehold flats in Scotland might also be accepted). For reversion schemes, your home generally needs to be worth at least £40,000.

You should be aware that equity release schemes invariably give you a very poor deal compared with your other option for releasing capital from your home – namely selling up and moving to a cheaper property. This is because the equity release company is advancing you money now that it will not get back until the scheme ends (usually on your death). The company charges you for that delay either through interest if it is a mortgage scheme, or by scaling down the cash it gives you if it is a reversion scheme. For example, you might give up 80 per cent of the value of your home but in return receive a lump sum equal to only 40 per cent. But the older you are when you start a scheme, the better the deal you should get.

Taking out an equity release scheme reduces the value of the estate you leave on death and so is sometimes recommended as a way to reduce a potential inheritance tax bill (see Chapter 15). However, you should bear in mind that the amount your heirs save in tax may be less than the loss of capital value inherent in the equity release scheme.

Where you took out a mortgage-based plan before 9 March 1999, interest on the mortgage qualifies for tax relief which, from 6 April 2000 onwards, is given at a set rate of 23 per cent on the first £30,000 of the loan. You will not lose the relief if you keep the plan going when you move home or if you switch to another mortgage lender without moving. Schemes taken out on or after 9 March 1999 do not qualify for tax relief.

More information

There is more about equity release schemes in *Money in retirement* from Which? Books★. You can also get a very good free factsheet (*12: Raising income or capital from your home*) from Age Concern★. Get in touch with SHIP★ for contact details of its members. If you are claiming means-tested state benefits (see below) and unsure how these might be affected if you take out an equity release scheme, get advice from your local Citizens' Advice Bureau★.

State benefits to boost your income

If your income is considered to be too low to live on, you may be eligible to claim various means-tested state benefits. The main benefits available are:

- **pension credit income guarantee** Available to anyone aged 60 or over whose income is less than a set amount (£109.45 a week for a single person and £167.05 for a couple in 2005–6). The guarantee tops up your pension to that level. Pension credit also includes a savings element for which you may qualify if you are aged 65 or more and have a limited amount of income over and above the state basic pension rate (i.e. above £82.05 a week for a single person or £131.20 for a couple in 2005–6)
- **income-based jobseekers allowance** Available if you are of working age and available for work. The amount payable depends on your circumstances, but it should normally bring your minimum income to at least £56.20 a week in 2005–6
- **income support** Available to people of working age who are not available for work; for example, because they are caring for a young child. Amounts payable are the same as for income-based jobseekers allowance
- **housing benefit** Help with your rent if you are a tenant
- **other housing costs** Housing benefit is not available to home-owners. However, if you are buying a home with a mortgage, you might qualify for help with the interest payments through pension credit, income-based jobseekers allowance or income support
- **council tax benefit** Waiving of part or all of your council tax bill.

Your eligibility for means-tested benefits depends on various factors, most importantly how much income and/or capital you have. Therefore, if you are getting means-tested benefits, any financial planning steps you take to boost your income or provide yourself with extra capital may cause a cut in your benefits.

More information

If you are over state pension age, contact The Pension Service★ to find out about state benefits for which you might qualify. If you are younger, get in touch with your local Jobcentre Plus★. Your local Citizens' Advice Bureau★ can also help you work out your entitlement.

Chapter 14

Planning for health issues in later life

The twentieth century saw great improvements in life expectancy. The table below shows how in recent times life expectancy at birth has been increasing by around one year every four or so. At the same time, healthy life expectancy has also been increasing, but more slowly. So, as we live longer, we can still expect more health problems and, as you might imagine, the older we get, the greater the likelihood of failing health. Many of us will eventually become

Life expectancy and healthy life expectancy

Year of measurement	Life expectancy at birth	Healthy life expectancy at birth	Expected number of years of ill health
Men			
1981	70.9	64.4	6.5
1985	71.8	65.3	6.5
1990	72.9	66.1	6.8
1995	74.2	66.4	7.8
1997	74.6	66.9	7.7
1999	75.1	66.6	8.5
Women			
1981	76.8	66.7	10.1
1985	77.6	67.6	10.0
1990	78.5	68.3	10.2
1995	79.4	68.7	10.7
1997	79.6	68.7	10.9
1999	80.0	68.9	10.9

Source: Government statistics

unable to cope on our own with normal daily activities and will require help and support from others.

This support might come from members of the family, though some experts predict that, as more women are now working, they will abandon their traditional role as carers of elderly parents and other relatives. And families are often geographically fragmented, making it harder for relatives to provide the regular support that might help an elderly person to stay in his or her own home. Some people need to move into a residential or nursing home, particularly in later life. Statistics are scant but a survey in 1995 found that just over one person in 100 aged 65 to 74 was living in a residential or nursing home. By age 75 to 84, nearly one person in 20 was living in a home. For people aged 85 and over, the proportion rose to one person in five.

Many people imagine that if they did need to move into a home, the state would look after them. In fact, this is not so, unless your income and savings are very low. In the main, you would have to foot the bill yourself – and the bill is high.

According to health research specialists Laing & Buisson, the average fees for a nursing home are £455 a week (£23,660 a year) and £329 (£17,108 a year) for a residential home. Laing & Buisson estimate that the average stay in a nursing home is from 18 to 30 months. This means that an average person could get through £25,000 to £59,000 – and that ignores fee increases, which tend to outstrip inflation. In your own particular case, the figure could range from nothing (if you did not need to move to a home at all) to a sum far in excess of £59,000.

Even if you do not move into a home, you might still need help and so receive care in your own home. Again, the state will not normally pick up the cost unless your income and capital are low, so over the years, you could run up substantial bills. On the other hand, you might remain healthy throughout and never need to use any on these services. So how do you plan sensibly for this phase of life?

One tool available is long-term care insurance. In return for a series of regular premiums or a lump sum, the insurance company pays out if you become too disabled to cope alone. The snag with this type of insurance is its high cost. Given this fact and the present rules about state provision of long-term care (see page 266), it is hard to view long-term care insurance as an essential part of most people's financial planning for health. However, it might figure in inheritance planning (see Chapter 15).

Help from the state

Local authorities are largely responsible for providing state support for elderly people whose physical or mental health is failing. The system works as follows.

Types of care

If you can no longer cope alone at home or your carer needs help, you can contact the social services department of your local authority. If you need financial help from the state, social services will carry out an 'assessment of needs'; they will also carry out an assessment of needs on request from people who do have enough money to pay for care themselves. Based on this assessment, a care plan will be drawn up. This sets out the level of care which social services reckon you need and the ways in which your needs can be met. There are three main options:

- **staying in your own home** Social services might suggest special equipment to make life easier – for example, grab rails and bathroom aids – and services such as a home help, meals-on-wheels, care assistance (such as someone calling each morning to help you get washed and dressed), home visits from the community nurse and a place at a day centre. The cost of services varies but, for example, personal care typically costs around £10 an hour.
- **moving to a more suitable home** Social services cannot force you to move, but they might suggest it as something worth considering. For example, you could move to sheltered housing with a resident warden available to give emergency assistance, or to a bungalow, say, if you have trouble with stairs, or somewhere closer to relatives who can help.
- **going into a care home** Again, you cannot be forced to go into a home, and social services will generally try to help you stay in your own home for as long as possible. If their recommendation is that you move into a residential or nursing home, you will need to be realistic about your ability to carry on if you

are determined to stay in your own home. Where possible, you will be offered a choice of homes, although if the local authority is paying in full for you cost will be a constraint.

Who pays?

Disability benefits

If you are aged 65 or over and need frequent care or supervision, you may qualify for attendance allowance. This is a non-means-tested tax-free state benefit paid at one of two rates depending on the degree of care you need (£40.55 or £60.60 a week in 2005–6). (People under age 65 might instead qualify for an alternative benefit called disability living allowance.)

You can spend your attendance allowance in any way you want, but it is intended to help you cope with the additional costs you incur as a result of your disability, such as paying for carers or buying special equipment. Not surprisingly, therefore, if you have to move into a care home and the state picks up part or all of the cost of the home fees (see below), you lose the attendance allowance. However, if you move into a home and pay all of the fees yourself, you keep the attendance allowance.

Care in your own home

You can organise your own help and equipment to make life easier at home. Alternatively, your local authority social services★ department might make the arrangements. Either way you might be using services provided by the local authority or by independent contractors.

Some equipment and services provided or arranged by your local authority may be free or offered at a minimal charge. But usually you will be expected to pay for personal carers, domestic help, and so on unless your income and savings are low.

Nursing care that you receive in your own home is funded by the National Health Service (NHS) and so free from your point of view.

Living in a care home

If you move into a nursing home, perhaps after a hospital stay, in order to receive ongoing medical care, the NHS may pick up the tab. In other cases, who pays depends on the type of care you receive and what financial resources you have.

Nursing care provided in hospital, your own home or a residential home has always been an NHS service free at the point of use. However, this used not to be true of nursing care you received in a nursing home. This anomaly has now been addressed and, where you receive care from a registered nurse, this is free up to certain limits (figures as for 2004–2005):

- £40, £77.50 or £125 a week in England depending on whether your nursing needs are assessed as low, medium or high
- £65 a week in Scotland
- £105 a week in Wales.

In Scotland, personal care (for example, help with washing, dressing, going to the toilet and so on) up to £145 a week is also free if you are aged 65 or over regardless of your financial situation. This does not apply in the rest of the UK where you will get help with the cost of personal care only if you pass a means test.

Throughout the UK, you are expected to pay the living costs (bed and board and so on) of living in a care home unless you pass the means test.

Local authorities set a 'standard rate' which is the amount they will pay for a place in a care home. Different authorities can set different rates, reflecting the varying costs around the country. The means test (see below) determines whether you have to pay part or all of that cost yourself.

In general, the means test is based just on your own income and savings. If you are married, it can't be based on your husband's or wife's income and savings as well (although joint amounts are apportioned between you). However, the local authority can ask your husband or wife to help with the cost of your care home fees. It cannot demand any information about your spouse's financial situation and the amount your husband or wife might pay is a matter initially for negotiation. If no agreement is reached, the local authority can refer the matter to court. Only a court can order your husband or wife to help with your care home costs. The same treatment is likely to be extended to same-sex partners in a registered civil partnership.

No-one else – for example, an unmarried partner (or same sex partner where the relationship has not been registered as a civil partnership), son or daughter, other relative – can be asked to pay towards your care home fees. However, they can volunteer to help – this is called a 'third party contribution'. This could be useful if you have chosen a home with fees which are higher than the standard rate and your local authority will not pay the extra.

The means test

The rules for assessing your income and savings are set nationally. Local authorities have some limited discretion, but broadly speaking the same rules apply wherever you live.

In working out whether or not you have enough income to pay for long-term care yourself, all your income will be taken into account, including pensions and any state benefits. Instead of actual income you get from your savings you are assumed to receive £1 a week of income from each £250 (or part) of your capital. If someone else is dependent on your income, the assessment will allow enough to cover that person's reasonable living costs. There is an exception to this approach: if you get a pension from a former employer's occupational scheme, half of it will be disregarded as belonging to your husband or wife (or, from a future date, a same-sex partner in a registered civil partnership) provided you normally share your pension with them.

This means an unmarried partner (or same-sex partner where the relationship has not been registered as a civil partnership) or anyone else you shared your house with (say, a carer or sibling) could be left with too little to live on, so you should plan how they might cope in this situation – for example, by putting extra savings into either their name or joint names and considering what state benefits, such as income support, might be claimed.

A small personal expenses allowance is deducted from your income for the purpose of the means test. This is intended to cover your incidental and personal expenses while living in a home. The local authority has discretion to increase this allowance; for example, to enable you to pay something towards the ongoing costs at home that an unmarried partner might be struggling to cope with.

If your capital (i.e. your savings and other assets) come to no more than a lower capital limit, it is ignored altogether. If it comes to more than an upper limit, then regardless of your income, you get no help with the means-tested part of the care home fees (but would still qualify, for example, for free nursing). Once your savings had run down to below the upper limit, state help could kick in. See the table below for the capital limits that applied in mid-2004.

Capital limits in mid-2003 used to determine whether you must pay towards care home fees

	Lower limit	Upper limit
England	£12,250	£20,000
Scotland	£11,750	£19,000
Wales	£13,500	£20,500
Northern Ireland	£12,250	£20,000

The value of your home is included as part of your capital unless your stay in the care home is only temporary or one of the following people will still be living in the home:

- your husband or wife or a partner who lives with you as husband or wife (this is likely to apply in future also to same-sex couples who are in a registered civil partnership or living together as if they were in such a partnership)
- a relative who is aged 60 or more or is incapacitated
- a relative under the age of 16 for whom you are legally responsible.

The local authority has discretion to ignore the value of your home in other circumstances: for example, if a younger relative or friend lives with you and would face hardship if they had to move.

If none of these exceptions applies, the value of your home (or if applicable your part-share of the home) counts as part of your capital. However, its value is ignored for the first 12 weeks to give you a breathing space while you find out whether moving into care is the right solution for you. After the 12-week period, you may find that you need to sell your home in order to meet the fees. However, there are other options. You might be able to rent out your home and use the rental income towards the fees. And you can ask the local authority to pay your fees for now but to take a 'charge' on your home so that it recoups the money it is in effect lending you when the home is eventually sold. The local authority cannot charge you interest on this loan.

You might be tempted to give away some of your capital or make some expensive purchases before being assessed, but if the social services department thinks you've done this deliberately to manipulate the rules, it can treat you as still owning the capital.

Helping yourself

If your income and/or capital are above the limits for state help, you will have no choice but to rely on your own resources. Family members can be an important source of private care. Currently, one in five men and one in four women aged 45 to 64 is caring for a relative, friend or neighbour; over a third of these are looking after a parent.

If you would not have help from family or friends, you will have to pay for professional care either in your own home or in an institutional setting. This could quickly run down your assets, but that should not necessarily be viewed as a problem. There are two main questions to consider:

- If you have a husband, wife or partner, would he or she be financially insecure if you had to move into a residential or nursing home? Similarly, would you have too little to live on if he or she went into a home?
- Are you particularly keen to preserve your assets, for example to hand on to your children? (This is an issue which perhaps you should discuss with your family. In a poll by Mintel, eight out of ten adults said that their parents should spend their money on looking after themselves in old age rather than storing it up to be passed on in inheritance.)

If your answer to either of these questions is 'yes', long-term care insurance could be worth looking at.

Long-term care plans

What is long-term care insurance?

This type of insurance pays out an income – often after a waiting period, such as 90 days – if you become unable to cope on your own. The income can be used to pay fees to a nursing or residential care home or to provide help in your own home. The income is tax-free. Typically, you'll have a valid claim if you are unable to carry out two or three out of five 'activities of daily living' (ADLs) – such as personal hygiene, dressing, feeding yourself, mobility and continence.

Although aimed mainly at paying for care in old age, this type of plan pays out whatever your age if you meet the disability test. But bear in mind that you might need care even though you are not so

Who needs long-term care insurance?

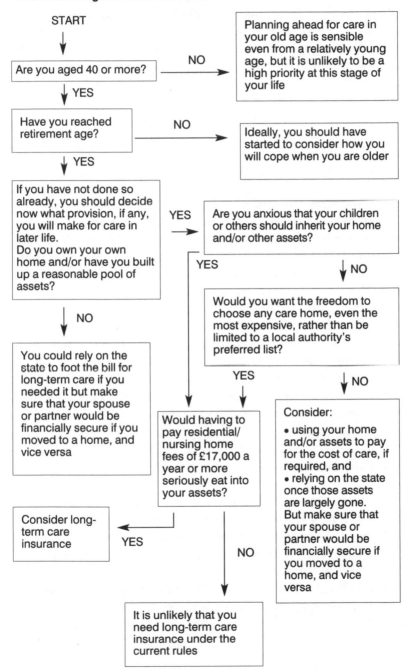

START

Are you aged 40 or more? — NO → Planning ahead for care in your old age is sensible even from a relatively young age, but it is unlikely to be a high priority at this stage of your life

↓ YES

Have you reached retirement age? — NO → Ideally, you should have started to consider how you will cope when you are older

↓ YES

If you have not done so already, you should decide now what provision, if any, you will make for care in later life.
Do you own your own home and/or have you built up a reasonable pool of assets?

YES → Are you anxious that your children or others should inherit your home and/or other assets?

↓ NO (from assets box)

You could rely on the state to foot the bill for long-term care if you needed it but make sure that your spouse or partner would be financially secure if you moved to a home, and vice versa

YES ↓ (from anxious box) / ↓ NO

Would you want the freedom to choose any care home, even the most expensive, rather than be limited to a local authority's preferred list?

↓ YES / ↓ NO

Would having to pay residential/nursing home fees of £17,000 a year or more seriously eat into your assets?

Consider:
• using your home and/or assets to pay for the cost of care, if required, and
• relying on the state once those assets are largely gone.
But make sure that your spouse or partner would be financially secure if you moved to a home, and vice versa

Consider long-term care insurance ← YES

↓ NO

It is unlikely that you need long-term care insurance under the current rules disabled as to qualify under the long-term care insurance tests, in which case the policy would not pay out.

There are two main types of long-term care insurance: pure insurance plans and investment-based plans. Pure insurance simply pays out if you have a valid claim and otherwise returns nothing. Investment-based plans combine an investment bond with the insurance. Provided the investment grows at a target rate, it provides enough to pay the premiums for the insurance and hopefully to return your original investment when you die. Investment-based insurance generally costs more but could be reassuring if your main concern is to preserve assets to hand on to your heirs.

What long-term care insurance costs

Premiums vary with your age, sex and health, the payout you choose and the number of ADLs you must fail to have a claim (the fewer the ADLs, the more expensive the policy). There is huge variation from one company to another, so you should shop around. For example, in 2001, a 60-year-old woman might pay anything from £30 to £170 a month or a single premium from £7,500 to £29,000 for a pure insurance policy providing cover of £1,000 a month. An investment-backed policy could cost her from £14,500 up to £34,000. Rather than paying the full cost of care, the payout is used typically to top up your other resources to the required level. So £1,000 a month would not be enough on its own to cover nursing home fees, but could be when combined with, say, pension income.

Insuring for a secure future

Mr X is 74 years old and recently widowed. He owns his own house and has no children. Taking out a long-term care insurance policy is not likely to be the best bet for Mr X – he has no dependants so is probably less worried than he might otherwise be about protecting his assets. Also, if he takes out a policy at his age, the premiums will be extremely high. If he does want to take precautions, Mr X would be better off with an equity release scheme. Otherwise, he may as well just pay for any care he ends up needing from his assets.

Which? February 1997

Alternative strategies

Insurance-based long-term care plans are a tool for planning ahead for your possible care needs. Other types of long-term care plan aim to meet an immediate need for care. Essentially, they require you to use a lump sum to buy an annuity (in other words, an income for life). The annuity rate may be particularly favourable taking into account the fact that your illness or disability may be shortening your life expectancy. Unlike ordinary annuities, the monthly payout is usually tax-free provided it is paid direct to the care provider.

Immediate-need plans may take the form of an equity release scheme (see Chapter 13) under which you sell all or part of your home (while keeping the right of your spouse, say, to live there) and use the capital raised to buy an annuity to pay for care. You could separately arrange an equity release scheme and use the money raised for any purpose including paying for care, but immediate-care plans have advantages in that the annuity rate may be higher and the income is tax-free if paid direct to the care home.

The advantage of immediate-need plans over simply paying for care out of whatever savings you have to hand is that, for a cost which is fixed at the outset, you can be confident that the monthly payments will continue however long you live. Therefore, you reduce the risk of running down your capital completely.

More information

You can find out what help is available from your local authority by contacting its social services department (look in the local telephone directory. You can also get information from a wide range of voluntary bodies, such as Citizens' Advice Bureaux★, Age Concern★ and Help the Aged★. Check *Yellow Pages* and leaflets in your library for locally based organisations that signpost enquirers to support services.

For details of the income and capital assessment rules, see *Charging for residential accommodation*, a manual which you can inspect at any social services department and many local advice centres (such as a Citizens' Advice Bureau). Long-term care insurance is developing only slowly in the UK and there are as yet relatively few plans on offer. *Which?*★ and money magazines, such as *Money Management*★, publish surveys of the long-term care plans available.

Chapter 15

Passing your money on

An integral part of financial planning as you get older is deciding what you want to happen to your wealth when you have died, and then ensuring that your wishes will actually be put into practice. But even when you are younger, you should give thought to this, especially if you have a family dependent on you. There are two aspects to your planning:

- setting out your wishes formally in a will
- ensuring that your assets do not disappear in unnecessary tax bills.

Below, we look at what happens if you don't make a will and how to go about drawing one up. On page 281, we look at the tax aspects of inheritance.

What happens if you don't make a will?

Everything you leave when you die, less anything you owe, is called your 'estate'. A will sets out what is to happen to your estate. It is a legal document which, although it can be changed after your death (see page 285), will normally be followed. A survey by NOP found that only one in three adults in Great Britain has made a will. Dying without a will (called dying 'intestate') can cause unnecessary hardship for your survivors:

- delays in trying to find out whether or not you did in fact leave a will and in tracing your possessions
- delays in the formalities required before your estate can be distributed

- your next of kin will usually be appointed to sort out your estate, and he or she might not be the best person to do the job
- the law dictates who will inherit your estate and in what proportions. The rules do not recognise unmarried partners (although a partner may be able to make a claim on your estate; see overleaf)
- the law may require legally binding trusts to be set up. These may be unnecessarily restrictive and expensive, especially where only small sums are involved
- there may be inheritance tax on the estate which could have been avoided.

Another very important reason for making a will is so that you can say who you want to look after your children if you have a young family.

Who gets what if there is no will?

Dying intestate means that the intestacy rules state who will inherit your estate when you die. The charts on pages 275–7 show the effect of the intestacy rules on those living in England and Wales – although other people might also have a claim under the Inheritance (Provision for Family and Dependants) Act 1975: see overleaf. For Northern Ireland and Scotland, see the box on page 278.

Same-sex couples

In 2004 new laws were passed which will give a same-sex couple who register their relationship as a civil partnership the same rights as an opposite-sex couple who marry. The government has said it expects to take about a year to bring the new laws into effect, so changes can be expected to take place from around late-2005. The changes will include:

- throughout the UK, a same-sex registered partner will have the same rights as a husband or wife to automatically inherit under the intestacy rules
- in England, Wales and Northern Ireland, an unregistered same-sex partner who has been living in a relationship as if it were a civil

---

partnership will be able to claim under the Inheritance (Provision for Family and Dependants) Act 1975 in the same way as an unmarried opposite-sex partner

- in England, Wales and Northern Ireland, a will will become automatically invalid when you enter a civil partnership unless it was made in contemplation of that partnership. If the civil partnership is dissolved, bequests to the former civil partner will become invalid though the rest of the will should stand.

Other claims on your estate

Your dying intestate can pose particular problems for an unmarried partner, because he or she has no automatic rights under the intestacy rules. But, in England and Wales, if the partner can show that he or she lived with you as man or wife throughout the two years prior to your death, he or she can claim a share of your estate under the Inheritance (Provision for Family and Dependants) Act 1975. If your partner had not been with you for the two years, he or she may still have a claim on your estate by proving financial dependence on you. In either case, the claim must be made within six months of permission to distribute the estate being granted. It will then be considered by the courts. The whole procedure could take a long time, so it is much better that you make a will in the first place.

Similarly, if you write a will and use it to disinherit someone who is financially dependent on you, that person can (following your death) go to court and challenge the will. The court decides whether that person should have a share of your estate and how much this should be.

Equivalent legislation applies in Northern Ireland but not in Scotland. An unmarried partner in Scotland does not have any claim on the estate of the partner who has died. However, husbands, wives and children have legal rights which they can claim through the courts if you have tried to disinherit them.

Who gets what if you die intestate and you are married with no children (England & Wales)

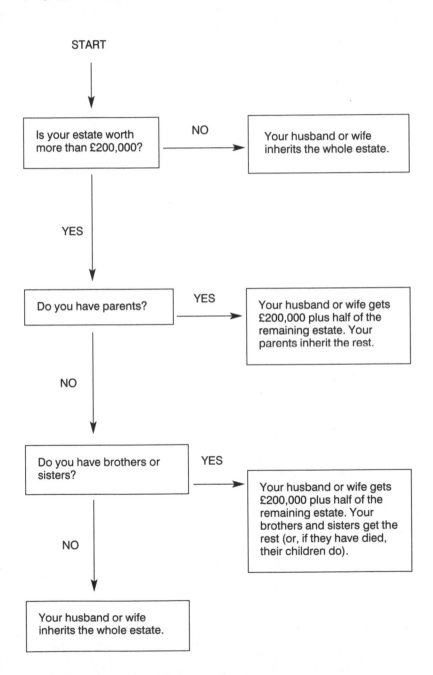

START

Is your estate worth more than £200,000?

NO → Your husband or wife inherits the whole estate.

YES

Do you have parents?

YES → Your husband or wife gets £200,000 plus half of the remaining estate. Your parents inherit the rest.

NO

Do you have brothers or sisters?

YES → Your husband or wife gets £200,000 plus half of the remaining estate. Your brothers and sisters get the rest (or, if they have died, their children do).

NO

Your husband or wife inherits the whole estate.

Who gets what if you die intestate and you have children (England & Wales)

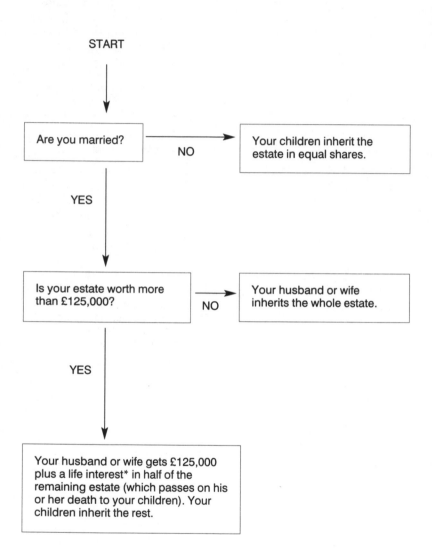

* A life interest gives you the right to the income produced by an asset or to use the asset during your lifetime, but you do not own the asset itself.

Who gets what if you die intestate and you have no close family (England & Wales)

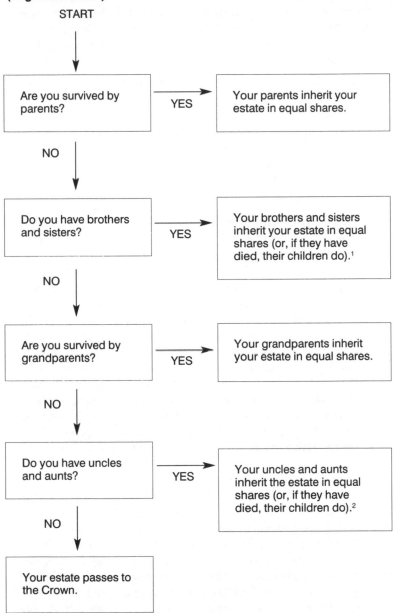

START

Are you survived by parents? — **YES** → Your parents inherit your estate in equal shares.

NO

Do you have brothers and sisters? — **YES** → Your brothers and sisters inherit your estate in equal shares (or, if they have died, their children do).[1]

NO

Are you survived by grandparents? — **YES** → Your grandparents inherit your estate in equal shares.

NO

Do you have uncles and aunts? — **YES** → Your uncles and aunts inherit the estate in equal shares (or, if they have died, their children do).[2]

NO

Your estate passes to the Crown.

[1] If you have no full brother and sisters, any half-brothers and half-sisters inherit instead (or, if they have died, their children do).
[2] If you have no full uncles and aunts, any half-uncles and half-aunts inherit instead (or, if they have died, their children do).

Northern Ireland

The intestacy rules for Northern Ireland are broadly the same as those for England and Wales. But there are some important differences where you are married, have children and your estate is worth more than £125,000:

- If you have one child, your husband or wife gets half of any excess over £125,000. But, if you have two or more children, your husband or wife gets only one-third of the excess.
- Your husband or wife receives the excess over £125,000 outright rather than just a life interest.

Scotland

The rules are as follows:

- **married no children** Your husband or wife has 'prior rights' to the family home up to the value of £130,000 (or £130,000 cash if the home is worth more), furniture and household effects up to £22,000 and a cash sum up to £58,000. He or she has 'legal rights' to half the remaining 'moveable estate' (that is, excluding land and buildings). See below for the remaining estate.
- **married with children** Your husband or wife has prior rights to the family home up to the value of £130,000 (or £130,000 cash if the home is worth more), plus furniture and household effects up to £22,000 and a cash sum up to £35,000, plus legal rights to one-third of the moveable estate. The children also have legal rights to one-third of the moveable estate. See below for the remaining estate.
- **children but no husband or wife** The children have legal rights to half the moveable estate. See below for the remaining estate.
- **the remaining estate** Whatever remains after any prior and legal rights have been met passes to your survivors or relatives in the following order of priority: 1) any children or, if they have died, their children; 2) if there are no children but there are parents and/or brothers and sisters, half to the parents and half to the siblings; if a sibling has died, his or her place is taken by his or her children, if any; 3) if no parents, everything to the brothers and/or sisters; 4) if no brothers or sisters, parents take everything; 5) a surviving spouse; 6) uncles and aunts or, if they have died, their children; 7) grandparents; 8) brothers and/or sisters of grandparents or, if they have died, their children; 9) remoter ancestors. If you are survived by no family at all, the estate passes to the Crown.

How to make a will

If your affairs are straightforward, you might consider making your own will using one of the d-i-y guides available. But be warned – solicitors claim they make more money out of unravelling d-i-y wills than they do drawing up professionally prepared ones! It is essential that the will makes your intentions absolutely clear. According to *The Guinness Book of Records*, the shortest-ever UK will simply said 'All for mother'. However, the gentleman concerned meant his wife, not his own mother. The will was contested in court (though eventually accepted), which goes to show that you need to take care over the wording of even the simplest will. Do not choose the d-i-y route if any of the following applies to you:

- your permanent home is outside England or Wales
- you have young children by a former marriage
- you run your own business or farm
- you are leaving 'heritage property' for the public benefit
- you have been married more than once and your ex-partner is still alive
- you want to set up complicated trusts, for example for a disabled person
- you are involved with family trusts.

In any of these instances, go to a solicitor. For a straightforward will, a solicitor will charge around £60 or so. You will pay more for a more complicated will. Will-writing services are often cheaper, but a survey by *Which?* found that overall they offered the worst service when compared with solicitors, banks, building societies and insurance companies. Over a third of the wills drawn up by will-writing services were rated as poor, being overly reliant on standard formats and often failing to get the detail right. Some banks,

---

Warning

If you do not make a will, your possessions will not necessarily be passed on in the way you would choose. This is a particular risk if you live with an unmarried partner – see page 274.

---

building societies and insurance companies offer will preparation services, which came out consistently adequate in the *Which?* survey but were often lacking in depth and so failing to cover all eventualities. Wills from this source can also work out expensive later on if you have to use the organisation as executor.

Be wary of appointing a bank or solicitor to act as executor of your will. Another survey by *Which?* found that this can result in problems which your survivors may find hard to resolve. If you do appoint a bank or solicitor, you are their client and the beneficiaries of your will have no direct contract with the executor. This makes it hard, when you have passed away, for anyone to put pressure on a professional executor who is slow or unduly costly in administering your estate. Instead, consider appointing a couple of the beneficiaries, or other friends or relatives, as executors. In many cases, administering your estate will be a relatively straightforward procedure. If your executors do need professional help, they can always hire a solicitor. In that event, they – not you – will have a contract with the solicitor and can take action if they are not satisfied with the service they receive.

Make sure you keep your will up to date. Review it whenever your circumstances change and, in any case, every couple of years or so. An out-of-date will can cause terrible problems, with the 'wrong' people inheriting, and distressing and costly battles between your survivors, especially if you have divorced and remarried. In England and Wales, a will is usually automatically invalid if you subsequently marry. If you divorce (but not if you merely separate), any bequests to your former husband or wife automatically lapse but are instead subject to the intestacy laws with all the problems that they can entail, although the rest of the will still stands. In Scotland, neither marriage nor divorce invalidates your will, although a new husband or wife can claim 'legal rights' from your estate.

Warning

You can alter a will by adding a 'codicil' – a written amendment which must be signed and witnessed and should be kept with the will. But codicils can be lost, so unless the amendment is very slight it is better to draw up a fresh will when changes are needed.

Tax planning

Many people worry unnecessarily about tax taking a large slice of the inheritance they hope to leave to their families. In fact, at present only about five deaths out of every hundred trigger an inheritance tax bill. However, this proportion has been increasing steadily over the last few years and many families who would not consider themselves to be wealthy are being drawn into the inheritance tax net largely because of increases in the value of their home. Nevertheless, there might not be any inheritance tax to pay on your estate, because:

- tax is payable only if the value of your estate plus any taxable or potentially taxable gifts made in the preceding seven years come to more than a set 'tax-free slice', which is £263,000 in 2004–5
- some bequests are tax-free and are deducted from the value of your estate for tax purposes; these include bequests to charity and to your husband or wife. (From a future date yet to be announced, bequests to a same-sex partner where your relationship is registered as a civil partnership are also due to become tax-free.)

If it does look likely that there will be inheritance tax on your estate, you can take certain steps during your lifetime to reduce or avoid the tax bill on death. But always bear in mind that ultimately inheritance tax is a problem for your heirs, not you. Do not jeopardise your present financial security simply to save your heirs some tax on their inheritance in the future. In particular, consider what resources you might need if you require specialist care in your old age – see Chapter 14.

Inheritance tax tips

Use your tax-free slice

If you are married, you may be tempted to leave everything tax-free to your husband or wife. But because bequests to children and other relatives or friends are *not* tax-free, there could be a hefty tax bill when your husband or wife then dies and everything passes to other members of the family. If your husband or wife does not need all your money and assets, consider sharing them between your spouse and other family members, making sure that the bequests which are not tax-free fall within your available tax-free slice.

If you are not sure at this stage what your husband or wife might need, you could rewrite your will so that on death an amount up to the amount of your tax-free slice is bequeathed to a 'discretionary will trust'. A trust is a legal arrangement where one or more people (the trustees) hold property for the benefit of other people (the beneficiaries). Your spouse and other heirs should be named as the beneficiaries and the trustees (who you can appoint in your will – for example, the same people who are your executors and who can also be beneficiaries) can decide how the trust money and assets or income produced by them are given out (or even lent interest-free). This is a complex area so get advice from a solicitor*.

Make lifetime gifts

Provided you can afford to make gifts during your lifetime, this is a good way to reduce the value of your estate, because many gifts are completely tax-free. Most other gifts between individuals count as potentially exempt transfers (PETs) and become taxable only if you die within seven years of making them (and, even then, only if the total of gifts made over the seven years up to the PET comes to more than the tax-free slice). Tax-free lifetime gifts include:

- gifts between husband and wife (and from a date yet to be announced gifts between same-sex registered partners)
- gifts to charities
- a regular pattern of gifts – for example, premiums for a life insurance policy – which count as normal spending out of your income
- any number of small gifts up to £250 per person
- wedding gifts up to certain limits
- up to £3,000 of any other gifts each year (or up to £6,000 if you did not use up the limit in the previous year).

Take care to ensure that gifts are genuinely made. If you give away something but continue to use or benefit from it, this will be a 'gift with reservation'. Although the person to whom you gave the item will legally own it, a gift with reservation is not recognised for inheritance tax purposes and continues to be treated as part of your estate.

Over the years, various clever schemes have been developed to get around the gift with reservation rules. Some were becoming fairly popular as people who were being drawn into inheritance tax because of rising house prices sought to give away their homes tax-efficiently while continuing to live in them. The government has decided to clamp down on all such schemes and, from 6 April 2005 onwards, if you are benefiting or using something you have given away on or after 18 March 1986 you will have a choice: either the gift must be within the gift with reservation rules and so ineffective for inheritance tax, or you must pay a new income tax (called the 'pre-owned assets tax') on the amount of benefit you are deemed to receive each year from your use or benefit of the asset. For example, if you have given away your home but still live there, the benefit to be taxed each year is the open-market rent you would pay for such a property less anything you actually pay. However, the pre-owned assets tax is waived where the total benefit from such assets (before deducting any rent or similar payment from you) come to less than a set amount (£5,000 in 2005–6).

Give away things whose value will rise
The increase in value then benefits the person to whom you make the gift rather than swelling your estate.

Use life insurance
You can pay the premiums (using one of the lifetime gift exemptions) on an insurance policy to benefit someone else. In this way, you can make an outright gift or you can ensure that the proceeds of the policy are available to pay an expected inheritance tax bill. Seven-year decreasing term insurance can be used to cover the potential tax bill on a PET.

More complex schemes
If you have a large estate, you might be attracted to schemes which use loans, trusts and businesses to reduce the value of your estate. These can become complicated and the government has now become very aggressive in attacking schemes that seek to avoid tax. The new pre-owned asset tax (see above) is retroactive in that it introduces a tax charge now on arrangements that were legally set up and previously appeared to be effective in saving tax. The government has made clear that it is prepared to use further retroactive measures in future to stop tax avoidance. So, before entering into any complex arrangement, get professional advice.

Write life insurance policies in trust

If you have a life policy on your own life, on death the pay-out will be part of your estate unless the policy is written in trust. By writing the policy in trust, you can specify that the proceeds go direct to named people, such as your husband, wife or children. The proceeds then bypass your estate completely which may save tax and also saves having to wait for probate before the money can be released. You can get a form for setting up the trust from the insurance company with whom you have a policy and usually the process is free. For more about life insurance, see Chapter 6.

Think about your pension arrangements

With most pension arrangements, you do not directly own the assets building up in your pension fund so, on death, it is up to the trustees or similar organisers to decide who should receive any lump sum or survivor's pension from your scheme or plan. Nearly always, you will be asked to complete a form nominating the people you would like to benefit and in most cases the trustees/organisers will follow your wishes. (However, they may consider claims from other people – for example, a former spouse who has not remarried – if they have a valid claim that they were financially dependent on you.) Payments made in accordance with such nominations bypass your estate and so are not subject to inheritance tax or probate delays.

On death after you have started to draw a pension, usually survivors might qualify for a pension from your scheme or plan but not usually a lump sum. However, in some cases, money purchase schemes (see Chapter 12) give your survivor(s) the option of taking a lump sum instead. Although there is no inheritance tax on the lump sum, there will be an income tax charge to claw back tax relief previously given on the pension savings.

Long-term care planning

As described in Chapter 14, if you need personal or nursing care, the state will cover the full cost only if you have capital below a fairly low threshold. If you have more capital, you'll be expected to pay all or part of the cost yourself. This will run down your capital and eventually the state will take over the payments but, by that stage, you will not have much left to bequeath to your heirs. To avoid completely running down your capital in this way, you could consider taking out a long-term care plan – see page 269. These are expensive so will take a large chunk out of your estate – meaning you have less to leave and also possibly reducing a potential inheritance tax bill – but serve to limit the reduction in your estate to a known amount. Once the care plan has been purchased, the rest of your assets remain intact to be passed on.

Equity release schemes

Equity release schemes – see Chapter 13 – are a way in which homeowners can use the capital tied up in their property to boost their income in retirement and/or provide a cash lump sum. They work by either mortgaging or selling part of the home. You then spend the money released, invest it in, say, an annuity (see page 308) if you want income, or use the money to make lifetime gifts. The value of your estate is reduced (by either the amount of the mortgage or the value of the part of your home you have sold, less any of the proceeds that you keep). Therefore, some financial advisers have been promoting these schemes as a method of inheritance tax planning.

Certainly, equity release schemes can reduce a potential inheritance tax bill, but bear in mind that you give up a much larger share of your home than you get back as a lump sum or income. (see Chapter 13). If you do not mind moving, a more efficient plan would be to sell your home and move to somewhere smaller. That way you would realise a sum much closer to the full value of equity previously locked in your home.

Altering a will after death

If all the beneficiaries of your will agree, they have two years following your death within which they can alter the bequests made under the will by drawing up a 'deed of variation'. This could be done to reduce or eliminate an onerous tax bill (though it is possible that the Inland Revenue might challenge a variation whose only effect was a tax saving without also, for example, any change in the beneficiaries).

Limiting inheritance tax

Pat and Ken are both in their 60s. Their home is worth £230,000 and they have a second property worth £80,000 which they let. They have £55,000 in savings and each has a life insurance policy. In total their estate is worth £393,000. If Pat and Ken had died in 2004–5 and their estate passed to their children, the inheritance tax due would be 40 per cent of everything over £263,000. That's a tax bill of £52,000.

Like most couples, Pat and Ken own most of their assets jointly. This means that when the first of them dies, everything passes to the survivor. Their wills are also set up so they leave everything first to each other and then to their children. There is normally no IHT to pay if you inherit from your husband or wife. So in Pat and Ken's case, the tax bill won't arise until the surviving spouse dies.

We asked two independent advisers to help Pat and Ken cut their inheritance tax liability.

The first and simplest thing our experts suggest is for Pat and Ken to put the life insurance policies under trust for the children. Policies paid out under trust aren't counted when valuing the estate for inheritance tax. If both policies are taken out of the equation, the value of Pat and Ken's estate is reduced to £365,000.

Both our experts thought that Pat and Ken have some scope for inheritance tax planning by using their wills. The problem with leaving everything to each other is that one partner's tax-free slice is wasted and the big tax liability is stored up until the second death. Pat and Ken could restructure their wills so that some assets pass directly to the children on the first death. Provided that such gifts don't exceed the tax-free slice applicable at the time of death, the children won't have any inheritance tax to pay. The remaining estate passing to the surviving spouse will be reduced and may well be below the level of the tax-free slice applicable at the time of the second death. This method could eliminate Pat and Ken's tax bill, but our experts warned that it could leave the survivor with problems. For example, if some of the cash savings went straight to the children when the first partner died, this could leave the survivor without enough capital to cope in an emergency or if, say, they needed to pay for long-term care.

Which? July 2003

More information

To find out more about wills, see *Wills and Probate*, published by Which? Books*. For a more detailed look at making gifts and bequests and the tax position, see *The Which? Guide to Giving and Inheriting*, also published by Which? Books*. For anything beyond the simplest will or tax-saving scheme, get professional advice from a solicitor* or accountant*. Consider choosing a member of the Society of Trust and Estate Practitioners (STEP)*. The Capital Taxes Office – part of the Inland Revenue* – produces a number of useful booklets about inheritance tax (see table below).

Useful leaflets about inheritance tax

Leaflet code	Leaflet name
IHT2	Inheritance tax on lifetime gifts
IHT3	Inheritance tax. An introduction
IHT15	Inheritance tax. How to calculate the liability
IHT16	Inheritance tax and settled property
IHT17	Inheritance tax. Businesses, farms and woodlands
IHT18	Inheritance tax. Foreign aspects

Chapter 16

Lower-risk investments

This chapter gives you basic information about those investments that do not involve any risk of losing your original money. However, you should bear in mind that most of them are vulnerable to the impact of inflation and, over the long term, their return generally lags behind returns available elsewhere. This makes them unsuitable as the only home for long-term saving and investing, although they might form part of a more widely invested portfolio. The investments described here are usually the most suitable for short- and many medium-term saving and investment goals.

Bank and building society savings and investments

Current accounts

What they are Current accounts are the prime tool for basic money management. You deposit money – often your main source of income – and have various ways of instructing the bank or building society to make payments from the account: cheque, debit card, standing order, direct debit, for example. ('Basic bank accounts' have fewer features and are designed to prevent you going overdrawn.) Access to cash is usually through visits to a branch or an automated teller machine, so convenience of these to your home/work may be a key factor in your choice of account. Small sums can also be obtained through 'cashback' arrangements at supermarkets. In some areas or for some banks, there are arrangements to bank through post offices. Most bank current accounts and a few building society accounts allow you to borrow through your current account in the form of an overdraft.

Minimum investment Often none, although the minimum investment in high-interest current accounts may be thousands of pounds.

Maximum investment None.

Type of return Many personal current accounts pay a very small rate of interest on balances which are in credit. The amount is so small that it should not be a major factor in your choice of account. High-interest accounts pay better rates but usually require you to keep a substantial minimum balance; you might do better to invest surplus funds in a proper savings product. The best returns are often to be had with Internet-based accounts.

Tax treatment Interest is taxable and usually paid with tax at the savings rate (20 per cent in 2004–5) already deducted. Non-taxpayers can reclaim tax overpaid, or, better still, arrange for interest to be paid gross by completing Form R85 from the bank, building society or the Inland Revenue★. Starting-rate taxpayers can reclaim part of the tax. There is no further tax for basic-rate taxpayers to pay. Higher-rate taxpayers must pay extra.

How long you invest for No set time. You can withdraw your money whenever you like, though there may be an upper limit on cash and/or withdrawals in any one day.

Charges With most personal current accounts, there are no charges if the account is in credit. If the account is overdrawn, there may be charges for each transaction credited to and debited from the account. Usually, there are charges for overdrafts, which are much higher if you do not arrange the overdraft in advance. A few accounts let you overdraw by a small, set limit without charge. Current accounts aimed at students and new graduates normally have a large interest-free overdraft.

Risk No capital risk. Vulnerable to inflation, so do not keep surplus funds idle in a current account. Risk rating: one.

More information Regular surveys in *Which?*★, personal finance magazines and the personal finance pages of newspapers, summaries in *Moneyfacts*★, fax services★, Ceefax★ and Teletext★ (for high-interest accounts).

How to open an account For a branch-based account, visit the local branch. Internet accounts can be opened online. Open a telephone banking account by phoning the number given in advertisements or *Yellow Pages*.

All-in-one mortgage accounts

What they are A mortgage, current account and savings facility combined. This is a holistic approach to handling your finances. You overpay your mortgage either by paying off larger amounts than the contractual minimum or by arranging to have your whole salary or other earnings paid into your mortgage account. Using normal current account tools – cash card, debit card and chequebook, for instance – you draw against the overpayment whatever money you need to cover your normal living expenses and other spending. Any surplus remains in the mortgage account, so reducing the mortgage debt. This in effect means that the difference between your overpayment and your spending – that is, your savings – earns whatever is the current mortgage rate (since it reduces the mortgage debt on which you pay the rate).

Minimum investment Not relevant. You must take out a mortgage and there may be a minimum for this – for example, £50,000 – and you must agree to have your earnings paid into the account. As is normal practice, the lender will usually restrict the maximum mortgage to a given multiple of your earnings.

Maximum investment In effect, the size of your mortgage.

Type of return Saving in interest on the mortgage loan if you pay off more than the minimum required. In effect, your savings are earning the mortgage rate, which is usually significantly higher than the rate on a comparable deposit account.

Tax treatment You do not receive interest as such; instead you save the interest which would otherwise be paid on the mortgage loan. Therefore, there is no tax – in effect, the return on your savings is tax-free.

How long you invest for The mortgage term, or a shorter period if you pay off your mortgage at a faster rate.

Charges Normal charges associated with taking out a mortgage (see Chapter 9).

Risk No capital risk. Inflation has both positive and negative effects, since it erodes the value of your mortgage loan as well as the value of your income/savings. If you have a variable-rate mortgage, the account is vulnerable to rising interest rates and although this in effect increases the return on your 'savings', rising rates increase the cost of the mortgage and leave a smaller surplus from your income to be 'saved'. Risk rating: one.

More information Summaries in *Moneyfacts*★. Occasional articles in personal finance magazines★ and personal finance sections of newspapers.

How to open an account Contact providers direct or through a financial adviser. Some of these accounts are available by Internet.

Instant access/easy access accounts

What they are Instant access accounts let you withdraw your money at any time without notice or penalty. However, there may be limits on the amount of cash or cheque withdrawals you can make in any one day. Easy access accounts give you rapid, though not necessarily instant, access to your money – for example, they include postal accounts where you have to wait for a cheque to be sent and telephone accounts where transfers to your current account may take, say, a few days. Both instant access and easy access accounts make a suitable home for an emergency fund. National Savings & Investments (NS&I) includes an easy access account in its range – the Easy Access Savings Account. The NS&I cash ISA is also an easy access account.

Minimum investment Often none. £100 with the NS&I account.

Maximum investment Usually none. £2 million for the NS&I account.

Type of return Interest, which is variable. Usually tiered accounts, meaning that small balances earn little or no interest, and higher rates are paid as your balance reaches set thresholds.

Tax treatment Interest is taxable and usually paid with tax at the savings rate (20 per cent in 2004–5) already deducted. Non-taxpayers can reclaim tax overpaid, or, better still, arrange for interest to be paid gross by completing Form R85 from the bank, building society or the Inland Revenue★. Starting-rate taxpayers can reclaim part of the tax. Basic-rate taxpayers have no further tax to pay. Higher-rate taxpayers have extra to pay. Interest from the NS&I Easy Access Savings Account is taxable but paid out without any tax deductions. Some cash ISAs (see Chapter 11) are available as easy access accounts, in which case return is tax-free.

How long you invest for No set period.

Charges No explicit charges. The provider's costs are one factor influencing the interest rates offered.

Risk No capital risk. Vulnerable to inflation. Vulnerable to falling interest rates. Risk rating: one.

More information Regular surveys in *Which?*★, personal finance magazines and the personal finance pages of newspapers, summaries in *Moneyfacts*★, fax services★, Ceefax★ and Teletext★. Post offices or NS&I★ for NS&I products.

How to invest For branch-based accounts, contact your local branch. For postal or telephone accounts, contact the telephone number (or address) in advertisements or *Yellow Pages*. Register for Internet-based accounts through the Internet. For NS&I products, via post offices or deal direct with NS&I★.

Stakeholder deposit product

From April 2005, new stakeholder deposit products are due to become available. These will be savings accounts that meet certain government rules:

- the interest offered must not be less than 1 per cent below the Bank of England base rate and must increase within one month of any rise in the Bank of England rate
- the minimum investment must not be higher than £10
- you can make unlimited withdrawals
- there must be no extra charge for transfers in or out of the product
- the product can be set up as a cash ISA (in which case the return would be tax-free – see Chapter 11).

Notice accounts

What they are Savings accounts which let you withdraw your money without penalty only if you give a specified period of notice, such as a month or 90 days, depending on the account. Earlier withdrawal is usually (but not always) possible on payment of an interest penalty. NS&I includes a notice account in its range: the Investment Account.

Minimum investment Varies from, say, £500 to £10,000. The minimum sum for the NS&I Investment Account is just £20.

Maximum investment Usually none. £100,000 for the NS&I account.

Type of return Interest, which is variable. Often tiered accounts, paying higher rates if the amount you have invested exceeds specified thresholds.

Tax treatment Interest is taxable and usually paid with tax at the savings rate (20 per cent in 2004–5) already deducted. Non-taxpayers can reclaim tax overpaid, or, better still, arrange for interest to be paid gross by completing Form R85 from the bank, building society or the Inland Revenue★. Starting-rate taxpayers can reclaim part of the tax. No further tax for basic-rate taxpayers, but higher-rate taxpayers pay extra. Interest from the NS&I Investment Account is taxable but paid without any tax deducted. Some cash ISAs (see Chapter 11) are available as notice accounts, in which case return is tax-free.

How long you invest for No set term, but you should aim to give the full notice period when you want to make withdrawals.

Charges No explicit charges, apart from penalties or notice periods on withdrawal. The provider's costs are one factor influencing the interest rates offered.

Risk No capital risk. Vulnerable to inflation. Vulnerable to falling interest rates, especially since you cannot readily switch to another investment. Risk rating: two to three, depending on length of notice period.

More information Regular surveys in *Which?*★, personal finance magazines and the personal finance pages of newspapers, summaries in *Moneyfacts*★, fax services★, Ceefax★ and Teletext★. Post offices or NS&I★ for NS&I products.

How to invest At a local branch. By post or phone, if postal or phone-based account. For NS&I products, via post offices or direct with NS&I★.

Term accounts and bonds

What they are You invest for a set period – one or two years, say – and either cannot get your money back earlier or withdrawals are subject to strict rules: for example, you must leave a certain sum invested, or make only one withdrawal of up to ten per cent of the value of the account, and so on. There are many variations: with some, the return is paid at the end of the term when the account or bond matures; with others, you can take a monthly income. The NS&I range includes several Fixed Rate Savings Bonds and also a Capital Bond.

Minimum investment Varies: £2,500 or £10,000, for example. £500 for the NS&I Fixed Rate Bonds; £100 for NS&I's Capital Bond.

Maximum investment Usually none. £1 million for the NS&I bonds.

Type of return Interest, which may be fixed or variable, depending on the particular account or bond. The return on NS&I Fixed Rate Savings Bonds is fixed but Capital Bonds pay a variable rate.

Tax treatment Interest is taxable and usually paid with tax at the savings rate (20 per cent in 2004–5) already deducted. Non-taxpayers can reclaim tax overpaid, or, better still, arrange for interest to be paid gross by completing Form R85 from the bank, building society or the Inland Revenue★. Starting-rate taxpayers can reclaim part of the tax. No further tax for basic-rate taxpayers, but higher-rate taxpayers have extra to pay. Interest from the NS&I Capital Bond is taxable but paid without any tax already deducted. Some cash ISAs (see Chapter 11) are available as term accounts or bonds, in which case the return is tax-free.

How long you invest for The specified term.

Charges No explicit charges. The provider's costs are one factor influencing the interest rates offered.

Risk No capital risk. Vulnerable to inflation. Variable rates are vulnerable to falling interest rates, but you would lose out if locked into fixed rates when other interest rates were rising. Risk rating: three.

More information Regular surveys in *Which?*★, personal finance magazines and the personal finance pages of newspapers, summaries in *Moneyfacts*★, fax services★, Ceefax★ and Teletext★. Post offices or NS&I★ for NS&I products.

How to invest At local branch. By post or phone, if postal or phone-based account. For NS&I products, via post offices or deal direct with NS&I★.

Monthly income accounts

What they are These can be based on several types of deposit: for example, instant access or notice account, term account or bond. Most commonly they are notice accounts. Instead of accumulating interest within the account or bond, the interest is paid out monthly as income. This form of investment is popular with pensioners seeking to boost their income. NS&I offer two monthly income products: Pensioners Bonds (for people aged 60 and over) and

Income Bonds. Its Fixed Rate Savings Bonds (see page 293) also give you the option of having interest paid out as an income.

Minimum investment Varies: can be as low as £500, but is more often £5,000 to £10,000. £500 for the NS&I bonds.

Maximum investment Usually none. £1 for the NS&I bonds.

Type of return Interest, which may be fixed or variable, depending on the particular account or bond. The rate for NS&I Income Bonds is variable; the rate on NS&I Pensioners Bonds is fixed.

Tax treatment Interest is taxable and usually paid with tax at the savings rate (20 per cent in 2004–5) already deducted. Non-taxpayers can reclaim tax overpaid, or, better still, arrange for interest to be paid gross by completing Form R85 from the bank, building society or the Inland Revenue★. Starting-rate taxpayers can reclaim part of the tax. No further tax for basic-rate taxpayers, but higher-rate taxpayers have extra to pay. Interest from the NS&I Pensioners Bonds and Income Bonds is taxable but paid without any tax already deducted.

How long you invest for Depends on the type of account or bond. Most commonly, these are notice accounts where you can have your money back at any time provided you give the required notice – for example, 60 or 90 days – or alternatively pay an interest penalty.

Charges No explicit charges. The provider's costs are one factor influencing the interest rates offered.

Risk No capital risk. Vulnerable to inflation. Variable rates are vulnerable to falling interest rates, but you would lose out if locked into fixed rates when other interest rates were rising. Risk rating: one to three, depending on type of account or bond.

More information Regular surveys in *Which?*★, personal finance magazines and the personal finance pages of newspapers, summaries in *Moneyfacts*★, fax services★, Ceefax★ and Teletext★. Post offices or NS&I★ for NS&I products.

How to invest At a local branch. By post or phone, if postal or phone-based account. For NS&I products via post offices or direct with NS&I★.

Regular savings accounts

What they are Bank and building society accounts where you agree to pay in regularly – usually monthly – for a set period of time. The rate of interest is normally reduced if you miss any or more than a specified number of payments. The number of withdrawals you can make is also usually restricted.

Minimum investment Varies from, say, £10 a month to £100 a month depending on the account.

Maximum investment Varies from, say, £100 a month to £1,000 a month depending on the account.

Type of return Interest is usually variable, but occasionally fixed.

Tax treatment Interest is taxable and usually paid with tax at the savings rate (20 per cent in 2004–5) already deducted. Non-taxpayers can reclaim tax overpaid or register for gross interest by completing form R85 from the bank or building society or the Inland Revenue★. Starting-rate taxpayers can reclaim part of the tax. No further tax for basic-rate taxpayers to pay. Higher-rate taxpayers have extra to pay. A few cash ISAs (see Chapter 11) are available as regular savings accounts, in which case interest is tax-free.

How long you invest for The specified term, for example, one, three or five years.

Charges No explicit charges apart from loss of interest if you do not keep to any restrictions on payments in and out. The provider's costs are one factor influencing the rate of interest offered.

Risk No capital risk. Vulnerable to inflation. Variable rates are vulnerable to falling interest rates. Fixed rates lock you in so you would miss out on any rise in interest rates. You must stick to the various conditions to earn the interest offered. Risk rating: three.

More information Regular surveys in *Which?*★ and personal finance pages of newspapers, summaries in *Moneyfacts*★, fax services★.

How to invest At a local branch. By post or phone, if postal or phone-based account.

Children's accounts

What they are Accounts especially for children (variously defined: for example, up to age 16, 18 or 21), usually offering introductory gifts, magazines, money-boxes, etc. Some accounts include cash cards for older children (aged 11 and over, say). Children's accounts are useful as a way of getting children into the savings habit or introducing them to the rudiments of budgeting.

Minimum investment Often as low as £1.

Maximum investment Usually none.

Type of return Interest, which is variable.

Tax treatment Interest is taxable and, if you do nothing, it will be paid with tax at the savings rate (20 per cent in 2004–5) already deducted. However, non-taxpayers (which includes most children) can have interest paid gross if Form R85 from the bank, building society or the Inland Revenue is completed. Watch out for interest being treated as income of the parent (see Chapter 10).

How long you invest for Usually, these are instant access accounts, but some do not allow withdrawals before a given age.

Charges No explicit charges. The bank's or building society's costs are one factor influencing the interest rates offered.

Risk No capital risk. Vulnerable to inflation. Variable rates are vulnerable to falling interest rates. Risk rating: one.

More information Regular surveys in *Which?*★, personal finance magazines and the personal finance pages of newspapers, and summaries in *Moneyfacts*★.

How to invest At local branch.

National Savings & Investments tax-free products

NS&I certificates

What they are Two-year- or five-year-term investments producing a guaranteed tax-free return, which makes them attractive for taxpayers, especially those paying at the higher rate.

Minimum investment £100.

Maximum investment £15,000 per issue, plus a further unlimited amount if you are reinvesting the maturity proceeds of an earlier issue.

Type of return Interest, which is fixed and paid out at the end of the two-year or five-year term or on earlier encashment. The rate of interest increases each year you hold the certificates.

Tax treatment Tax-free.

How long you invest for You choose either a two-year or a five-year term. You can get your money back earlier, but you'll get interest only at the reduced rates which apply to the earlier years. If you cash in during the first year, you get no interest at all (except on reinvested certificates). At the end of two or five years, make sure you cash in the certificates or reinvest in a new issue, otherwise they usually revert to a standard rate of interest called the 'General Extension Rate', which is very low.

Charges No explicit charges. NS&I's underlying costs are one factor influencing the interest rates offered.

Risk No capital risk. Vulnerable to inflation. Because you are locked in at a fixed rate, you'll lose out if other interest rates rise. Risk rating: three.

More information Post offices, direct from NS&I★, occasional reviews of these products in *Which?*★, personal finance magazines and the personal finance pages of newspapers, and summaries in *Moneyfacts*★.

How to invest Via post offices or direct with NS&I★.

Index-linked NS&I certificates

What they are Investments producing a guaranteed tax-free return which is inflation-proofed. At the time of writing, available with either a three- or five-year term. Useful if you are concerned to protect your savings against rising prices (or if you want to take a gamble on inflation rising to high levels). The tax-free status makes them attractive for taxpayers, especially those paying at the higher rate.

Minimum investment £100.

Maximum investment £15,000 per issue, plus a further unlimited amount if you are reinvesting the maturity proceeds of an earlier issue.

Type of return Interest made up of two elements: first, you get interest at set rates which increase for each year you hold the certificates; second, you get the amount needed to protect your capital and the interest already earned against inflation as measured by changes in the Retail Prices Index. The return is paid out at the end of the two-year or five-year term or on earlier encashment.

Tax treatment Tax-free.

How long you invest for You choose either a three-year or five-year term. You can get your money back earlier, but you'll get only the extra interest at the reduced rates which apply to the earlier years. If you cash in during the first year, you get no interest at all (except on reinvested certificates). At the end of three or five years, make sure you cash in the certificates or reinvest in a new issue, otherwise they usually revert to a lower rate of interest (still index-linked) or just index-linking.

Charges No explicit charges. NS&I's underlying costs are one factor influencing the interest rates offered.

Risk No capital risk. Because you are locked in at a fixed rate, you'll lose out if other interest rates rise, though what is relevant here is 'real' interest rates, that is, interest less the inflation rate. Risk rating: two.

More information Post offices, direct from NS&I*, occasional reviews of these products in *Which?**, personal finance magazines and the personal finance pages of newspapers, and summaries in *Moneyfacts**.

How to invest Via post offices or deal direct with NS&I*.

NS&I children's bonus bonds

What they are Bonds bought by adults (defined as anyone over 16) on behalf of children up to the age of 16. The bonds can run until the child reaches age 21, building up a tax-free lump sum. The return is fixed for five years at a time and reviewed on each five-year anniversary.

Minimum investment £25.

Maximum investment £3,000 per issue per child.

Type of return Interest, at fixed rates guaranteed for five years at a time, including a bonus payable on each five-year anniversary.

Tax treatment Tax-free. Bearing in mind that children's income may be treated as income of the parents (see Chapter 10), the tax-free status means that these bonds can be particularly useful as gifts from parents to a child.

How long you invest for Money can remain invested in the bonds until the child reaches age 21, when the bonds stop earning interest. They can be cashed in before then. If you cash in a bond within one week after a five-year anniversary, you do not have to give any notice, and the money is paid over to the child's parent or guardian within a few days. If you cash in at any other time, you must give one month's notice, and you will forfeit the five-year bonus. If you cash in during the first year, you get no interest at all.

Charges No explicit charges. NS&I's underlying costs are one factor influencing the interest rates offered.

Risk No capital risk. Vulnerable to inflation. Being locked into fixed rates means the child could lose out if other interest rates rise. Risk rating: three.

More information Post offices, direct from NS&I*, occasional reviews of these products in *Which?**, personal finance magazines and the personal finance pages of newspapers, and summaries in *Moneyfacts**.

How to invest Via post offices or direct with NS&I*.

> **Tip**
> Because they offer a tax-free return, children's bonus bonds make a good gift for parents if they are worried that income from the child's investments would otherwise be taxed as the parents' income – see Chapter 10.

Premium bonds

What they are Strictly, these are a gamble rather than an investment. You buy the bonds, and they are entered into a monthly prize draw where each bond stands a 1-in-24,000 chance of winning a prize ranging from £50 to £1 million (figures for January 2005). Unlike most other forms of gambling, though, you never lose your stake money.

Minimum investment £100.

Maximum investment £30,000 (plus automatically reinvested prizes).

Type of return The money invested in premium bonds is placed in a prize fund from which prizes are paid out each month. Prizes range from £50 to £1 million. Small prizes (£50 to £1,000) can be automatically reinvested to buy new bonds. In January 2005, the prize fund represented 3.2 per cent of the total invested in the bonds.

Tax treatment Prizes are tax-free.

How long you invest for Up to you. Bonds must be held for one complete calendar month before they are eligible for the prize draws. You can withdraw your money at any time, though this is done by post and takes a few days.

Charges No explicit charges. NS&I's costs are one factor influencing the return on the prize fund (and hence the overall payout in prizes).

Risk No risk to capital. Vulnerable to inflation. Return can range from nil to £1 million. Risk rating: three.

More information Post offices, direct from NS&I*, occasional reviews of these products in *Which?*★, personal finance magazines and personal finance pages of newspapers.

How to invest Via post offices or direct with NS&I*.

> **Tip**
> Premium bonds are an interest lottery. You do not gamble with your capital, only the interest from it. You could set up your own interest lottery by investing a lump sum in a bank or building society account and using the interest to buy National Lottery tickets, back horses, and so on.

Summary of lower-risk investments

Investment	Minimum period for which you should aim to invest	Type of return	Risk rating
Bank and building society savings and investments			
Current accounts	No set period	Variable, taxed,* if interest paid at all	1
All-in-one mortgage accounts	Mortgage term or shorter	Tax-free interest	1
Instant access/easy access accounts	No set period	Variable, taxed*†	1
Notice accounts	No set period	Variable, taxed*†	2–3
Term accounts and bonds	The specified period, e.g. 1 or 2 years	Fixed or variable, taxed*†	3
Monthly income accounts	Varies	Fixed or variable, taxed*	1–3
Regular savings accounts	The specified period e.g. 1, 3 or 5 years	Variable (or occasionally fixed), taxed*†	3
Children's accounts	Usually, no set period	Variable, taxed*	1
National Savings & Investments (NS&I) tax-free products			
NS&I certificates	2 or 5 years	Fixed, tax-free	3
Index-linked NS&I certificates	3 or 5 years	Fixed, inflation-proofed, tax-free	2
Children's bonus bonds	5 years	Fixed, tax-free	3
Premium bonds	No set period	Tax-free prizes	3

* Income is paid out before deduction of tax, or non-taxpayers can arrange to receive income gross, that is, before deduction of tax.
† Some available as cash ISAs (see Chapter 11) in which case return is tax-free.

Chapter 17

Medium-risk investments

If you are looking at a long-term (say, ten years plus) savings or investment goal, you would be unwise to rely too heavily on the lower-risk products described in Chapter 16. Over long periods, their returns have tended to lag a long way behind the return from higher-risk investments and often have not even kept pace with inflation. Even with medium-term goals (five to ten years) it is often sensible to put part of your money into products that give you the chance of a better return. But pursuing higher returns means accepting additional risk, in particular capital risk. Not everyone is comfortable with the higher risks inherent in the investments described in Chapter 18. Often the answer is a portfolio which mixes some lower-risk investments with higher-risk ones to create an overall middling balance of risk and return. As part of such a portfolio, or on their own, the medium-risk investments described in this chapter help you to take this middle path.

This chapter also touches on the government's proposed new suite of 'stakeholder products' which are due to be launched from April 2005 (see page 326). These do not fall neatly into the description 'medium-risk' but rather are 'controlled-risk' products. The aim is that where you see the name 'stakeholder' you can be confident that the product is designed to avoid high risks and has certain other consumer-friendly features, such as a cap on charges.

Investments from the government

Gilts (British government stocks)

What they are Loans you make to the government in the form of bonds which usually have a fixed lifetime. You do not have to hold them for that set period because you can buy and sell them on the stock market. At the time of writing, there are around 30 different conventional British government stocks (as well as index-linked stocks – see page 306). Stocks are often described in terms of their 'nominal' or 'par' value of £100. This is a convenient way of dividing the stocks into units, but if you bought a nominal £100 stock, for example, what you pay could be more or less than that amount. British government stocks are called 'gilts' (or 'gilt-edged'), reflecting the very sound nature of these stocks because of the unlikelihood that the government would ever default on them.

Minimum investment There are two ways to buy. If you buy stock when it is newly issued, you can do so direct from the Debt Management Office (DMU)★ (which issues stock on behalf of the government). New stock is auctioned and you must bid for at least £1,000 of stock. There are no dealing charges on stock you buy this way.

Alternatively, you can buy stock which has already been issued and is traded on the stock market. You can buy this way through a stockbroker or through the DMO Gilts Purchase and Sale Service★. There is no set minimum investment, but dealing charges make buying small amounts (less than, say, £1,000) uneconomic. However, the DMO Service charges (see page 306) tend to be lower than a stockbroker's for smallish transactions.

Maximum investment None.

Type of return The return is made up of two parts: while you hold the stock, you are paid a fixed amount of interest every six months; when the stock is sold or comes to the end of its life, you make a capital gain or loss. Some stocks pay a very low amount of interest and are useful only for people who are mainly after capital gains. Other stocks pay a high level of interest and are particularly useful for people who need income immediately; it may even be worth reckoning on some capital loss (by buying the stock at more than its nominal value) if a high income is a major priority.

If you hold the stock until the end of its life (until it is 'redeemed'), you will get back a known amount of £100 for each nominal £100 of stock you hold. This means that you know from the time you buy exactly what return you will get overall if you hold the stock to redemption: that is, the return is fixed and guaranteed. Alternatively, you can sell the stock before redemption, in which case you cannot be certain in advance what capital gain or loss you stand to make. So the nature of the return depends on how you choose to use these stocks.

Since 1997, you have also been able to buy 'gilt strips'. A single gilt-edged stock provides a stream of income payments plus the capital payment at redemption. Some stock can now be split up ('stripped') into components, each producing one payment. For example, a gilt with two years until redemption would produce four interest payments and a redemption payment. This could be split into five strips, one for each payment. Each strip (which is in effect a 'zero coupon bond') is traded separately. Gilt strips provide a very flexible form of investment and can be used, for example, to design an income flow tailored to your needs.

Tax treatment The income from all gilts is normally paid gross – that is, without any deduction of tax – which is especially convenient for non-taxpayers. But the income is taxable, unless you are a non-taxpayer. You can request to receive the income from gilts net of tax, in which case you will receive interest after deduction of tax at the savings rate of 20 per cent. There is no further tax to pay if you are a basic-rate taxpayer. Higher-rate taxpayers have extra to pay. If you are a starting-rate taxpayer, you can reclaim part of the tax deducted but it would be more sensible for you to opt to receive gross interest. Before 6 April 1998, income from gilts was normally paid net of tax if you bought through a stockbroker. Under transitional rules, if you already held gilts on that date, you will continue to receive the income net unless you request to switch to gross payments.

Capital gains on gilts are tax-free. This means that stocks paying low interest, whose return is likely to be largely in the form of capital gain, can be particularly attractive for higher-rate taxpayers and people who would normally pay tax on their gains.

How long you invest for If you want to hold stocks until redemption, there is a large range of redemption dates, from stocks just about to mature up to lifetimes of 30 years or more. But, of course, you can sell at any time before then on the stock market, and some stocks, called 'irredeemables', have no redemption date at all, so you *have* to sell to cash in your investment.

Traditionally, gilts are divided into three groups:

- shorts (five years or less to redemption),
- mediums (five to fifteen years), and
- longs (over fifteen years).

The groups tend to behave in different ways. As short-dated stocks get closer to their redemption date, their prices tend towards the nominal value at which they will be redeemed; other short-dated stocks tend to react to changes in general interest rates. Longer-dated stocks are influenced more by the inflation outlook and wider-ranging economic factors.

Charges If you deal through a stockbroker. Typically, you might pay, say, 1 per cent on deals up to £7,000 with a minimum charge of £17.50. The DMO Gilts Purchase and Sale Service* is cheaper (see overleaf). There is also a 'spread' between the price paid by buyers and sellers, with buyers paying a little more than the quoted mid-market price and sellers getting a little less.

Risk This varies, depending on how you use the stocks. If you intend to hold them until redemption (or you invest in 'gilt strips'), you know exactly what will happen to your capital, and your total return is fixed – though you are not locked into this because you could change your mind and sell before redemption. If you are holding conventional gilts for their income, bear in mind that the income is vulnerable to inflation (though see the section below on index-linked gilts). You can also buy and sell gilts on a more speculative basis, though their price movements tend to be more modest than those of shares. Buying through the DMO Service, you deal by post and so cannot be certain of the price at which your deal will be struck, which makes buying and selling in this way more risky than buying through a stockbroker. Risk rating: around four when held as medium- to long-term investments.

More information The Debt Management Office* publishes an excellent booklet explaining how gilts work and how to invest, *Investing in gilts – the private investor's guide to British Government stock*. For stockbrokers (including many high-street banks and some building societies which run their own stockbroking arms), contact the Association of Private Client Investment Managers and Stockbrokers (APCIMS)* for a free directory of its members or the London Stock Exchange* for a list of brokers. Quality daily newspapers carry full lists of gilts, including their prices and returns.

How to invest Register with the Debt Management Office Gilts Purchase and Sale Service* to use the service. Otherwise, deal through a stockbroker*. If you are buying gilts within an ISA (see Chapter 11), you will have to buy through your ISA manager – who will usually be a stockbroker or the broking arm of a bank or building society. If you invest in new issues, do so via a stockbroker or by contacting the Debt Management Office* for a prospectus or look for a prospectus printed in the press.

Debt Management Office Gilts Purchase and Sale Service: charges for buying and selling gilts

Type of deal	Commission rate	Minimum charge	Example
Buy up to £5,000	0.7%	£12.50	• If you buy £1,000 of stock, commission costs £12.50 • If you buy £3,000 of stock, commission costs £21
Sell up to £5,000	0.7%	None	• If you sell £1,000 of stock, commission costs £7 • If you sell £3,000 of stock, commission costs £21
Buy or sell over £5,000	£35 plus 0.375% of the excess over £5,000	£35	• If you buy or sell £7,000 of stock, commission costs £42.50 • If you buy or sell £10,000 of stock, commission costs £53.75

Index-linked gilts

What they are Basically, these are much the same as conventional gilts (see above), but both the income and the amount you get back at redemption are increased in line with inflation (measured as changes in the Retail Prices Index, subject to an eight-month lag). Their stock-market prices will *tend* to increase along with the rising redemption value, but are, of course, subject to other forces as well, such as returns available on other investments, confidence in the economy, and so on.
Minimum investment As for conventional gilts.
Maximum investment As for conventional gilts.
Type of return Income is inflation-proofed, which is useful for, say, retired people wanting an income to supplement their pensions. Your capital would be inflation-proofed too if you bought a stock when it was first issued and held it until redemption, but this link to

inflation is weakened when you buy and sell on the stock market at prices which may be out of line with the indexation.

Tax treatment As for conventional gilts.

How long you invest for At the time of writing there were nine index-linked gilts with redemption dates ranging from 2006 to 2035.

Charges As for conventional gilts.

Risk In the main, as for conventional gilts, with one important exception: income and to some extent capital are protected against inflation. Risk rating: around three to four when held as a medium- to long-term investment.

More information As for conventional gilts.

How to invest As for conventional gilts.

Local authority bonds and stocks

What they are Loans to local government. Some loans are in the form of fixed-term bonds which must be held to redemption. Others are stocks, similar to gilts, which can be bought and sold on the stock market.

Minimum investment For bonds, this varies from, say, £200 upwards. With stocks, there is no set minimum, but dealing costs would make less than, say, £1,000 uneconomic.

Maximum investment None.

Type of return Fixed-term bonds give you fixed interest, which is usually paid every six months. Stocks are similar to gilts, paying you a fixed income plus a capital gain or loss, depending on the prices at which the stocks are bought and sold (or redeemed). The interest rate on local authority stocks tends to be higher than on gilts, reflecting the higher risk (see below).

Tax treatment Interest from both bonds and stocks is taxable and paid with income tax at the savings rate (20 per cent in 2004–5) already deducted. Non-taxpayers and starting-rate taxpayers can reclaim all or part of the tax respectively. Basic-rate taxpayers have no further tax to pay. Higher-rate taxpayers have extra to pay. Capital gains on stocks are tax-free.

How long you invest for Terms vary. Like gilts, stocks can be sold before redemption on the stock market. Bonds are typically for two to eight years, and you are locked in for the whole period as these cannot be traded and there is generally no way to get your money back early.

Charges None for bonds. Stockbroker's commission and a spread between buying and selling prices for stocks.

Risk Bonds: the only risk to your capital is that the local authority might default on the loan and be unable to repay it, but this risk is slight; vulnerable to inflation; the fixed term and return mean you could lose out if other interest rates rose. Stocks: similar to conventional gilts, except for possible problems buying and selling, since the market for these stocks is sometimes not very active; slight risk that the local authority might default. Risk rating for both: around five.

More information Bonds: direct from local authorities, and summaries in *Moneyfacts**. Stocks are listed in quality newspapers with details of their prices and returns.

How to invest Bonds: contact the relevant local authority. Stocks: via a stockbroker.

Investments from commercial organisations

Annuities

What they are Investments offered by insurance companies whereby you swap a lump sum for a regular income. You cannot get your original investment back as a lump sum, though you are treated as if part of each income payment is in fact a bit of your original capital coming back (see 'Tax treatment', opposite). Annuities can be for life ('lifetime annuity') or for a set period of years ('temporary annuity'). Pensions from money purchase pension schemes and plans (see Chapter 13) are usually a type of lifetime annuity and are called 'compulsory purchase annuities'. Non-pension annuities are called 'purchased annuities'.

Minimum investment Varies, but you would usually pay thousands of pounds for a lifetime annuity.

Maximum investment None.

Type of return Income, which can be fixed or can increase each year either by a fixed percentage or in line with prices – you decide on the type of return at the time you invest. You can also choose annuities which guarantee to pay out for a fixed period – for example, five or ten years – even if you die during that period. The return from lifetime annuities depends heavily on the average life expectancy for someone of your age, so rates are generally higher the older you are and are higher for men than for women. Some providers offer annuities for people in poor health ('impaired life annuities') and these pay higher than normal rates. See Chapter 13 for more about the different types of annuity available. Although that chapter focuses on pension annuities, the choices for non-pension annuities are the same.

Tax treatment With the exception of annuities used to provide a pension, part of each regular payment is deemed to be the return of part of your capital and is tax-free. The remaining part is income, which is usually paid with tax at the savings rate already deducted, but you may be able to arrange to have it paid gross if you are a non-taxpayer (if not, you can reclaim the tax). Starting-rate taxpayers can reclaim part of the tax. Basic-rate taxpayers have no further tax to pay. Higher-rate taxpayers must pay extra. The whole of the income from a pension annuity is taxable at your top rate of income tax and is generally paid with the correct amount of tax deducted using the PAYE system.

How long you invest for A lifetime annuity is literally for life: having made your decision to invest, you have no chance to reverse it. Temporary annuities are for set periods: for example, five years. You are committed to investing for the full period and cannot get your capital back as a lump sum.

Charges No explicit charges. The insurance company's costs are one factor determining the annuity rates on offer. (If you buy through a financial adviser, you may pay a fee for the advice – see Chapter 2).

Risk No access to your capital as a lump sum once you have invested. Annuities with no built-in increases are vulnerable to inflation: you are locked in at whatever annuity rates apply at the time you invest, and you will lose out if annuity rates subsequently rise. (However, the trend in recent years has been for annuity rates to fall.) Risk rating: around four for annuities paying a fixed income; around three for annuities which provide some protection against inflation.

Warning

The annuity rate at the time you invest determines the income you will get for the rest of your life in the case of a lifetime annuity or for the whole term in the case of a temporary annuity. Therefore, it is important to avoid investing at times when annuity rates are low. If you're not sure whether the timing is right, get advice.

More information Example annuity rates are listed in a wide range of personal finance magazines, some newspapers and in *Moneyfacts Investments Life & Pensions*★. A number of fax services★ also give up-to-date rates. A few IFAs specialising in annuities★, such as the Annuity Bureau and Annuity Direct, focus on finding the best annuities for clients. If you have access to the Internet, you can find annuity rate comparisons on some personal finance and IFA websites, for example www.moneyfacts.co.uk, www.annuity-bureau.co.uk and www.annuitydirect.co.uk.

How to invest Either contact the insurer offering your chosen annuity or use one of the IFAs which specialise in annuities.

Insurance company guaranteed income and growth bonds

What they are Investments based on either single-premium insurance policies and/or annuities which give you a fixed income or fixed rate of growth over a set period and then return your original investment at the end of the period.

Minimum investment Varies from £1,000 upwards.

Maximum investment None.

Type of return You get either fixed income from income bonds or a fixed rate of growth from growth bonds (paid when the bond matures).

Tax treatment Depends on the underlying investments which make up the bond, but usually there is no basic-rate tax for you to pay. The insurance company has often already paid tax on the underlying investment, but this is the company's own tax bill, so non-taxpayers and lower-rate taxpayers cannot reclaim any tax. Higher-rate taxpayers may have to pay extra, though, with some types of bond, tax is deferred until the end of the term and based on the taxpayer's tax position in that year.

How long you invest for Depends on the fixed term of the bond, which is generally from one year to ten years. You cannot usually get your money back early.

Charges No explicit charges, although the insurance company's costs are one factor taken into account when setting the rate of return.

Risk No risk to capital. Vulnerable to inflation. Being locked into a fixed return, you will lose out if returns on other investments rise. Risk rating: around four. Do not confuse with other types of insurance company bond where return of capital is not guaranteed – see pages 323 to 325.

More information Details of bonds available are included in many finance magazines, including *Money Management*★ and *Moneyfacts Investments Life & Pensions*★. Regular summaries are also given in the personal finance sections of quality newspapers. For information about specific bonds, contact the insurer direct or use an independent financial adviser (IFA)★.

How to invest Either contact the insurer direct or invest through an independent financial adviser.

Permanent income-bearing shares (PIBSs)

What they are Loans to building societies in the form of stocks which have no redemption date at all and which are bought and sold on the stock market. (Holding PIBSs often makes you a member of the building society. If the society converted to a bank or was taken over, you could be eligible for a cash or share windfall.)

Minimum investment Varies from £1,000 upwards.

Maximum investment None.

Type of return Fixed interest paid out twice a year, which makes PIBSs popular investments with people seeking an immediate income. The rate of interest is usually higher than it is on gilts, reflecting the higher risk you take with PIBSs (see below). Depending on the prices at which you buy and sell, you may make a capital gain or a capital loss.

Tax treatment Interest is taxable and, since 1 April 2001, paid before deduction of tax. Income tax is due at your highest rate, unless you are a basic rate tax payer, in which case tax is due at the savings rate (20 per cent in 2004–5). Capital gains are tax-free.

How long you invest for No set period, but this is not a suitable home for money you might need back at a particular time or at short notice because prices may be low at that time.

Charges Stockbroker's commission and spread between the prices at which you buy and sell.

Risk Capital risk on three counts: prices can fall, the market in these stocks is not very active (so you might have problems selling – and buying), and there is a small risk that the building society might go out of business (though in the past the few societies that have run into difficulties have been absorbed into other societies rather than allowed to go bust). There is also a slight risk to income, because the building society is allowed to waive the interest if it is facing financial difficulty. The fixed income is vulnerable to inflation. Risk rating: around five.

More information Stockbrokers★, the personal finance sections of some newspapers, occasional articles in personal finance magazines★.

How to invest Via a stockbroker.

Corporate bonds

What they are These work in a similar way to gilts, except they are loans to companies in the form of stocks which are bought and sold on the stock market. There are various types of corporate bond: for example, those which are 'secured' either against the general assets of the company or against specific assets which can be seized and sold if the company defaults on the loan (in contrast to 'unsecured' loans, which are not backed by specific assets). There are also 'convertibles', which can be swapped for shares in the company at a set price at or before some specified date.

Minimum investment No set minimum, but dealing charges would make less than, say, £1,000 uneconomic.

Maximum investment None.

Type of return Usually, corporate bonds offer a fixed rate of interest, paid half-yearly. You also stand to make a capital gain or loss, depending on the prices at which the bonds are bought and sold, redeemed or converted.

Tax treatment Interest is taxable and, since 1 April 2001, paid before deduction of tax. Income tax is due at your highest rate; unless you are a basic rate taxpayer, in which case tax is due at the savings rate (20 per cent in 2004–5). Capital gains are generally tax-free.

How long you invest for Most bonds have a fixed lifetime, after which they are redeemed by the company. But of course you can sell on the stock market before then. This is not the home for money you might need back at short notice because prices could be low when you want to sell.

Charges Stockbroker's commission: for example, 1 per cent on deals up to £5,000 or so, with a flat-rate minimum commission of £15–£20. There is also a spread between the prices paid by buyers and sellers.

Risk There is a risk to your capital because bond prices can fall. You also have the risk that the company might go out of business and be unable to repay the loan, in which case you would lose all your capital. This latter risk should be reasonably small if you invest in the bonds of a large, well-established company (though, as the collapse of Barings Bank showed, bondholders in even the most seemingly sound company can lose). The risk of default can be substantial if you pick new and/or struggling companies. Fixed incomes are vulnerable to inflation. Risk rating: from around five for the most sound ('blue chip') companies to ten for companies which are unproven or in difficulty.

More information Stockbrokers.

How to invest Via a stockbroker. If you invest in new issues, via a prospectus from the company's agents or printed in the press.

Preference shares

What they are Unlike loans to a company, buying shares gives you a stake in the ownership of a company. Ordinary shares are described in Chapter 18, but preference shares are included here because they have various characteristics which are more akin to corporate bonds. Preference shares usually offer a fixed income, which is paid before any dividends to ordinary shareholders. Some preference shares have a redemption date, at which time they are bought back by the company, while others are irredeemable. In either case you can buy and sell them on the stock market. Convertible preference shares give you the right to switch to ordinary shares in the company at a set price at or before some specified date, which gives you the option to switch from a fixed to a variable income and participate in the generally more volatile movement of ordinary share prices.

Minimum investment No set minimum, but dealing charges would make investing less than, say, £1,000 uneconomic.

Maximum investment None.

Type of return Income is in the form of dividends, usually at a fixed rate and paid half-yearly. You also stand to make a capital gain or loss, depending on the prices at which the shares are bought and sold.

Tax treatment Income is taxable. The dividends are paid net of income tax at a special 10 per cent rate. Non-taxpayers cannot reclaim the tax deducted. Both starting-rate and basic-rate taxpayers have no further tax to pay. Higher-rate taxpayers have further tax to pay. Capital gains are taxable, though you may have allowances to set against them (see Chapter 4).

How long you invest for No set period, because you can sell at any time on the stock market. But this is not the home for money you might need back at short notice or at a set time, since share prices might then be low.

Charges Stockbroker's commission and spread between the prices which buyers pay and sellers receive.

Risk Capital risk because of fluctuating share prices. You also have the risk that the company might go out of business. If it does, preference shareholders are in line for a payout ahead of ordinary shareholders, but the company might not have enough assets to stretch even to the preference shareholders, in which case you would lose all your capital. This should be a small risk with large, well-established companies, but a major consideration with companies struggling to get established or going through a bad patch. Fixed incomes are vulnerable to inflation. Risk rating: around five for 'blue chip' companies to ten for riskier ventures.

More information Stockbrokers and specialist magazines such as *Investors Chronicle*★. Prices and so on are included in share listings in daily newspapers.

How to invest Via a stockbroker. If you invest in new issues of shares, via a prospectus from the company's agents or published in the press or, more commonly, through a stockbroker which offers a new issues service.

Pooled investments

Pooled investments are ready-made portfolios of particular types of assets, such as shares of a particular country, or a range of different assets, such as shares, gilts and property. They give you a way of spreading risks, investing relatively small sums and keeping down dealing costs. Against these advantages you must weigh the charges levied by the managers who run these investments and whether you are happy that the investment policy of the managers fits sufficiently well with your own investment aims.

With-profits life insurance

What it is This is one form of investment-type life insurance offered by insurers and by friendly societies – organisations which started life as mutual self-help organisations to help people cope financially with crises such as illness and death. (Pension schemes – see Chapter 12 – can also be invested on a with-profits basis, in which case they work in basically the same way as outlined here.) Your premiums are invested by the insurer in gilts, shares, property, and so on to form a fund out of which it meets claims and the costs of running its business. But insurers tend to be prudent people and so, normally, the investments produce more than the amount needed to meet claims, costs, dividends to shareholders (if the insurer is set up as a company) and reserves. The excess is distributed to the with-profits policyholders as bonuses. The insurer's actuary advises on how much can be paid out in bonuses each year. Usually, some kind of smoothing is applied to avoid sharp variations in bonuses from year to year. This means that some of the profits from a good year are held back in reserve instead of being paid out as bonuses. The reserves are then used to maintain bonus levels in years when the with-profits fund does not perform well. In this way, a with-profits policy should normally give you reasonably steady growth from year to year. You should not expect to do as well in the boom years as you would investing directly in the stock market, but equally, you should be insulated to some extent from falls in the market. But watch out for market value reductions (MVRs) if you cash in or transfer early – see 'Charges' on page 317.

Minimum investment Varies, depending in part on the type of policy or plan you are looking at. But some regular-premium policies accept sums of less than £10 a month. Single-lump-sum premiums tend to start in hundreds of pounds.

Warning
The return from most investment-type life insurance is not tax-free because the insurer has had to account for tax (which you can't reclaim) on the underlying investments.

Maximum investment Insurers may set their own maxima, in particular limiting the amount of life cover they are willing to give. Tax rules may also play a part: for example, friendly societies cannot accept more than £25 a month (£270 a year) into their tax-exempt plans (see page 318).

Type of return There are two types of bonuses: reversionary bonuses are added regularly, usually every year. Once added to the value of your policy, they cannot be taken away provided you keep

> **Warning**
>
> With-profits life insurance policies are generally contracts designed to run for the long term. Their investment value builds up gradually. If you cash in the policy or stop paying premiums in the early years, your policy may be worth less than you have paid in premiums, or even worth nothing at all.

the policy going for its original term. But if you cash in or transfer your policy early, even reversionary bonuses can be reduced by MVRs (see opposite). A terminal bonus is paid when the policy matures or on death – but not if it is cashed in or transferred early. The terminal bonus can account for a large proportion – for example a half – of the total return.

Tax treatment The return you get counts as income. With a few exceptions, the insurer has to pay or allow for tax on the underlying investment fund. This is deemed to be equivalent to having had income tax at the savings rate (20 per cent in 2004–5) already paid when you get the bonuses, so basic-rate taxpayers do not have any tax to pay themselves. However, non-taxpayers cannot reclaim any of the tax deemed to have been paid. Higher-rate taxpayers do not have to pay any extra tax, provided the policy counts as a 'qualifying' one (this means that the policy meets certain rules and so qualifies for advantageous tax treatment; most regular-premium policies designed to last for at least ten years meet these rules). If the policy is not a qualifying one, there could be some higher-rate tax. 'With-profits bonds' often allow you to take up to a given level of income each year, but put off paying tax on the income until the policy eventually matures. The limit on the yearly income is one-twentieth of the premiums paid. Any amount not used up in one year can be carried forward to future years. The proceeds of the bond, including the earlier income withdrawals, are then taxed when you finally cash in the bond. Although only higher-rate taxpayers would then have tax to pay on the bond itself, the payout can also affect other taxpayers if they are claiming income-related allowances or benefits, such as age allowance or child tax credit. Friendly societies can offer plans which are invested in a partially tax-free fund (dividends and similar income are taxable at 10 per cent)

How long you invest for This depends on the type of policy or plan you have, because many different sorts of policy can be invested on a with-profits basis. The main ones are shown in the box overleaf. In general, though, with-profits life policies are long-term investments, often designed to last at least ten years, which will give you a very poor investment if you pull out early. Stopping a policy early crystallises charges (largely commission paid to advisers and salespeople) which would otherwise have been spread out over the lifetime of the policy. People are often taken by surprise by the fact that, once those charges have been taken into account in arriving at the surrender value, their policy may have a very low value indeed.

Charges An administration fee is usually deducted from each premium. If you give up the policy early, there will usually be surrender penalties. In addition, there may be a market value reduction (MVR) – sometimes also called a market value adjustment (MVA). These days, most with-profits insurers retain the right to impose an MVR if you cash in or transfer your policy before the end of its original term. Until recent years, not much attention was paid to MVRs. Insurers gave the impression that they would be imposed only in very exceptional market conditions. However, with a three-year slide in the stock market between 2000 and 2003, the exceptional conditions arrived and MVRs have become commonplace. The aim of an MVR is to ensure that policy-holders who quit do not take away more than their fair share of the with-profits fund to the detriment of policyholders who stay behind. The MVR reduces the cash-in value or transfer value of your policy (which is likely already to have been reduced by surrender charges), commonly by 5, 10 or even 20 per cent. MVRs are not levied if you hold your policy to the end of its term.

With a traditional with-profits policy, other charges are not explicit – they are simply one of the factors determining the bonus rates. However, many policies these days are 'unitised' with-profits plans – with these charges made explicit and usually expressed as an upfront charge deducted from the amount you invest plus an annual management fee ranging from, say, 1 to 3 per cent of the value of the money invested.

Risk Provided you do not have to cash in your investment early, there should be little or no capital risk. Because bonuses are linked to a

Investment-type life insurance

Investment-type life insurance is usually invested on either a with-profits basis (see page 314) or a unit-linked basis (see page 336). Here, the variations common to both the with-profits and unit-linked routes are described. See also page 340.

Endowment policies These are designed to run for a specified length of time (the 'endowment period'), during which you pay regular premiums (usually monthly) and at the end of which the policy pays out a cash sum. The policy also pays out if you die during the policy term but, if it's life cover you need, term insurance is a cheaper option. In the past, endowment policies have been used widely as an all-purpose way of building up your savings: for example, as part of an endowment mortgage, to pay for education, or to accumulate a nest egg for non-specific purposes. This made some sense, because premiums to most policies qualified for some tax relief, but that premium relief was abolished in 1984. Nowadays, individual savings accounts (ISAs) – see Chapter 11 – are a more tax-efficient route for tackling medium- to long-term savings objectives.

Friendly society tax-exempt plans and 'baby bonds' These are usually endowment policies, but, unlike most life insurance plans, the return on the invested premiums is partially tax-free. Before 6 April 2004, the return was completely tax-free which made the plans useful for taxpayers, but now dividend income is taxed at 10 per cent generally only higher-rate taxpayers gain any significant advantage from these plans.

'Baby bonds' are simply versions of the tax-exempt plans aimed at children, and they are useful as gifts from parents who would otherwise be taxed on their child's income (see Chapter 10). There is a snag: the government restricts the amount you can invest in these plans (in 2004–5 to just £25 a month or £270 a year). The low amount invested means that any flat-rate charges can eat heavily into the value of the plan. Some friendly societies offer lump-sum versions of the plans whereby your money is invested in, say, an annuity to meet the regular premiums for the tax-exempt plan.

Whole-of-life policies As the name suggests, these are designed to run for the whole of your life. Because the life cover element will inevitably have to pay out one day, such policies build up a cash value, which can be cashed in to provide an investment return. Whole-of-life plans, invested on a unit-linked rather than a with-profits basis, are used as **maximum protection plans** and **universal plans,** which package together life insurance, investment and often other types of insurance.

Single-premium bonds (including with-profits bonds) These are single-premium whole-of-life policies, though that doesn't mean you have to keep them for the rest of your life. With most bonds, you can invest for as long or as short a period as you like, but they are designed to run for the medium to long term (say, at least five to ten years) and you could face hefty surrender charges if you cash in during the first few years. They can be used to provide growth or income.

With-profits bonds (i.e. single-premium bonds that are invested on a with-profits basis) are especially popular with income-seekers. This is in part because the tax rules for single-premium bonds let higher-rate taxpayers take a limited income each year while putting off any tax bill until the year the bond is cashed in (see page 316). Investors who are not higher-rate taxpayers do not in any case have any tax to pay, though the equivalent of income tax at the savings rate has already been deducted and can't be reclaimed.

With-profits bonds' popularity with income-seekers stems also from the fact that the bonds generally offer a higher return than bank and building society accounts but are less risky than fully fledged stock-market investments (such as unit trusts). But the returns are not guaranteed and depend on the insurer's ability to maintain bonus levels (see 'Risk' on page 317). Although you may receive the advertised income, the full return of your capital usually depends on bonus rates throughout the life of the bond. If bonuses fall short of target, you will not get all of your capital back – which is, of course, a very different situation from investing in a bank or building society account.

broadly based investment fund, you stand a good chance of beating inflation. But bonuses are unpredictable, especially the terminal bonus. You should be wary of simply assuming that past bonus levels will be maintained, or improved on, for the future: in recent times, many companies have cut their reversionary bonuses. A useful indicator of an insurer's ability to keep up future bonus levels is some measure of their 'financial strength', which looks at factors such as the level of reserves, the nature of the assets held by the insurer, and so on. Insurers must give you information about this if you ask. You might want help from an independent financial adviser★ when assessing financial strength. Risk rating: about five provided you keep the policy going until the end of its term. If you are not sure you will be able to do this, your returns become much more uncertain and risk rises to around six to seven.

More information If you are interested in a particular insurer's or friendly society's products, the company or adviser must provide you with product details set out in a Key Facts document (see Chapter 3). *Money Management*★ publishes regular surveys of with-profits performance and financial strength. *Moneyfacts, Investments Life & Pensions*★ gives performance details and premiums for with-profits policies and a summary of insurers' bonus declarations.

How to invest If, from your research, you have picked out a particular insurer's products, deal with the insurer direct if it allows this. Otherwise, use an independent financial adviser (IFA)★.

Gilt and fixed-income unit trusts

What they are Unit trusts are discussed more fully in Chapter 18. The gilt and fixed-income versions are professionally managed funds investing at least 80 per cent of the fund in gilts and other investments offering a fixed income, such as corporate bonds and/or preference shares. You invest by buying units in the trust.

Minimum investment Varies from, say, £500 upwards as a lump sum and from £25 a month through a regular savings scheme run by the trust management company.

Maximum investment None.

Type of return Units earn income (called 'distributions'), which can either be paid out regularly or, if you hold what are called 'accumulation units', automatically reinvested in the fund. Gilt and fixed-income trusts are particularly useful for investors seeking a regular income immediately. It is important to note that, although the underlying investments produce fixed income, the income from the trust itself is variable, because of the changing mix of underlying investments. You also stand to make a capital gain or loss, depending on the prices at which you buy and sell your units.

Tax treatment Distributions are paid or credited with income tax at the savings rate (20 per cent in 2004–5) already deducted. You get a tax credit showing the amount of tax paid, which you use to reclaim tax if you are a non-taxpayer. If you are a starting-rate taxpayer, you can reclaim part of the tax. Basic-rate taxpayers have no further tax to pay. Higher-rate taxpayers have extra to pay. Capital gains count as taxable, but you may have allowances you can set against them (see page 63). Since April 1999, provided the bulk of the trust (taken to be 60 per cent or more of the marketable value of its investments) is invested in interest-bearing investments, such as corporate bonds or gilts, this tax treatment continues unchanged. However, if the trust does not meet this condition – for example, if it has sizeable investments in preference shares – the distributions will be treated as if they are made from a share-based unit trust – see page 342. Note, in particular, that non-taxpayers would not then be allowed to reclaim the tax already paid. If you invest through an ISA (see Chapter 11) the return is completely tax-free.

How long you invest for No set period, but this is not the home for money you might need back at a set time or at short notice when unit prices could be low. Treat as a medium- to long-term investment.

Charges There is an annual management charge (often around 1–1.5 per cent of the underlying fund) and usually a spread between the prices at which you buy ('offer price') and sell ('bid price') units. This spread incorporates what is called the 'initial charge' – often around 3–5 per cent of the amount invested – but the total you pay upfront is effectively the spread, which tends to be 1 or 2 per cent more.

Risk These trusts give you a stake in a spread of different fixed-interest investments, which is generally a lower-risk strategy than investing direct in just one or two such stocks. They are a particularly useful way of spreading risk if you want to invest in corporate bonds. Bear in mind that income is variable. Risk rating: about five.

More information For general information, contact the Investment Management Association (IMA)★. Performance of trusts is published daily in quality newspapers and in specialist magazines, such as *Money Management*★. *Which?*★, personal finance magazines and the personal finance pages of newspapers all run regular articles about unit trusts. Some personal finance websites★ have search tools to help you choose unit trusts. There are now numerous fund supermarkets★ which both help you choose and buy unit trusts. Having selected several trusts which interest you, contact the management companies for product details (see Chapter 3 for more about these).

How to invest If, having done your initial research, you know which trust(s) you want to invest in, you could contact the management companies direct. But you may get a better deal through a discount broker★, fund supermarket, or an IFA★.

Open-ended investment companies (OEICs)

Open-ended investment companies (OEICs) are, from the investor's point of view, basically the same as unit trusts, though technically they are different. They are a cross between investment trusts (see page 345) and unit trusts. Like investment trusts, OEICs are companies which invest in funds – you invest by buying the OEIC's shares. Like unit trusts, though, the size of the fund varies with the number of investors involved, because shares are created and cancelled as investors come and go. This means that the price of OEIC shares behaves more like the price of units in a unit trust than shares in an investment trust, being directly related to the value of the underlying fund.

OEICs were developed largely as a way of widening the appeal of UK pooled investments. Foreign investors are unfamiliar with the trust status of unit trusts and feel more comfortable with corporate status. There is just one price at which shares in an OEIC are both bought and sold; this is in line with the way in which most Continental and US funds are priced. The price is based directly on the value of the investments in the fund, with charges shown separately. OEICs are taxed in the same way as unit trusts.

At the time of writing, OEICs are still fairly novel, but newly created collective investment schemes are tending to adopt the OEIC model and some unit trust managers are converting existing trusts to the new OEIC structure. The views of existing unit trust investors have to be taken into account before this can happen, but in general your investment should be broadly unchanged.

Guaranteed equity investments

What are they A group of investments aimed at people who want better returns than the bank or building society can provide but do not want any risk of losing their capital. Guaranteed equity bonds can be based on deposit bonds (offered by banks, building societies and National Savings & Investments), insurance bonds or unit trusts, which all work in different ways (see the box on page 325). What they all have in common is that they offer a return linked to the stock market – typically, linked to the rise in the FTSE 100 Index or some other measure of stock-market performance – but aim to return your capital in full at the end of a set period. In the case of bank, building society and NS&I bonds, this aim usually takes the form of a guarantee to return your full capital. But, with the insurance- and unit-trust-based versions, the 'guarantee' generally holds only provided certain conditions are met, so it is important to read the terms and conditions thoroughly. For example, the guarantee may cease if the relevant stock-market indices fall more than a given amount and this can trigger large capital losses.

Minimum investment Varies from as little as £500 with some providers up to, say, £10,000.

Maximum investment Often none per investor. But many of these investments are offered for only a short period of time with a fixed limit on the amount that can be invested by all the investors in total.

Type of return Lump sum paid at the end of the guarantee period. If this is a deposit-based bond, the return counts as interest. The return from an insurance bond counts as income. The return from a unit trust will usually count as a capital gain.

Tax treatment Deposit bonds: the same as for bank and building society accounts (see Chapter 16) but some can be set up as cash ISAs in which case the return is tax-free (see Chapter 11). Insurance bonds: as for non-qualifying policies (see page 316) and mainly suitable for people who are higher-rate taxpayers or who usually use up their full capital gains tax allowance each year (see Chapter 4). Unit trusts: as for unit trusts (see page 341).

How long you invest for Deposit bonds have a set term, which is usually from one year up to five years and you can't normally get your money back early. You must normally hold an insurance bond for at least a minimum period – say, five or six years – for the return of your capital to be guaranteed. You can generally cash in earlier but in that case you probably will not get back all your capital. Usually you can leave your money invested beyond the initial guarantee period. With the unit trust versions, the guarantee generally runs for three months at a time and you can continue investing for further three-month periods for as long as you like.

Charges Deposit bonds: as for bank and building society accounts, though a few of these bonds have an upfront arrangement fee. Insurance bonds: as for unit-linked insurance policies. Unit trusts: as for unit trusts.

Risk Deposit bonds: in general, no capital risk provided you invest for the full guarantee period or term. Unit trust versions aim to return your full capital but generally do not give an absolute guarantee. Check the small print of insurance bonds carefully – with some, you are guaranteed a full return of your capital only if the stock market does not fall by more than a set amount (say, 27 per cent). If it does fall by more, you could lose a substantial sum. All these guarantees come at a price. Although you share in stock-market growth, you usually get only a proportion of the growth and you do not get any of the income that shares and share-based investments generally produce. If the stock market falls you get no return at all beyond return of your capital. Risk rating for bank and building society guaranteed investments: around five. Risk rating for unit trust versions: five to six. Risk rating for insurance bonds: five to seven depending on the small print. Do not confuse the guaranteed version of unit trusts with protected unit trusts (which are much higher-risk) – see the box overleaf.

Warning

The whole proceeds of both bank or building society guaranteed equity bonds and insurance guaranteed equity investments count as income for the year the bond comes to an end or is cashed in. If you are then aged 65 or over, the return from the bond could take you over the income limit for age allowance (see page 63). In that case, you would lose some or all of the allowance and have to pay extra tax as a result. Ways to avoid this problem include opting for an ISA version of a bank or building society bond or choosing a unit trust guaranteed investment instead.

How guaranteed equity investments work

Bank and building society guaranteed and National Savings & Investments equity bonds These are fixed-term deposit accounts. The bond earns interest which is paid out when the bond comes to an end, together with the full return of your capital. The amount of interest you get depends on the performance of a stock-market index, such as the FTSE 100, a group of several stock-market indices or a basket of shares. For example, you might get 50 per cent of the growth in the FTSE 100 Index, or a return of 6.5 per cent a year provided the FTSE 100 Index rises or stays at the same level, or growth in a basket of five specific shares up to a maximum return of 30 per cent.

Insurance guaranteed equity investments You take out a single-premium life insurance policy and your money (less any upfront charges) is put in an investment fund. Provided you invest for the full guarantee period, you get back your capital plus the growth of the fund or alternatively growth linked to one or more stock-market indices – for example 100 per cent of the average growth of the FTSE 100, S&P 500, Nikkei 25 and Eurostox 50, or growth in the FTSE 100 up to a maximum return of 30 per cent. A few of these insurance bonds invest in a fund which works in the same way as the unit trust versions described below.

Guaranteed unit trusts When you pick the trust, you choose the level of protection you want. Only a '100-per-cent fund' tries to return your capital in full. Typically, the investment is divided into three-month periods. At the end of each three-month period, the trust aims to return at least the amount you invested at the start of the period, by investing the bulk of your money to earn interest. It also aims to give you a proportion of any increase in a stock-market index by investing in financial futures.

Not all protected unit trusts are 100-per-cent funds. For example, a '95-per-cent fund' aims only to ensure you get back at least 95 per cent of your original investment at the end of the three-month period. But this allows more of your money to be put into futures, so increasing the amount you stand to gain if the market rises. These types of protected funds are not guaranteed investments and expose you to higher risks.

More information From banks, building societies, National Savings & Investments*, insurance companies and unit trust management companies that offer these investments and from IFAs. *Moneyfacts Investments Life & Pensions*★ lists many of the bonds available. The IMA's★ information service includes details of guaranteed and protected funds. See occasional articles in *Which?*★ and *Money Management*★.

How to invest If you've identified specific guaranteed investments you want to invest in, contact the providers directly. Otherwise, consult an IFA★. Note that the deposit bonds and insurance bonds are often on sale only for a short period of time. The unit trust versions are continuously available.

Stakeholder products

From April 2005, a full range of 'stakeholder products' is due to become available. These are products which meet certain conditions set by the government aimed at ensuring the products are straightforward, good value and not unduly risky. The conditions vary according to the type of product and include for example, a cap on charges and ban on extra charges if you want to transfer to another product. There are five stakeholder products in all:

- **deposit product** – see page 292
- **medium-term investment product (MTIP).** This can be set up as a unit trust (see pages 320 and 341) or similar investment or as a unit-linked insurance policy (see page 336). It must be invested in a broad spread of investments, of which no more than three-fifths are shares and property and the rest in bonds, desposits and so on. The value of your investment will go up and down with the stock market but because of the wide spread of investments you should normally be shielded from very large swings in value. Charges are capped at 1.5 per cent a year for the first ten years and 1 per cent a year thereafter. The MTIP can be set up as a stocks-and-shares ISA – see Chapter 11
- **smoothed MTIP.** This is invested as already described for the MTIP but some of the return in good years is put into a 'smoothing fund' which is used to top up the return in bad years – in a similar way to the working of a with-profits fund (see page 314)

- **stakeholder pension** – this is based on the existing stakeholder pension which has been available since 2001 (see Chapter 12) with the following changes for new schemes: charges are capped at 1.5 per cent during the first ten years falling to 1 per cent thereafter; the default fund must be a lifestyle fund and, even if you choose another type of fund, it must be lifestyled so that you are automatically shifted into lower-risk bonds and deposits in the last few (probably five) years before you reach the selected retirement age
- **child trust fund** – see Chapter 10.

All the stakeholder products except the smoothed MTIP can be sold through the basic advice regime described in Chapter 2.

Summary of medium-risk investments

Investment	Minimum period for which you should aim to invest	Type of return	Risk rating
Investments from the government			
Gilts	a) Until redemption	a) Fixed income, taxed or taxable; fixed capital gain or loss, tax-free	4
	b) No set period	b) Fixed income, taxed or taxable; capital gain or loss, tax-free	4–5
Index-linked gilts	a) Until redemption	a) Fixed income, inflation-proofed, taxed or taxable; capital gain or loss, ignoring the increases in line with inflation, is fixed at the time you invest, tax-free	3–4
	b) No set period	b) Fixed income, inflation-proofed, taxed or taxable; capital gain or loss, tax-free	4

Investment	Minimum period for which you should aim to invest	Type of return	Risk rating
Local authority bonds	Set period – usually 1–8 years	Fixed, taxed	5
Local authority stocks	As for gilts	As for gilts	5
Investments from commercial organisations			
Annuities	For life or for a set period	Fixed or with built-in increases, taxed	3 or 4
Insurance company income and growth bonds	Set period – usually 1–10 years	Fixed, taxed	4
Permanent income-bearing shares (PIBS)	No set period	Fixed, taxable	5
Corporate bonds	As for gilts	Fixed income, taxable; capital gain or loss, tax-free*	5–10, depending on quality of issuing company
Preference shares	No set period	Fixed income, taxed; capital gain or loss, taxable*	5–10, depending on quality of issuing company
Pooled investments			
Bank and building society guaranteed investments	Set period, usually 1–5 years	Growth, taxed as interest*	About 5
With-profits life insurance	Set period, often 10 years or more	Bonuses, effectively taxed*	About 5
With-profits friendly society tax-exempt plans	Set period, often 10 years or more	Bonuses, partially tax-free	About 5
Stakeholder - smoothed medium-term investment product	Full details not available at time of writing*	Full details not available at time of writing*	Likely to be around 5
Gilt and fixed-income unit trusts and OEICS	No set period	Income, variable, taxed; capital gain or loss, taxable*	About 5

Stakeholder medium-term investment product	Full details not available at time of writing*	Full details not available at time of writing*	Likely to be around 6
Guaranteed unit trusts	No set period (but multiple of 3 months)	Capital Gain, taxable	5–6
Insurance guaranteed equity investment	Set period – after 5 or 6 years	Income, variable taxed	5–7

* You can invest in these through an ISA (see Chapter 11), in which case the return will be tax-free.

Chapter 18

Higher-risk investments

When it comes to any serious longer-term savings targets, you should consider putting at least part of your money into investments whose returns are linked in some way to shares. This does not mean you have to buy shares in individual companies yourself (although this is one option, of course): a number of pooled investments give you cheaper and often more convenient access to a well-balanced portfolio. This chapter looks at the mainstream ways of investing in shares in the context of basic financial planning; it does not look at more esoteric investments, such as traded options, the Enterprise Investment Scheme, venture capital trusts, and so on. These may well have a place in your personal finances but, given their inherently higher risks, they should perhaps be viewed as fun investments rather than ways of achieving particular financial objectives. On that basis, they fall outside the scope of this book.

Direct investment in shares

Ordinary shares

What they are The shareholders of a company are its owners and share in the profits of the company. Your shares also give you the right to have a say in how the company is run (by exercising your voting rights at shareholder meetings) – but see page 335.

Minimum investment No set minimum, but dealing charges mean that buying less than, say, £1,000–£1,500-worth of a company's shares at a time is usually uneconomic.

Maximum investment None.

Type of return This can come in two forms. An established company usually pays dividends every six months (with some companies, every three months) to its shareholders. The amount paid is variable, although most companies are reluctant to reduce or miss a dividend payment. Companies still establishing themselves or those facing difficulties might not pay any dividends at all. Shareholders might be quite happy to accept this, if they can see profits being ploughed back into the growth of the company, giving the promise of future rewards.

Because shares are traded on the stock market, you also stand to make a capital gain or loss if you sell your shares, depending on the prices at which you bought and sold them.

Tax treatment Dividends count as income for tax purposes. They are paid after deduction of tax at a special rate of 10 per cent, and you receive a tax voucher along with the dividend cheque showing how much tax has been deducted. Both starting-rate and basic-rate taxpayers have no further tax to pay. Non-taxpayers cannot reclaim the tax. Higher-rate taxpayers have further tax to pay, bringing their total tax rate on dividends to 32.5 per cent – see Example below. Capital gains on shares are taxable, though you can set your capital gains tax allowances against them (see Chapter 4). Gains on employee shares and unquoted shares in trading companies – including those listed on the Alternative Investment Market (AIM) qualify for the higher rates of taper relief that apply to business assets, so reducing the tax you pay.

How long you invest for No set period, but this is not the home for money you might need back at a set time or at short notice, when share prices might be low.

Example

In 2004–5, Jules receives £540 in share dividends. These have already had tax at 10 per cent deducted. The before-tax value of the dividends is £600 (which equals £540 plus a £60 tax credit).

Since Jules is a higher-rate taxpayer, he is liable for tax at 32.5 per cent on the £600 dividends. This comes to 32.5% × £600 = £195. But £60 tax has already been deducted from the dividend payout, so Jules just has the excess to pay, in other words £195 – £60 = £135.

Charges For the purchase of newly issued shares, no charges. For other shares, stockbroker's commission; the table on page 335 gives an indication of the amount you might pay. Stamp duty of 0.5 per cent on purchases but not sales. The spread between the prices at which you buy and sell: say, 1.5 per cent for large, well-established companies, but a much higher percentage for small companies whose shares are not often traded. In addition, on a purchase or sale of £10,000 or more, you have to pay a small PTM levy, which helps fund the City's Panel on Takeovers and Mergers. Some brokers also make a separate 'compliance charge', which goes towards the cost of meeting the regulatory rules for the industry.

You may be encouraged to hold your shares in electronic form through your broker's 'nominee account' (see page 334). Using a nominee account might be free or there could be charges: for example, on a regular basis or each time the broker hands over dividends. With nominee accounts, watch out too for extra charges if you want to receive company reports and accounts or to attend a company's AGM. (You could avoid a charge for company accounts by getting them direct from the company registrar or through a free service such as that available through the *Financial Times* – see 'More information' opposite.) As an alternative to using a nominee account, you could become a 'sponsored member' of Crest*, in which case you directly hold your electronic shares. You must be sponsored usually by a broker who will make a charge. You do not have to hold shares electronically but, if you choose to hang on to paper share

---

Warning

Beware of stock-market 'bubbles'. Throughout the centuries, there have been periods when investors get overly enthusiastic about a particular company or sector. One of the most notorious incidents was the South Sea Bubble in the 1700s; one of the most recent has been the passion for 'dotcom shares'. If you get in on a bubble early and sell your shares before the bubble bursts, you can make a real killing. But don't be the last one left holding the shares when their price suddenly plunges back to reality. Chasing stock-market bubbles must be viewed as a high-risk 'fun investment' – not a tool of financial planning.

> **Tip**
> Gains from shares will be tax-free if you invest through an individual savings account (ISA) – see Chapter 11.

certificates, you will probably face higher charges when you sell or buy. Also, you will probably need to deal under a slower system than normal or else face fines if your money or certificates do not reach your broker in time. For more details see overleaf.

Risk Capital risk, because the value of your shares can fall as well as rise. In addition, there is the risk that a company you invest in goes out of business, in which case you would lose all your capital. On the inflation front, shares offer a good chance of keeping abreast of, or bettering, inflation over the long term – but no guarantee of doing so. Income can vary. You can reduce risk by investing in shares of different companies from different sectors. Risk rating: from around seven for shares in a single, sound, well-established company to ten for a high-risk venture.

More information One of the best ways to keep abreast of company information and share prices is via the Internet. Numerous websites and many online dealing services now exist which can help you do this – see Shares Websites★ in the Addresses section. Share prices are listed in many daily newspapers, on Ceefax★ and Teletext★ and on the Internet. ProShare★ is an independent organisation set up to promote direct investment in shares; it produces information packs, runs conferences, and so on.

> **Warning**
> Many small investors buy shares as new issues, attracted by the simplicity of the transaction and the fact that there are no charges. Privatisation issues, which were attractively priced at issue and have on the whole produced good profits, have fuelled this interest. However, companies try to launch their new issues when stock-market conditions look set to raise the maximum possible money for the company. That is the worst time at which investors should buy. Waiting and buying 'second-hand' might be a better deal.

Among other perks, membership of ProShare gives you access to a telephone share information service. The *Financial Times*★, *Investors Chronicle*★, other specialist magazines such as *Shares*★ and *Growth Company Investor*★ and, to a lesser extent, the financial pages of newspapers give reports and analysis of a wide range of individual companies. A number of fairly costly, but comprehensive, company guides is available, for example *The Pinsent Communications Company Guide*★; these give you essential statistics about companies and summaries of stockbrokers' recommendations. Company reports and accounts can be obtained direct from companies, and the *Financial Times*★ and *Investors Chronicle*★ offer a report and accounts service for readers. Numerous books have been written about how to analyse shares and how to make a million – try your local bookshop. Consult a traditional stockbroker★ for advice on which shares to buy and sell or the timing of deals.

How to invest To buy new issues, register with a broker offering a new-issue service or, in the case of privatisations, see details in the press. For other shares, buy and sell through a stockbroker. If you need advice, choose a traditional stockbroking 'execution-and-advice' service. If you are confident about dealing without advice, opt for an 'execution-only' (also called 'dealing-only') service. The latter should be cheaper than a service which includes advice.

There are now numerous websites through which you can buy and sell shares. Most are execution-only. They work in two ways:

- **via a direct link to the dealing facility** The trading computer supplies you with a real-time share price at which you can trade. You generally have 15 to 20 seconds to accept or reject it. If accepted, your trade is executed instantaneously.
- **via a link to the broker's dealing desk** Your order is delivered by email. A human dealer picks it up and carries out the trade in the normal way. This is essentially the same as placing an order by phone. Price information may be supplied on the website but it will not necessarily be real-time.

Three-day trading, nominee accounts and all that

In order to compete with stock markets around the world, the London Stock Exchange has been speeding up the pace at which deals are completed. On 5 February 2001, 'three-day trading' was

Stockbrokers' commissions when you invest in shares

	Typical traditional stockbroker's service including advice	Example of a dealing-only service
Commission levels	• 1.5% on first £7,000 • 0.55% on next £8,000 • 0.5% on anything above £15,000. Minimum £20	1% Minimum £14
For example, commission on:		
Small deal (£500)	£20	£14
Medium deal (£2,500)	£37.50	£25
Large deal (£10,000)	£121.50	£100

introduced, meaning that payment takes place just three working days after shares are bought or sold. Three-day trading is no problem for professional investors, but it is near impossible for those small investors who are generally reliant on the postal system to receive transfer documents and deliver share certificates or cheques within just three days. Therefore, many brokers encourage their smaller clients to hold their shares through 'nominee accounts' and to open deposit accounts with the broker from which payments for deals can be made. With a nominee account, you cease to be the direct owner of your shares; instead, the broker owns the shares on your behalf. There are a number of potential drawbacks with this arrangement:

• As you are no longer the direct owner, you often lose your automatic right to receive reports and accounts, to attend company meetings, to vote, and also the right to any share perks. Whether or not you can still exercise these rights depends on the services the broker offers as part of the nominee account.
• You may have to pay an annual fee for the nominee account, and there may be extra charges for collecting dividends, passing on information about company meetings, and so on.
• Deposit accounts with brokers typically pay less interest than a comparable building society account.

You do not have to hold your shares through a nominee account. You can carry on dealing outside the three-day trading system, allowing longer for settling your deals – usually, this means using the old ten-day system instead. However, you may have to pay higher charges and/or accept a worse deal on share prices if you use the slower ten-day system. If you deal only occasionally, the slower system is likely to be best for you.

If you are a very active trader, consider the nominee route, but shop around for a service which suits you. Alternatively, consider becoming a 'sponsored member' of Crest (an electronic share settlement system). With this route, you have your own Crest account (in the same way that stockbrokers do), in which you hold your own shares electronically, which means they can be rapidly delivered when you sell them. Ask your stockbroker for details or contact Crest*.

Warning

If investing directly in shares, you should ideally invest a minimum of around £15,000 to £20,000 in a dozen or more different companies to protect yourself adequately from risk and to avoid dealing charges eating too heavily into your profits. For many investors, pooled investments, such as unit trusts, OEICs, investment trusts and exchange-traded funds, will be the better option.

Pooled investments

Unit-linked life insurance

What it is This is a form of investment-type life insurance. (Pensions can also be invested on a unit-linked basis – see Chapter 12.) The bulk of your premiums buys units in one or more funds investing in shares and/or other investments. The value of your policy depends directly on the value of these underlying fund(s), so if the prices of the shares in a share-based fund fall, so too will the value of your units. There is usually a very wide range of different investment funds to choose from, including:

- **deposit-based fund** (often called 'money fund', 'cash fund' or 'deposit administration') This invests in high-interest bank and building society accounts and/or money market funds. Like the underlying deposits, the value of these funds cannot fall, so a deposit-based fund is useful to switch into if you want to consolidate gains on a policy or you want to switch out of a falling stock market.
- **unitised with-profits fund** This works in a similar way to traditional with-profits insurance, with bonus units being added to the plan, but the charges are explicit and the insurer usually reserves the right to adjust unit values downwards in exceptional investment conditions (although there may be a value below which the fund is guaranteed not to fall).
- **fixed-interest fund** This invests in gilts, corporate bonds, and so on.
- **property fund** investing in, say, shopping centres and office blocks which provide rental income.
- **managed fund** investing in a wide range of assets which might include gilts, shares and property.
- **share fund** – for example, those in the UK, Europe, the United States, Japan or Australia, or shares in companies which are in the doldrums but expected to grow strongly in future.
- **tracker fund** whose value rises and falls in line with a selected stock-market index – most commonly the FTSE 100 or FTSE All Share Index. Tracker funds (also called 'passively managed funds) tend to buy and sell shares in the fund less frequently than other ('actively managed') funds, so should benefit from lower costs.
- **commodities and metals**.

Minimum investment Varies, depending on the type of policy. But for regular-premium policies, payments start at under £10 a month. For single-premium policies, you might need a lump sum of at least, say, £500.

Maximum investment As for with-profits policies – see page 315.

Type of return Your policy builds up a value according to the value of the underlying investment funds. How this value is used depends on the type of policy: for example, a maximum investment plan is designed to pay out a lump sum at the end of ten years, but a single-premium bond can be used to provide an income. See 'Tax treatment' overleaf for more detail.

Tax treatment As for with-profits policies (see page 316). Special rules apply to single-premium bonds used to provide income. Each time you take any 'income' you are treated as cashing in part of the policy. Provided you cash in no more than a given limit, you can put off paying any tax due (which would be only higher-rate tax anyway) until the policy eventually comes to an end, and tax would be charged according to your tax status at that time. The limit on the amount you can cash in each year is one-twentieth of the premiums paid so far; any amount not used up in one year can be carried forward to future years. The proceeds of the bond, including the earlier income withdrawals, are taxed when you finally cash in the bond. Although only higher-rate taxpayers would then have tax to pay on the bond itself, the payout can also affect other taxpayers if they are claiming income-related allowances or benefits, such as age allowance or child tax credit.

How long you invest for This depends on the type of policy or plan – see the boxes on pages 317 and 340. Many unit-linked life insurance products are designed to be long-term investments and will give you a very poor return if you pull out early. Stopping a policy early crystallises charges (largely commission paid to advisers and salespeople) which would otherwise have been spread out over the lifetime of the policy. As a result, the surrender value of your policy could be less than you have paid in premiums, or even nothing at all.

Tip and warning

If you are currently a higher-rate taxpayer, but expect to pay tax at a lower rate later on, a single-premium insurance bond can be a tax-efficient way of providing income because no tax is charged at the time you take out any income (provided this is below a certain limit). When the policy matures, only higher-rate tax is levied, so if you are a basic-rate or starting-rate taxpayer by then, there will be no tax at all to pay on the proceeds. But beware: if you are aged 65 or more when your single-premium insurance bond comes to an end and you qualify for age-related tax allowances (see page 63), you could lose some or all of the extra allowance and have extra tax to pay as a result.

> **Warning**
> Make sure you understand the nature of the unit-linked life insurance policy or plan you are investing in. If it is designed for the long term, you could get a very poor return if you pull out early.

Charges There are several charges to consider. First, there will be some form of policy or administration fee deducted from each premium; this will often be a flat-rate fee, so it can eat heavily into small payments. Next, you need to consider the 'unit allocation', which tells you what proportion of the remaining premiums will be used to buy units; this proportion might be low in the first year or two when the bulk of the costs (commissions, for example) are being paid by the insurer. Don't be too impressed by unit allocations of more than 100 per cent: this does not mean that more than you have paid in is being invested; the policy fee has already been deducted, so you are in effect getting a refund of part of the fee. Watch out for what are called 'capital units'; the distinctive feature of these is that they have a higher-than-usual annual management fee which persists for the lifetime of the policy. There is a spread between the offer price at which you are allocated units and the bid price at which you cash them in; typically, this is around 5 to 6 per cent. Finally, there is the annual management fee of around 1 per cent.

Assessing the impact of this hotchpotch of charges would be a difficult task. Fortunately, nowadays the work is done for you, as insurers are required by law to tell you about the impact of charges on your investment (see Chapter 3). They must also tell you what happens if you cash in or stop your policy early, when surrender charges can heavily dent the value of your policy. If you switch between investment funds, the first switch or two might be free; you will be charged for subsequent switches (though the charge is usually fairly low).

Risk There is a risk to your capital because the value of the underlying investments can fall as well as rise. On the other hand, by investing in a fund you are spreading your risks and reducing the impact that any one company's share collapse could have on your overall investment. Your choice of fund affects risk: a UK managed fund (see page 337), for example, is far less likely to see sharp swings

---

Unit-linked life insurance plans

The box on pages 318–19 looks at the broad types of insurance policy which can be invested on either a with-profits or unit-linked basis. Here, two further plans, which are usually set up as unit-linked insurance, are considered briefly.

Single-premium bonds   These are usually a form of whole-of-life insurance policy (see page 319) which provide minimal life cover and are intended to be used for investment purposes. There may be as many as 20 or so different funds to which you can link. You can invest in more than one fund simultaneously and switch between them at any time. The insurance company has to account for tax on both income and gains from the underlying investment funds, and you cannot reclaim any of that tax. This makes the bonds unattractive for basic-rate, starting-rate and non-taxpayers and anyone with unused capital gains tax allowances, who would do better generally to invest in unit and investment trusts. These bonds are therefore most suitable for higher-rate taxpayers and those who particularly want to switch funds regularly.

Maximum investment plans   These are ten-year endowment policies designed to build regular savings into a lump sum. Life cover is kept to a minimum, and you can choose from a wide range of investment funds. As with single-premium bonds, the tax treatment means that these plans are generally not suitable unless you are a higher-rate taxpayer or particularly need a cheap route for switching between different investment sectors.

---

in value than a small companies or commodities fund. By investing in shares and similar investments, you stand a good chance of keeping pace with or beating inflation (but if you choose a deposit-based fund, this would not be the case). Risk rating: deposit-based funds, around three; other funds, from six upwards.

More information Price and performance details of insurance funds are included in quality daily newspapers and various personal finance magazines, such as *Money Management*★, and *Moneyfacts Investments Life & Pensions*★, which publishes annual surveys of fund managers' performance. Articles in *Which?*★ and the personal finance pages of newspapers are also useful sources of information. For individual policies and plans, the insurer or adviser will provide product details (see Chapter 3).

How to invest If you are interested in a particular product, deal directly with the insurer or friendly society if they allow this. Otherwise, buy through an independent financial adviser (IFA)★.

Unit trusts

What they are These are professionally managed funds investing in shares and/or other stock-market investments. They can also (though only a few do this) invest in other assets, such as property and futures and options (the last two let you speculate on which way the future prices of shares and other assets will move without your actually holding the shares or assets themselves). The fund is divided up into units, and you invest by buying these units. The value of your holding depends on how the price of those units moves. Often, the unit trust management company operates a range of different trusts, for example:

- **UK all companies**, investing in shares of UK companies and aiming to produce a mixture of income and growth
- **UK growth**, again investing in UK companies, but specialising in shares expected to produce capital gains
- **UK equity income**, concentrating on shares with high dividend yields; the income can be reinvested rather than paid out
- **'index' or 'tracker' funds**, which mimic the movement of a particular stock-market index, such as the FTSE 100, and which often have lower annual management fees because the underlying investments are less actively traded
- **gilt and fixed-interest**, investing in gilts (see page 302), corporate bonds (see page 312), preference shares (see page 313) and similar investments
- **convertibles**, investing in convertible corporate bonds (see page 312)
- **balanced**, investing in a mixture of shares and fixed-interest
- **international funds**, investing in shares etc. from a wide range of stock markets around the world
- **smaller companies**
- **particular countries**, for example European countries or Japan
- **fund of funds**, investing in other unit trusts.

Minimum investment Varies, but could be as low as £25 a month if the management company runs a regular-savings scheme, and from, say, £250 as a lump sum.

Maximum investment None.

Type of return You can use most unit trusts to provide either growth or income, though some are better for one purpose than the other, and a few trusts can be used only for growth. Income is in the form of distributions, which are similar to dividends from shares. If you want to receive an income, choose 'distribution units'; if you do not, choose 'accumulation units', whose income is automatically used to buy you further units.

Tax treatment Distributions count as income for tax purposes. Distributions from unit trusts investing wholly or mainly in shares are taxed in the same way as dividends from shares. In other words, you receive the distributions with tax at a special rate of 10 per cent already deducted. If you are a non-taxpayer, you cannot reclaim the tax. Starting-rate and basic-rate taxpayers have no more tax to pay. Higher-rate taxpayers must pay extra tax, bringing the total rate they pay on the distribution to 32.5 per cent. Capital gains on units are taxable, though you may have allowances to set against them (see page 63).

How long you invest for No set period, but this is not the home for money you might need back at a set time or in a hurry, as unit prices might be low when you come to sell.

Charges There is an annual management charge (usually around 0.75–1.5 per cent of the underlying fund) and a spread between the prices at which you buy ('offer price') and sell ('bid price') units. This spread incorporates what is called the 'initial charge' – commonly 5 per cent of the amount invested – but the total you pay upfront is effectively the spread, which tends to be 1 or 2 per cent more. Some trusts have reduced or scrapped their initial charge and make an 'exit charge' instead if you sell within, say, five years. The initial charge is reduced or waived altogether if you buy through a discount broker★ or fund supermarket★.

Risk There is a risk to your capital because the price of units can fall as well as rise. Your choice of trust affects this risk: a UK all-company trust, for example, is far less likely to see sharp swings in value than a smaller-companies or trust. By investing in shares and similar investments, you stand a good chance of keeping pace with or beating inflation. Risk rating: from six upwards.

More information The IMA★ produces leaflets and has a useful website explaining how unit trusts work, the types of trust available and how you can use them. The information service also publishes a directory of its members. Price and performance details of unit trusts are included in quality daily newspapers and personal finance magazines, such as *Money Management*★ and *Moneyfacts Investments Life & Pensions*★. Articles in *Which?*★ and the personal finance pages of newspapers are also useful sources of information. For individual trusts, the management company or adviser will provide product details (see Chapter 3). If you are an Internet user, you can find many sites producing performance statistics and risk ratings – see Investment Fund websites★ in the Addresses section.

Exchange traded funds (ETFs)

Exchange traded funds have been available in the USA for some years. In April 2000, the first ETF went on sale in the UK. An ETF is an investment fund set up as a company. You invest by buying its shares, which are traded on a stock exchange. You buy ETF shares in the same way as any other stocks and shares – see page 334.

Investment trusts (see page 345) are also traded on the stock exchange, but ETFs are different because, like unit trusts and OEICs, they are 'open-ended funds'. This means that extra ETF shares are created when there are more buyers than sellers, and shares are cancelled when sellers outnumber buyers. Because the size of the ETF adjusts with supply and demand, its price is not affected by demand for and supply of the shares (unlike an investment trust). So the ETF's price reflects just the value of the investments in the fund.

In the USA, ETFs are very popular and as a result the spread between the buying and selling price of the shares has been driven as low as 0.1 per cent. So far, all ETFs have been tracker funds (though ETFs in managed funds are also under consideration). As tracker funds, they have low management costs too – for example, 0.35 per cent of the fund per year for the UK's first ETF. But, as with other shares, you'll have to pay dealing charges when you buy and sell (though there is no stamp duty on purchases). This makes ETFs suitable only if you have a lump sum of, say £1,000 or more to invest. To find out about ETFs, visit the website www.ishares.net.

> **Open-ended investment companies (OEICs)**
>
> You may come across funds which are set up as OEICs rather than unit trusts. From the investor's point of view, there is little difference between the two investments. See page 322 for details.

How to invest If you have already selected the trusts you want to invest in, you might be tempted to go directly to the trust management company. But often this will not be the cheapest way to buy. Typically, you'll pay less if you buy through a discount broker★ or a fund supermarket★ because, with both, the initial charge is reduced or cut completely so that more of your money is invested. If you need advice choosing a fund, contact an independent financial adviser (IFA)★.

> **Pound-cost averaging**
>
> Some advisers suggest, when buying unit trusts and similar funds, there is an advantage in choosing regular saving over investing a lump sum because of 'pound-cost averaging'. The essence of the argument is that, when unit prices are low, your set regular sum buys more units than when unit prices are high. Therefore, the average price you pay for your units is less than the average unit price.
>
> For example, suppose you invest £100 a month. If the unit price is 100p, you get £100 / 1.00 = 100 units. If next month the unit price is 50p, you would get £100 / 0.50 = 200 units. In total you would have 300 units at a price of £200, i.e. an average price to you of £200 / 300 = 66.7p per unit. This compares with an average price over the two months of (100 + 50) / 2 = 75p. Sounds like a bargain.
>
> But there is nothing magic about the sums. They merely show how regular saving takes the 'timing risk' out of your investment: you avoid the problem of investing all your money when unit prices are high, but equally you lose the opportunity of investing all your money when unit prices are low. So pound-cost averaging may reduce your potential losses but it also reduces your potential gains. Whether that appeals to you depends on your attitude towards risk. Bear in mind that you still have to worry about the timing when you come to sell your units.

Investment trusts

What they are Investment trusts are companies that are quoted on the stock market. Their business is managing funds invested in shares and other assets. You invest by buying the shares of the investment trust. There are different types of investment trust, specialising in different areas of investment, in much the same way as unit trusts. But there are some important differences between unit trusts and investment trusts:

- Unit trusts are open-ended, meaning that when there are more people wanting to invest than to cash in, new units are created, expanding the size of the trust, and this new money is used to buy further investments in the fund. By contrast, investment trusts are closed-ended funds, because there is a finite pool of shares in the company. If more people want to buy than to sell, this drives up the share price. The unit price of a unit trust will, then, largely reflect the value of the underlying assets in the trust. But the underlying assets are only one factor influencing the share price of an investment trust.
- Investment trusts, but not unit trusts, can borrow money to invest. This has what is called a 'gearing effect', which magnifies gains on a successful investment but also magnifies losses on a poor one.

Minimum investment Varies from, say, £25 a month through a savings scheme run by the investment trust management company; savings schemes also accept *ad hoc* lump sums as small as, say, £250. Otherwise you buy through a stockbroker, and dealing charges would tend to make deals under £1,000 uneconomic.

Maximum investment None.

Type of return With some investment trusts, just one class of shares will automatically give you income (in the form of dividends) and growth (if the share price rises). But 'split capital trusts' give you a choice of shares. A split capital trust is set up for a fixed period. During that time, some of its shares (the 'income shares') receive all or most of the income from the trust; when the trust is wound up, the 'capital shares' receive all or most of the growth. There are some exotic variations on this theme: for example, zero dividend preference shares (see page 346) and capital indexed shares, both of which require some homework before you use them. Income shares can be useful for investors seeking a high income immediately, provided they are prepared to sacrifice capital growth.

Tax treatment The same as for direct investment in shares. Capital shares in split capital trusts can be particularly useful for higher-rate taxpayers.

Charges The same as for direct investment in shares – see page 332 – if you buy through a stockbroker. The cost of investing is generally lower if you use a savings scheme run by many of the investment trust management companies (because they can then buy and sell in bulk and pass on cost savings to investors). There is a spread between the price at which you can buy shares and the price at which you can sell them. The management company's annual charge for its services is usually fairly low: for example around 0.5 per cent.

Risk There is a risk to your capital because share prices can fall as well as rise. A trust which has a high level of borrowing – that is, it is

---

Investment trust zero-dividend preference shares ('zeros')

Zeros can be a useful way of investing for growth over periods of, say, five to ten years.

Zeros are capital shares in a split-capital investment trust. They do not receive any income but, when the trust is wound up on a pre-set maturity date, they receive part of the capital growth of the assets held by the trust. The longest available periods to maturity are usually ten years.

Because zeros are preference shares (see page 313), they are among the lower-risk types of shares which you can hold. When the investment trust is wound up, the zeros receive a set share of the capital growth before any ordinary shareholders get a look-in.

In a complex investment trust, there may be many different classes of shares, including several types of preference share. Before investing, check that the zeros you have chosen are high up in the pecking order – 'first order preference shares' would get the first cut.

Bear in mind that, if you need to sell before maturity, you cannot be sure of the share price at which you can sell.

On a one-to-ten risk scale, zeros would generally score about five or so.

highly geared – will tend to have a more volatile share price than a less highly geared trust. Similarly, if the trust invests in inherently more risky companies – smaller companies or emerging markets, for instance – the share price can be expected to vary more widely and your risk will be greater. In recent times, some high-risk versions of split-capital trusts have appeared, which rely on complicated arrangements for borrowing and/or investing in the shares of other split-capital trusts. If you are not happy taking high risks, you should avoid these types of trust. To help you assess the risks, the Association of Investment Trust Companies (AITC)★ has started to publish information about trusts' investment in other trusts. As with all share-based investments, you stand a good chance of keeping pace with or beating inflation over the long term. Risk rating: from six or seven upwards.

More information The AITC★ produces a number of useful explanatory booklets and a directory of investment trust

---

However, risk can vary enormously. In particular, investment trusts that are highly geared (i.e. are borrowing a high proportion of the money they invest) and/or have large amounts invested in the shares of other split-capital investment trusts have proved very high risk and vulnerable to the slide in the stock market during 2000 to 2003. Many small investors were mis-sold these trusts since neither the marketing literature nor their adviser (where they used one) had made the risks clear. At the time of writing, the Financial Services Authority (FSA) had just finished negotiating a compensation package with the investment trust companies concerned to pay some redress to investors who lost money as a result of these mis-sales. Contact the FSA★ for details.

Understandably, the recent history of these split-capital investment trusts has given all such investments, including zeros, a bad name, but it would be wrong to tar them all with the same brush. The zeros of those split-capital trusts that are not highly geared and do not invest in other trusts' shares are still worth considering as a useful growth investment.

Unit trust or investment trust?

Having decided to invest in a fund, should you go for a unit trust (or OEIC) or an investment trust? You will have to weigh up a variety of factors:

- Investment trusts that borrow money to invest in the fund are more risky (i.e. there is more risk of losing money but also a greater opportunity for gain) than the equivalent unit trust (which is not allowed to use borrowed money).
- Investment trusts tend to be more risky/offer the opportunity for greater return than unit trusts because the value of your investment does not just reflect the value of the underlying fund but also the relative demand for the investment trust shares.
- The different charges: for example, with investment trusts, you usually have dealing costs when you buy and sell the shares. On the other hand, the annual management charge is sometimes lower than for an equivalent unit trust.
- How well the return is tailored to your goals: in particular, split-capital investment trusts offer different shares particularly suited to either capital growth or regular income.

companies. Price and performance details of investment trusts are included in quality daily newspapers and various personal finance magazines, such as *Money Management**. Articles in *Which?** and the personal finance pages of newspapers are also useful sources of information. Like all quoted companies, investment trusts must produce an annual report and accounts; you can get these direct from the trust management company or, for example, through the *Financial Times** service to readers. You can also get advice from stockbrokers offering a traditional dealing and advice service. Useful investment fund websites* include Trust Net and, for split-capital investment trusts, Splits Online.

How to invest Through a stockbroker or, if there is one, through a savings scheme run by the investment trust management company: contact the company directly (details from the AITC* directory). Some fund supermarkets offer investment trusts as well as unit trusts and OEICs.

Other investments

Buy-to-let property

What it is Buying residential property, not to live in yourself, but to let out in order to earn rental income. Most people do not have enough spare capital to buy a second or subsequent property outright, but in recent years it has become fashionable to take out a mortgage to buy such property. It is important to choose properties that are likely to attract a strong supply of tenants – for example, in a university town or large urban area with good employment opportunities.

Minimum investment No specific minimum, but usually the maximum mortgage is 60 to 85 per cent of the property's value, so you will need to find a sizeable chunk of the purchase price yourself.

Maximum investment None.

Type of return Provided the rental income exceeds any mortgage payments and other charges, this can be a source of income. In addition you may make a capital gain from any rise in property prices.

Tax treatment Income is taxable – broadly, you are treated as if you are running a business and you can deduct all business-related expenses when working out your profits. A gain when you sell the property could be subject to capital gains tax but you can claim various allowances (see page 63).

Charges Cost of the mortgage (see Chapter 9): the interest rate for buy-to-let mortgages is generally slightly higher than on a mortgage to buy your own home. Costs associated with being a landlord: for example, maintenance and repairs. Cost of an agent if you pay one to look after the property and to find tenants.

Risk A portfolio of many properties would generally be a medium-risk investment – historically, residential properties have produced higher returns than gilts or equities with less variation in the returns (in other words, less risk). However, ready-made portfolios of residential property are not generally available to private investors (although they can invest in property unit trusts and investment trusts which are invested in commercial properties such as offices and shops). Investing in a single property carries a much higher risk. You might pick a property that you find is hard to rent out – perhaps because of its condition or the area it is in. The economic or social climate of the area might change, damaging your rental prospects. You might get a difficult tenant and incur substantial legal costs enforcing the terms of the lease or removing them. And house prices might have fallen at the time you want to sell. Worse still, you might not be able to find a buyer and so be unable to cash in your investment when you want to. Taking out a mortgage to buy a rental property is a form of gearing. It has the effect of magnifying both any profits you make and also any losses. In other words, borrowing increases the risks you are taking. Risk rating: varies from, say, seven upwards.

More information To find out about suitable properties, consult estate agents. For information about buy-to-let mortgages, see the free booklet *Buying to Let* from the Council of Mortgage Lenders★, contact lenders direct or check the summary tables in *Moneyfacts*★. Occasional articles are published in magazines such as *Which?*★ and *Money Management*★. For guidance on the tax position, see Inland Revenue★ leaflets IR150 *Taxation of rents – a guide to property income* and CGT1 *Capital gains tax – an introduction*. Consider joining the Residential Landlords Association★ to access information, advice, legal documents and so on.

How to invest Purchase properties through estate agents. Many lenders currently offer buy-to-let mortgages – contact them direct or use a mortgage broker.

Summary of higher-risk investments

Investment	Minimum period for which you should aim to invest	Type of return	Risk rating
Direct investment in shares			
Ordinary shares – direct investment	No set period, but generally at least 5 years	Variable income and/or growth, taxable[†]	7 and above

Summary of higher-risk investments *(contd)*

Investment	Minimum period for which you should aim to invest	Type of return	Risk rating
Pooled investments			
Unit-linked life insurance – regular-premium plans	Usually at least 10 years	Growth, effectively taxed at equivalent of basic-rate income tax[†]	6 and above (but 3 for deposit-based funds)
Unit-linked life insurance – single-premium plans	Varies	Growth, but you can use partial withdrawals for income, effectively taxed at equivalent of basic-rate income tax[†]	6 and above (but 3 for deposit-based funds)
Unit-linked friendly society tax-exempt plans	Set period, often 10 years or more	Growth, tax-free*[†]	6 and above (but 3 for deposit-based funds)
Unit trusts, OEICs and exchange traded funds (ETFs)	No set period, but generally at least 5 years	Income, taxed; growth, taxable; or just growth[†]	6 and above
Investment trusts	No set period, but generally at least 5 years	Income, taxed; growth, taxable; or just growth; or just income[†]	6/7 and above
Investment trust 'zeros'	Up to ten years	Growth, taxable[†]	About 5 (but some may be higher)
Buy-to-let property	No set period	Income, taxable; growth, taxable	7 and above

* Except dividends and similar income taxable at 10 per cent from 6 April 2004 onwards.
† You can hold these investments through an ISA (see Chapter 11) in which case the return is partially tax-free.

Addresses

Accountants

Look in *Yellow Pages* under 'Accountants', or for a list of members in your area contact:

- Association of Chartered Certified Accountants,
  29 Lincoln's Inn Fields,
  London WC2A 3EE.
  Tel: 020 7396 5700
  Website: www.acca.co.uk
- Institute of Chartered Accountants in England and Wales,
  PO Box 433,
  Chartered Accountants' Hall,
  PO Box 433,
  London EC2P 2BJ.
  Tel: 020 7920 8100
  Website: www.icaew.co.uk
- Institute of Chartered Accountants in Ireland,
  Chartered Accountants' House,
  83 Pembroke Road,
  Dublin 4,
  Republic of Ireland.
  Tel: (00 353) 1 637 7200
  Website: www.icai.ie
- Institute of Chartered Accountants of Scotland,
  CA House,
  21 Haymarket Yards,
  Edinburgh EH12 5BH.
  Tel: 0131 347 0100
  Website: www.icas.org.uk

Age Concern Information Line
Freepost (SWB 30375)
Ashburton
Devon TQ13 7ZZ
Tel: 0800 00 99 66 (freephone)
Website: www.ace.org.uk

Association of British Insurers
51 Gresham Street
London EC2V 7HQ
Tel: 020 7600 3333
Website: www.abi.org.uk

Association of Consulting Actuaries
Website: www.aca.org.uk

Association of Investment Trust Companies (AITC)
24 Chiswell Street
London EC1Y 4YY
Brochureline: 0800 707 707
Website: www.itsonline.co.uk

Association of Private Client Investment Managers and Stockbrokers (APCIMS)
114 Middlesex Street
London E1 7JH
Tel: 020 7247 7080
Website: http: www.apcims.co.uk

British Bankers' Association (BBA)
Pinners Hall
105–108 Old Broad Street
London EC2A 1EX
Tel: 020 7216 8840
Website: www.bba.org.uk

British Insurance Brokers Association (BIBA)
For a list of brokers in your area, contact BIBA at:
14 Bevis Marks
London EC3A 7NT
Tel: 020 7623 9043
Website: www.biba.org.uk

Ceefax
* BBC1 for share prices
* BBC2 for city news, share prices and stock exchanges

Citizens' Advice Bureaux
Look in The Phone Book under 'Citizens' Advice Bureau'.
Websites –
www.citizensadvice.org.uk
www.adviceguide.org.uk

Consulting actuary
See separate entries for:
* Association of Consulting Actuaries
* Society of Pension Consultants

Consumer Credit Counselling Service
Wade house
Merrion Centre
Leeds LS2 8NG
Tel: 0800 138 1111
Website: www.cccs.co.uk

Council of Mortgage Lenders
3 Savile Row
London W1S 3PB
Tel: 020 7440 2255 (request publications)
Website: www.cml.org.uk

County Court
* Look in *The Phone Book* under 'Courts'
* Website – (England & Wales) : www.courtservice.gov.uk
(Northern Ireland): www.courtsni.gov.uk

Crest
CRESTCo Limited
33 Cannon Street
London EC4M 5SB
Tel: 020 7849 0000
Website: www.crestco.co.uk

Debt Management Office (DMO)
Eastcheap Court
11 Philpot Lane
London EC3M 8UD
Tel: 0800 376 9232 (publications)
Website: www.dmo.gov.uk

Debt Management Office Gilts Purchase and Sale Service
Computershare Investor Services plc
PO Box 2411
The Pavillions
Bridgwater Road
Bristol BS3 9WX
Tel: 0870 703 0143
Website:
www-uk.computershare.com

Department for Education and Skills
Information Line: 0800 731 9133
Website: www.dfes.gov.uk

Department for Work and Pensions (DWP)
* **Benefit Enquiry Line**
Tel: 0800 88 22 00
Website: www.dwp.gov.uk
* **For a state retirement pension forecast**
State Pension Forecasting Team,
Tyneview,
Whitely Road,
Newcastle upon Tyne
NE98 1BA
Tel: 0845 3000 168
Website:
www.thepensionservice.gov.uk
* **For free pensions leaflets**
Pensions-Info Line:
0845 7 31 32 33
Websites:
www.pensionguide.gov.uk and
www.thepensionservice.gov.uk

Designated Professional Bodies (DPB)

- Professional bodies for accountants – see separate entry for 'Accountants' above
- Professional bodies for lawyers – see separate entry for 'Solicitors' below
- Institute of Actuaries – see separate entry below.

Discount brokers (examples)

- Hargreaves Lansdown,
  Kendal House,
  Brighton Mews,
  Clifton,
  Bristol BS8 2NX
  Tel: 0117 900 9000
  Website:
  www.hargreaveslansdown.co.uk
- The ISA Shop,
  Star House,
  6 Garland Road,
  Stanmore,
  Middlesex HA7 1NR
  Tel: 0870 870 8558
  Website: www.hcf.co.uk

Ethical consumer magazine

Unit 21
41 Old Birley Street
Manchester M15 5RF
Tel: 0161 226 2929
www.ethicalconsumer.org

Ethical Investment Research Service

80–84 Bondway
London
SW8 1SF
Tel: 020 7840 5700
www.eiris.org.uk

Ethical saving & investing

See separate entries for:
- Ethical consumer magazine
- Ethical Investment Research Service
- Independent financial advisers specialising in ethical investments

Fax services

Giving information provided by Moneyfacts (calls cost maximum 75p per minute)
Guaranteed income bonds
090 607 607 14
Mortgages 090 607 607 01
National Savings & Investments
090 607 607 12
Offshore savings 090 607 607 13
Pension annuities 090 607 607 31
Purchased life annuities
090 607 607 32
Savings accounts 090 607 607 11
Stocks and shares ISA funds
090 607 607 60
Term insurance (non-smokers)
090 607 607 52
With profits bonds
090 607 607 56 and 090 607 607 59

Finance and Leasing Association

Imperial House
15–19 Kingsway
London WC2B 6UN
Tel: 020 7836 6511
Website: www.fla.org.uk

Financial Ombudsman Service

South Quay Plaza
183 Marsh Wall
London E14 9SR
Tel: 0845 080 1800
Website:
www.financial-ombudsman.org.uk

Financial Services Authority (FSA)

25 The North Colonnade
London E14 5HS
Tel: 020 7066 1000
FSA Consumer Helpline: 0845 6061234 (calls charged at local rates)

FSA Register

(to check whether a firm is authorised):
Consumer Helpline as above or use the Firm Check Service on the consumer website below:
Website: www.fsa.gov.uk

Consumer website:
www.fsa.gov.uk/consumer
Comparative tables:
www.fsa.gov.uk/tables

Financial Services Compensation Scheme
7th Floor
Lloyds Chambers
1 Portsoken Street
London E1 8BN
Tel: 020 7892 7300
Website: www.fscs.org.uk

Financial Times
* From newsagents
* Website: www.ft.com
* Company report and accounts service
  Tel: 020 8391 6000
  Website: http: ft.ar.wilink.com

FSA Register
See Financial Services Authority above

Fund supermarkets (examples)
www.chasedevere.co.uk
www.egg.com
www.fidelity.co.uk (Funds Network)
www.hargreaveslansdown.co.uk
www.tqonline.co.uk

Funeral Planning Authority
Harelands
22 Bentsbrook Park
North Holmwood
Dorking
Surrey RH5 4JN
Tel: 01306 740878
E-mail:
enquiries@funeralplanningauthority
.com
Website: http:
www.funeralplanningauthority.com

Go Private
Tel: 0845 604 0333
Website: www.goprivatehealth.co.uk

Growth Company Investor
95 Aldwych
London WC2B 4JF
Tel: 020 7430 9777 (subscriptions)
Website:
www.growthcompany.co.uk

Healthcare Navigator
Tel: 0870 727 0140
Website:
www.healthcarenavigator.co.uk

Help the Aged
207–221 Pentonville Road
London N1 9UZ
Tel: 020 7278 1114
SeniorLine: 0808 800 6565
(Mon–Fri 9am –4pm)
(for factsheets and booklets, written requests preferred)
Website: www.helptheaged.org.uk

HM Treasury
www.hm-treasury.gov.uk

IFA Promotion
Tel: 0800 085 3250
Website: www.unbiased.co.uk

Independent financial adviser (to find one)
See separate entries for:
* IFA Promotion
* The Institute of Financial Planning
* Matrix Data UK IFA Directory
* Personal Finance Society (PFS)

Independent financial advisers specialising in annuities (examples)
* The Annuity Bureau,
  The Tower,
  11 York Road,
  London SE1 7NX.
  Tel: 0845 602 6263
  Website:
  www.annuity-bureau.co.uk
* Annuity Direct,
  32 Scrutton Street,
  London EC2A 4RQ

Tel: 0500 50 65 75
Website:
www.annuitydirect.co.uk
• William Burroughs Annuities
Tel: 020 7421 4545
Website:
www.williamburrows.com

Independent financial advisers specialising in ethical investments (to find one)
www.ethicalinvestment.org.uk

Independent money advice centre (to find one)
• **Community Legal Service Direct**
Can direct you to local solicitors and advice organisations in England and Wales that can give advice about legal and debt problems.
Tel: 0845 345 4 345
Website: www.clsdirect.org.uk
• **See also separate entries for:**
Citizens' Advice Bureaux, Consumer Credit Counselling Service, National Debtline

Inland Revenue (due to be renamed in 2005: Her Majesty's Revenue and Customs- HMRC)
• For local tax enquiry centres look in *The Phone Book* under 'Inland Revenue'.
• For your own tax office, check your tax return, other tax correspondence or check with your employer or scheme paying you a pension.
• Website:
www.inlandrevenue.gov.uk
• To get Inland Revenue leaflets, phone the Orderline:
0845 900 0404
• ISA Helpline: 0845 604 1701
• Inheritance Tax and Probate Helpline: 0845 302 0900
• Self Assessment Helpline:
0845 900 0444

• Tax Credits Helpline:
0845 300 3900
(Northern Ireland:
0845 603 2000)

Inland Revenue (Capital Taxes)
• Forms and leaflets: 0845 234 1000
• (England and Wales)
Ferrers House,
PO Box 38,
Nottingham NG2 1BB
• (Northern Ireland)
Level 3, Dorchester House,
52–58 Great Victoria Street,
Belfast BT2 7QL
• (Scotland)
Meldrum House,
15 Drumsheugh Gardens,
Edinburgh EH3 7UG
• Website:
www.inlandrevenue.gov.uk/cto

Institute of Actuaries
Staple Innn Hall
High Holborn
London WC1V 7QL
Tel: 020 7632 2100
Website: www.actuaries.org.uk

The Institute of Financial Planning
Whitefriars Centre
Lewins Mead
Bristol BS1 2NT
Tel: 0117 945 2470
Website:
www.financialplanning.org.uk

Insurance broker (to find one)
• See *Yellow Pages*
• See separate entry for British Insurance Brokers Association above

Investment fund websites
www.itsonline.co.uk
www.eiris.org
www.fsa.gov.uk/tables
www.ishares.net
www.investmentuk.org

www.splitsonline.co.uk
www.funds-sp.com
www.trustnet.co.uk

Investment Management Association (IMA)
65 Kingsway
London WC2B 6TD
Tel: 020 7269 4639
Website: www.investmentuk.org

Investors Chronicle
* From newsagents
* Subscriptions:
  PO Box 423,
  Sittingbourne,
  Kent ME9 8FA
  Tel: 0870 240 6663
  Website:
  wwwinvestorschronicle.co.uk
* Company report and accounts
  service
  Tel: 020 8391 6000
  Website: http: ft.ar.wilink.com

Jobcentre Plus
For local office, look in *The Phone Book* under 'Jobcentre Plus' or 'Social security'.
Website: www.jobcentreplus.gov.uk

Local authority planning department
Look in *The Phone Book* under 'Councils' or the name of your District, Metropolitan, London Borough or Unitary Council.

Local authority social services department
Look in *The Phone Book* under 'Councils' or the name of your County, Metropolitan, London Borough or Unitary Council.

London Stock Exchange
10 Paternoster Square
London EC4M 7LS
Tel: 020 7797 1000
Website:
www.londonstockexchange.com

Matrix Data UK IFA Directory
Website:
http: www.ukifadirectory.co.uk

Money Management
* From newsagents
* Subscriptions/ back issues:
  WDIS,
  Units 12 & 13,
  Cranleigh Gardens Industrial Estate,
  Southall,
  Middlesex UB1 2DS
  Tel: 020 8606 7545

Money Observer
* From newsagents
* Subscriptions:
  FREEPOST LON21183,
  Manchester, M3 9LS
  Tel: 0870 870 1324
  Website:
  www.moneyobserver.com

Moneyfacts and Moneyfacts Investments Life & Pensions
* Try larger public reference libraries
* Subscriptions:
  Moneyfacts House,
  66–70 Thorpe Road,
  Norwich NR1 1BJ
  Tel: 0870 2250 100
* Website:
  http: www.moneyfacts.co.uk

National Debtline
Tel: 0808 808 4000
Website: www.nationaldebtline.co.uk

National Health Service (NHS)
* NHS Direct Tel:
  (England and Wales) 0845 46 47;
  (Scotland) 08454 24 24 24
* Website: www.nhs.uk
* To find an NHS dentist:
  (England)
  www.nhs.uk/england/dentists;
  (Wales) www.wales.
  nhs.uk/dentistlocalservices.html;

(Scotland) www.show.scot.nhs.
uk/findnearest/healthservices/;
(NorthernIreland)
www.centralservicesagency.com/
display/dentala/

National Savings & Investments

- For Easy Access Savings Account,
  Investment Account, Ordinary
  Account, Children's Bonus
  Bonds, Capital Bonds, contact:
  National Savings and
  Investments,
  Glasgow G58 1SB
- For Premium Bonds, Guaranteed
  Equity Bonds, Pensioners Bonds,
  Income Bonds, contact: National
  Savings and Investments
  Blackpool FY3 9YP
- For Cash mini ISA, TESSA ISA,
  Fixed Interest Savings
  Certificates, Index-linked Savings
  Certificates, Fixed Rate Savings
  Bonds, Deposit Bonds, contact:
  National Savings and
  Investments,
  Durham DH99 1NS
- Tel: 0845 964 5000
- Website: www.nsandi.com

NS&I Independent Adjudicator
1st Floor, South Quay Plaza
183 Marsh Wall
London E14 9SR

Office of Fair Trading
Fleetbank House
2–6 Salisbury Square
London EC4Y 8JX
Tel: 08457 22 44 99
Website: www.oft.gov.uk

Pensions administrator (occupational pension scheme)
See pension statement, scheme
handbook, recent benefit statement,
annual report or noticeboard at work
for contact details of pension scheme
administrator or trustees.
Alternatively, contact your personnel
department.

Pension Schemes Registry
PO Box 1NN
Newcastle upon Tyne NE99 1NN
Tel: 0191 225 6316
Website: www.opra.gov.uk

Pension scheme trustees
See pension statement, scheme
handbook, recent benefit statement,
annual report or noticeboard at work
for contact details of pension scheme
administrator or trustees.
Alternatively, contact your personnel
department.

Pensions Advisory Service (OPAS)
11 Belgrave Road
London SW1V 1RB
Tel: 0845 6012 923
Website: www.opas.org.uk

Pensions Management
Subscriptions/ back issues:
WDIS
Units 12 & 13
Cranleigh Gardens Industrial Estate
Southall
Middlesex UB1 2DS
Tel: 020 8606 7545

The Pension Service
For local office, look in The Phone
Book under 'The Pension Service' or
'Social security'.
Tel: 0845 60 60 265
Website:
www.thepensionservice.gov.uk

Pensions Ombudsman
11 Belgrave Road
London SW1V 1RB
Tel: 020 7834 9144
Website:
www.pensions-ombudsman.org.uk

Personal finance magazines (examples)
- Bloomberg Money (investments) –
  from newsagents or for
  subscription
  Tel: 01795 414936

- *Growth Company investor* (small cap shares) – see separate entry
- Investors Chronicle (mainly shares) – see separate entry
- *Money Management* (most areas of personal finance) – see separate entry
- *Money Observer* (personal finance generally but particularly investments) – see separate entry above
- *Moneywise* (personal finance generally) – newsagents or for subscription
  Tel: 0870 458 4436
- *Mortgage Magazine* – from newsagents or for subscription
  Tel: 01509 844 333
- *Pensions Management* – see separate entry
- *Personal Finance & Savings* – from newsagents of for subscription
  Tel: 020 7827 5454
- *What Investment Trust* – from newsagents or for subscription
  Tel: 020 7827 5451
- *What ISA* – from newsagents
- *What Mortgage* – see separate entry above
- *Your Mortgage and Remortgage* – from newsagents

Personal Finance Society (PFS)
20 Aldermanbury,
London EC2V 7HY
Tel: 020 8530 0852
Website: www.thepfs.org

Personal finance websites
www.fsa.gov.uk/consumer
www.ft.com/yourmoney
www.moneyextra.com
www.moneyfacts.co.uk
www.moneynet.co.uk
www.moneysupermarket.com
www.which.co.uk

The Pinsent Company Guide
HS Financial Publishing Ltd
Arnold House
36–41 Holywell Lane

London EC2A 3SF
Tel: 020 7827 5678
Website: www.company-guide.co.uk

Proshare
Centurion House
24 Monument Street
London EC3R 8AQ
Tel: 020 7220 1730
Website: www.proshare.org

Residential Landlords Association
1 Roebuck Lane
Sale
Manchester
M33 7SY
Telephone : 0845 666 5000
Website: www.rla.org.uk

Safe Home Income Plans (SHIP)
PO Box 516
Preston Central PR2 2XQ
Tel: 0870 241 6060
Website: www.ship-ltd.org

Shares *magazine*
- From newsagents
- Subscriptions:
  FREEPOST SEA 8221,
  Haywards Heath RH16 3BR
  Tel: 01444 475661
  Website: www.moneyam.com/holding/sharesmag.php/

Shares websites
www.freequotes.co.uk
www.ft.com
www.ftse.com
www.hemscott.net
www.londonstockexchange.com
www.nasdaq.com
www.proshare.org
www.sharepages.com

Sheriff's Court
- Look in *The Phone Book* under 'Courts'
- Website: www.scotcourts.gov.uk

Social security office
Look in *The Phone Book* under 'Social security', 'Jobcentre Plus' or 'The Pension Service'.

Society of Pension Consultants
St Bartholomew House
92 Fleet Street
London EC4Y 1DG
Tel: 020 7353 1688
Website: www.spc.uk.com

Society of Trust and Estate Practitioners (STEP)
26 Grosvenor Gardens
London SW1W 0GT
Tel: 020 7838 4890
Website: www.step.org

Solicitor (to find one)
- (England and Wales)
  Law Society,
  113 Chancery Lane,
  London WC2A 1PL
  Tel: 020 7242 1222
  Website: www.lawsoc.org.uk
- (Scotland)
  Law Society of Scotland
  26 Drumsheugh Gardens,
  Edinburgh EH3 7YR
  Tel: 0131 226 7411
  Website: www.lawscot.org.uk
- (Northern Ireland)
  Law Society of Northern Ireland,
  Law Society House,
  98 Victoria Street,
  Belfast BT1 3JZ
  Tel: +44 (0) 28 90 231 614
  Website: www.lawsoc-ni.org

Stockbroker (to find one)
See separate entries for:
- Association of Personal Client Investment Managers and Stockbrokers
- London Stock Exchange

Switch with Which?
www.switchwithwhich.co.uk

Teletext
- C4 for bonds, borrowing, city news, mortgages, savings and share prices
- Website: www.teletext.com

Tax office
See *Inland Revenue* above

What Mortgage?
- From newsagents
- Subscriptions: Tel: 020 7827 5454
  Website:
  www.whatmortgageonline.co.uk

Which? *and Which? Books*
- Tel: 0845 307 4000
  Website: www.which.co.uk
- Online mortgage calculator:
  www.switchwithwhich.co.uk

Index